SEDONA HIKES

REVISED
THIRD EDITION

By
Richard K. Mangum
and Sherry G. Mangum

HEXAGON PRESS, INC.
FLAGSTAFF, ARIZONA

NONLIABILITY STATEMENT

While we have expended considerable effort to guarantee accuracy and have personally taken every one of these hikes, errors in field notes, transcription and typesetting can occur. Changes also occur on the land and some descriptions that were accurate when written may be inaccurate when you read this book. One storm, for example, can block a road, or the Forest Service can change a trail. In addition to the problems of accuracy, there is the problem of injury. It is always possible that hikers may sustain harm while on a hike. The authors, publishers and all those associated with this book, directly or indirectly, disclaim any liability for accidents, injuries, damages or losses whatsoever that may occur to anyone using this book. The responsibility for good health and safety while hiking is that of the user.

Produced by Northland Graphics, Flagstaff, AZ, on recycled paper
Cover Design by Joan Carstensen, Northland Graphics
Cover Photo by Sherry G. Mangum
Twilight at Red Rock Crossing

TABLE OF CONTENTS

ABOUT THE AUTHORS

D ick was born in Flagstaff and has lived there all his life. When his family acquired a second home in Back O' Beyond, south of Sedona, in 1951, he began his love affair with the Sedona area. He learned that by driving 25 miles (the distance between Flagstaff and Sedona) the hiking enthusiast can hike year around: in cool Flagstaff in the summer and warm Sedona in the winter—and in either place in between.

After graduating from Flagstaff High School in 1954, he became a lawyer. He practiced law in Flagstaff for 15 years, then became a Superior Court Judge for Coconino County in 1976, retiring in 1993 to devote full time to hiking and writing.

S herry has lived in Flagstaff since she was seven years old. The daughter of hiking parents, she has enjoyed getting into the outdoors from the time she was a toddler. She loves the scenic beauties of Sedona.

She also inherited a love of photography from her parents, who are both professional photographers. She has refined her skills to produce the photographs you will see in this book. Adept at all aspects of photography, she prefers landscapes. Her work has been published in books and periodicals since 1978. Sherry likes to work with a Nikon F4.

TIPS ON SEDONA HIKING

ACCESS
Many of these hikes can be reached on paved roads. For hikes on unpaved roads, you need to pay attention to conditions. Some of the roads become slippery and impassable when they are wet. Some, such as the upper part of Schnebly Hill Road, are officially closed during the winter by locked gates.

ROCK CLIMBING
We do not provide any rock climbing information in this book. If you want to go rock climbing, you are on your own. Much of the rock around Sedona is sandstone, a notoriously unstable substance.

THORNS
It seems sometimes that every plant along the hiking paths in the Sedona area has thorns, spines or sharp-edged leaves. Pay attention. Learn to identify the fanged plants and avoid them.

VARMINTS
Sedona is in a life zone favorable to rattlesnakes. Even so, we have only seen one on all our hikes and he was just warning us from several feet away. There are also some scorpions and black widow spiders in the area, though we have never seen either. Pests like mosquitoes are scarce. There are no chiggers nor swarming insects like black flies. Our advice about varmints is: be watchful but not paranoid.

WATER
Do not count on finding water anywhere. Take your water with you. In Sedona's hot dry climate you will need plenty of it.

WEATHER
Sedona is in a high desert location, at an altitude of about 4,000 feet. Its finest weather is from October to May. During the summer it can be quite hot, with many days over 100 degrees F. Some of the strenuous hikes can be exhausting in this kind of heat, so be prepared.

How to Use This Book

Alphabetical arrangement. The 127 hikes in this book are arranged from A-Z.

Index. The index starts at page 252. It groups the hikes by geographical area and by special features.

Layout. The text describing a hike and the map of the hike are on facing pages so that you can take in everything at once.

Maps. The maps are not to scale but their proportions are generally correct. The main purpose of the maps is to get you to the trailhead. The maps show mileage point-to-point. The text gives cumulative mileage.

Larger scale maps. For the big picture, buy a Forest Service map or *Experience Sedona.*

Bold type. When you see a trail name in bold type it means that the hike is described in this book.

Ratings. We show hikes rated as easy, moderate and hard. We are middle-aged hikers in normal condition, not highly conditioned athletes who never tire. Hikers should adjust our ratings for their own fitness level. The hike-in-a-box on each map may best show how hard a hike is.

Mileage. Driving distance was measured from the Sedona Y, located at the junction of Highways 89A and 179. All hikes start from this point. Milepost locations are also shown on the maps (as MP) on highways that have them. Hike mileage was measured by a pedometer.

Access roads. To reach many of these hikes, you will have to travel unpaved roads, some of them rough. Our Tercel has 4-wheel drive but not much clearance. Our access ratings were based on how well the Tercel handled the roads. Some drives require a high clearance vehicle.

Safety. We avoid taking risks on hikes. None of these hikes requires technical climbing.

Wilderness Areas. The Sedona area is blessed by having many of its hiking places included within federally designated Wilderness Areas. This is great for the hiker. Please read the Rules of the Trail on page 256.

Cairns. These are stacks of rocks used as trail markers. Some are officially placed, while others are made by hikers.

Mileposts. Major Arizona highways are marked every mile by a sign about three feet high on the right side of the road.

Handy Charts and Data

Hours of Daylight

☀☽	JAN	FEB	MAR	APR	MAY	JUN	JUL	AUG	SEP	OCT	NOV	DEC
SUNRISE	7:35	7:26	6:57	6:14	5:36	5:14	5:16	5:35	5:59	6:21	6:48	7:16
SUNSET	5:26	5:55	6:22	6:48	7:12	7:35	7:45	7:30	6:54	6:11	5:33	5:15

Normal Precipitation—Inches ☁

JAN	FEB	MAR	APR	MAY	JUN	JUL	AUG	SEP	OCT	NOV	DEC
2.22	2.19	2.78	1.23	0.82	1.31	1.30	2.26	1.97	1.31	1.72	2.00

☀ *Normal Temperatures F°—High and Low*

JAN	FEB	MAR	APR	MAY	JUN	JUL	AUG	SEP	OCT	NOV	DEC
57	61	65	74	81	93	96	93	88	77	64	56
32	35	38	45	51	60	65	65	59	50	38	33

Converting Feet to Meters ✌

Meters	910	1212	1515	1818	2121	2424	2727	3030	3333	3636
Feet	3000	4000	5000	6000	7000	8000	9000	10000	11000	12000

Average Walking Rates

Time	1 Hour	30 Min.	15 Min.	7.5 Min.
Miles	2.0	1.0	0.5	0.25
KM	3.2	1.6	0.8	0.4

Hike Locator

B5
A. B. Young Trail
Cookstove Trail
Harding Spring Trail
Pink Sand Canyon
Pumphouse Wash
Purtymun Trail
Telephone Trail
Thomas Point
West Fork

C1
Black Mountain
Casner Mtn. South
Dogie Trail
Loy Butte
Loy Canyon
Mooney Trail
Robbers Roost
Sugarloaf at Black Mountain

C2
Bear Mountain
Red Canyon

C3
Boynton Canyon
Boynton Vista
Fay Canyon
Long Canyon
Mescal Mountain
Mushroom Rock
Rachel's Knoll

C4
Bear Sign Trail
Dry Creek Trail
HS Canyon
Lost Canyon
Lost Canyon Ruins
Lost Wilson Mtn.
Secret Canyon
Van Deren Cabin
Vultee Arch

C5
Brown House Canyon
Slide Rock
Sterling Pass
Wilson Mountain North

D3
Cockscomb, The
Doe Mountain

D4
Angel Falls
Brins Mesa East
Brins Mesa West
Capitol Butte
Chimney Rock
Cibola Mittens
Coffee Pot Trail
Devils Bridge
Shooting Range Ridge East
Shooting Range Ridge West
Soldier Pass Arches
Soldier Pass Trail
Sugarloaf in Sedona

D5
Allens Bend
Casner Canyon North
Hermit Ridge
Old Jim Thompson Trail
Steamboat Rock
Wilson Canyon
Wilson Mountain South

E3
Scheurman Mountain

E4
Airport Saddle Loop
Carroll Canyon
Cathedral Rock

E5
Battlement Mesa
Broken Arrow
Cow Pies
Damfino Canyon
Little Horse Trail
Margs Draw
Merry-Go-Round
Mitten Ridge
Munds Mountain
Schnebly Hill Buttes
Schnebly Hill Trail
Snoopy Rock
Submarine Rock
Twin Buttes

F1
Packard Mesa Trail
Parsons Trail

F2
Page Springs

F3
Apache Fire Trail
Eagles Nest
Goosenecks
Hidden Cabin
Javelina Trail
Kisva Trail
Smoke Trail
Turkey Creek
Yavapai Ridge Trail

F4
Cathedral Ridge
Cathedral Rock, Back O'
Little Park Heights
Twin Pillars

F5
Bell Rock
Bell Rock Pathway
Courthouse Butte
Hot Loop
Jacks Canyon

G1
Gaddes Canyon Trail
General Crook Trail P 5-7
Grief Hill
Oak Creek-Verde Conf.
Woodchute Trail

G3
Deer Pass Trail
House Mountain

G5
Beaverhead Trail
Rattlesnake Canyon
Woods Canyon Trail

G6
Apache Maid Trail
Bell Trail
Blodgett Basin
Casner Canyon South
Chasm Creek Trail
Flume Road
General Crook Trail V 13
Long Canyon #63
Red Tank Draw
Sacred Mountain
Towel Creek Trail
Verde Hot Spring
Walker Basin
Weir Trail
West Clear Creek Trail

Location Map

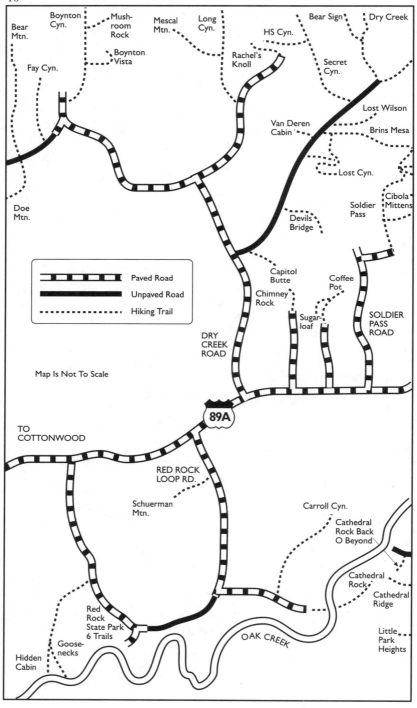

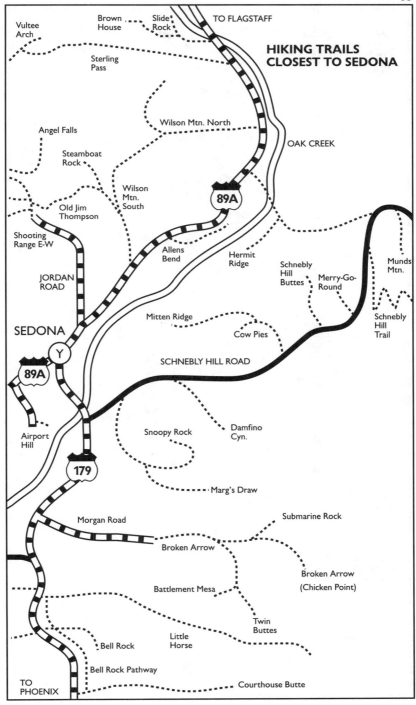

HIKING TRAILS
CLOSEST TO SEDONA

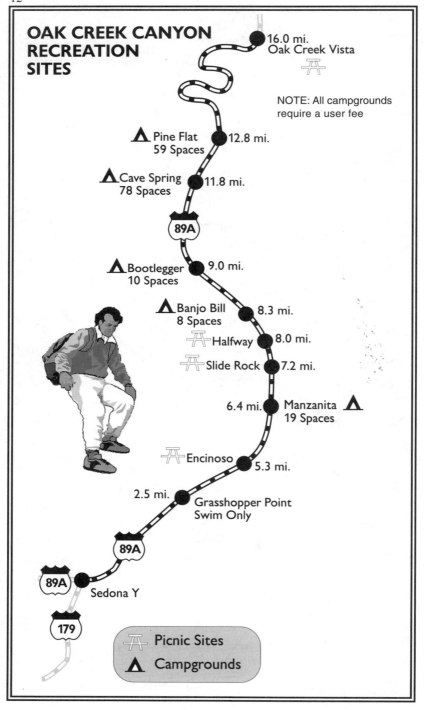

OAK CREEK CANYON RECREATION SITES

16.0 mi.
Oak Creek Vista

NOTE: All campgrounds require a user fee

Pine Flat
59 Spaces — 12.8 mi.

Cave Spring
78 Spaces — 11.8 mi.

89A

Bootlegger
10 Spaces — 9.0 mi.

Banjo Bill
8 Spaces — 8.3 mi.

Halfway — 8.0 mi.

Slide Rock — 7.2 mi.

6.4 mi. — Manzanita
19 Spaces

Encinoso — 5.3 mi.

2.5 mi. — Grasshopper Point
Swim Only

89A

89A
Sedona Y

179

Picnic Sites
Campgrounds

Changes For This Edition

New hikes for this edition:

1. Bell Rock Pathway
2. Broken Arrow
3. Chasm Creek
4. Deer Pass
5. Gaddes Canyon
6. General Crook Trail P 5-7
7. General Crook Trail V 13-14
8. Goosenecks
9. Grief Hill
10. Hidden Cabin
11. Packard Mesa
12. Page Springs
13. Rachel's Knoll
14. Woodchute Mountain

Changes to trails still in the book

Airport Saddle Vortex—New trails established
Cockscomb—New, easier access
Courthouse Butte—Trailhead changed
Hot Loop—New access, first part of trail changed
Jacks Canyon—New trailhead
Old Jim Thompson—New trailhead
Scheurman Mountain—Original trailhead restored
Soldier Pass Arches—New trail alignment
Soldier Pass Trail—New trail alignment

Hikes we removed from the book:

Chinup—Not interesting enough
Devil's Dining Room—Now a waypoint on Broken Arrow Trail
Devil's Kitchen—Now a waypoint on Soldier Pass Trail
Harding Mountain—Difficult to reach
Kushman's Cone—Difficult to reach
Old Highway 79—Access problems
Schnebly To-Marg's Draw—Has become an access trail
Windmill Mountain—Difficult to reach

A. B. YOUNG TRAIL #100

Location Map B5
Munds Park and Wilson Mt. USGS Maps
Coconino Forest Service Map

Driving Distance One Way: 8.8 miles *14.0 km* (Time 20 minutes)
Access Road: All cars, Paved all the way
Hiking Distance One Way: 1.6 miles *2.56 km* (Time 80 minutes)
How Strenuous: Hard
Features: Views

NUTSHELL: This is a steep trail up the west wall of Upper Oak Creek Canyon near Bootlegger Campground, 8.8 miles *14.0 km* north of Sedona.

DIRECTIONS:
From the Sedona Y Go:
  North on Highway 89A for 8.8 miles *14.0 km* (MP 383). Parking is scarce, with no official parking area for the trail. Sometimes you can park in the Bootlegger campground, but don't count on it. Seek a place on the shoulder of the highway.

TRAILHEAD: Walk through Bootlegger Campground, where you will see a set of steps going down to the creek. Go to the creek, which you must wade or try to hop across on boulders. There is a marked trailhead on the other shore, for this is a maintained trail; its sign reads, "A B Young #100."

DESCRIPTION: Once you get across the creek you will see an old road running parallel to the creek. This old road was formerly the main road through Oak Creek Canyon and it is not the hiking trail. Your trail goes uphill.
  The trail is broad at the beginning. It started its life as a cattle trail, but was improved during the 1930s with CCC labor; so it is better engineered than many of the former cattle trails that are now hiking trails. It was widened and the grades were moderated so it is not as vertical as it was originally.
  An interesting thing about the hike is that you pass through three life zones. Down at the creek, there is the lush riparian life zone. As you begin to climb, you get into a high desert life zone. At the top, you are in a pine forest. Once you rise above the trees at creekside, you are on an exposed face with no shade. This can be a very hot hike in the summer though it is in the cool upper canyon.

The hike is steep, so although the trail is a good one, it is a hard climb. You get some fine views as you go. At the top, you will notice that the trail continues. For the purposes of this book, we have ended the trail at the top, but you can continue southwest about 1.25 miles *2.0 km* to the East Pocket fire lookout tower. If this tower is occupied, the ranger may be willing to have you come up and share the tremendous views. This part of the rim is called East Pocket.

From many vantage points both above and below the A. B. Young Trail you can see it zigzagging up the face of the west canyon wall. It makes sharp diagonal turns at the end of each zag and is so obviously a route cut into the face of the canyon wall that some people mistake it for Highway 89A when they see it from a distance.

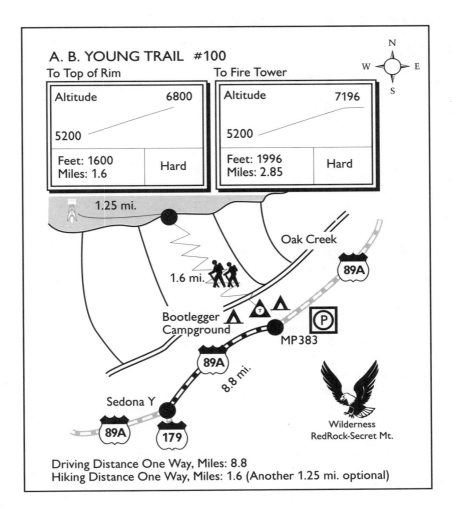

A. B. YOUNG TRAIL #100

To Top of Rim

Altitude	6800
5200	
Feet: 1600 Miles: 1.6	Hard

To Fire Tower

Altitude	7196
5200	
Feet: 1996 Miles: 2.85	Hard

N
W ─ E
S

1.25 mi.

Oak Creek

89A

1.6 mi.

Bootlegger Campground

MP383

P

89A

8.8 mi.

Sedona Y

89A   179

Wilderness RedRock-Secret Mt.

Driving Distance One Way, Miles: 8.8
Hiking Distance One Way, Miles: 1.6 (Another 1.25 mi. optional)

AIRPORT SADDLE LOOP TRAILS

VORTEX

General Information
Location Map E4
Sedona USGS Map
Coconino Forest Service Map

Driving Distance One Way: 1.5 miles *2.4 km* (Time 10 minutes)
Access Road: All cars, Paved all the way
Hiking Distance Complete Loop: 0.7 miles *1.12 km* (Time 45 minutes)
How Strenuous: Easy to Hard
Features: Vortex Spot, Views

NUTSHELL: This is the easiest and most accessible Sedona Vortex spot.

DIRECTIONS:
From the Sedona Y Go:
   Southwest on Highway 89A for 1.0 mile *1.6 km,* to Airport Road. Turn left onto Airport Road and drive uphill half a mile, to the 1.5 miles *2.4 km* point. Here you will see a parking lot to the left big enough for 12 cars.

TRAILHEAD: A cable fence marks the boundary of the parking lot on the east side. There is a gap in the fence, where you enter. Just beyond is a sign post showing a map of the trails, and a flight of natural stairs.

DESCRIPTION: Responding to the high number of visitors who were coming to this spot, the Forest Service has designated several trails and viewpoints to help guide the visitor. You can mix and match.
   Yavapai Route: Take one step through the cable fence and turn left on a narrow footpath. You will move north toward a bald red knob. In 0.1 mile *0.16 km* you will see a path going to your right. This is a connector that can be used as a shortcut.
   Coconino Loop: Keep going ahead from the place where the Yavapai Route meets the connector. As you reach the red knob, the trail turns to the right (E). You make a short climb to a gap and then go down to a red ledge at 0.3 miles *0.48 km.* You will probably find a medicine wheel here, for this is regarded as one of Sedona's vortex spots. You will see a path going off to the north here, but don't take it. It is not one of the loop trails. Instead head back south on a path that you will see well-worn into the redrocks. In 0.4 miles *0.64 km* you will meet the connector trail that you saw on the other side of the ridge. Keep going forward and in a few yards you will come to a place where the Overlook Trail goes uphill.
   Overlook Trail: This trail is very short, taking off from the Coconino

Loop. It makes a steep climb to the top of a red knob, and is worth doing if you have the energy. It climbs 70 feet in 0.05 miles *0.08 km.* From the top, known as Overlook Point, you will enjoy the views. You can climb down the front face of the rock, but it is pretty scary for some people, as you must scale down bare rock. Some people like to go back down the way they came up and take a path that is unnamed, parallel to the Yavapai Route but a few feet higher. It is well worn and takes you back to the top of the "stairs." If you do this, you will have hiked about 0.6 miles *0.96 km.* It's about another 0.1 mile *0.16 km* back down to the parking lot.

If you go down the front of Overlook Point, you come to a point at the top of the "stairs," a natural walkway up from the parking lot. Here you have a chance to take the last of the loop trail, to Courthouse Butte Vista.

Courthouse Butte Vista: This little trail really needs a sign. It is a very short trail to the south, which climbs up about 25 feet in less than 0.1 miles *0.16 km* to a viewpoint.

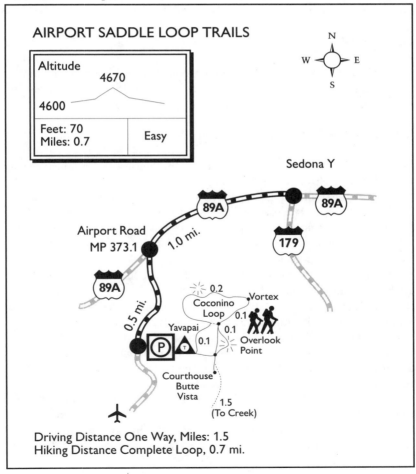

AIRPORT SADDLE LOOP TRAILS

Altitude
4670
4600
Feet: 70
Miles: 0.7
Easy

Sedona Y

Airport Road
MP 373.1
1.0 mi.

Coconino Loop
0.2
Vortex
0.1

Yavapai
0.1
Overlook Point
0.1
0.5 mi.

Courthouse Butte Vista
1.5 (To Creek)

Driving Distance One Way, Miles: 1.5
Hiking Distance Complete Loop, 0.7 mi.

ALLENS BEND #111

General Information
Location Map D5
Munds Park USGS Map
Coconino Forest Service Map

Driving Distance One Way: 2.3 miles *3.7 km* (Time 10 minutes)
Access Road: All cars, Paved all the way
Hiking Distance One Way: 0.5 miles *0.8 km* (Time 30 minutes)
How Strenuous: Easy
Features: Creekside walk, Small Indian ruin

NUTSHELL: This trail, located 2.3 miles *3.7 km* north of Sedona, provides an easy, yet delightful creekside ramble.

DIRECTIONS:
From the Sedona Y Go:
   North on Highway 89A 2.3 miles *3.7 km* (MP 376.5) to the Grasshopper Point Recreation Area. There is fee parking at the lot. A few spaces are available on nearby road shoulders.

TRAILHEAD: Rusty sign at north end of creek-level parking lot.

DESCRIPTION: The parking lot is open only during the summer season, roughly May 1-November 1. If it is open, you can drive down a paved road to a loop parking lot that has capacity for a couple of dozen cars. It also has a toilet. If the gate is closed, you will have to try to find parking off the shoulder of the road as near to the driveway as you can get. There is no longer an upper parking area. It's about 0.33 miles *0.5 km* to walk to the trailhead from the beginning of the driveway.
   The trail does not go down toward Oak Creek. Instead, it hugs the west wall of the canyon. The trail is easy. For about the first 0.15 miles *0.25 km*, it moves along a redrock ledge. In some spots stones have been mortared into place to pave the trail and to make steps. You walk along the base of a 100 foot tall red cliff, which is undercut and is very interesting. The cliff is not nearly so towering as many in the Sedona area, but it has its own charm and is more human sized and intimate. The creek is to your right (E) at all times, anywhere from 20 to 100 yards away.
   At 0.19 miles *0.3 km* you reach a fork. The main trail is the left fork. The right one goes to the creek, to a scenic spot that is well worth a short detour. The trail is shaded all the way and the creek—if by nothing other than its sound—offers refreshment.

Just beyond this fork take a look to your left and you will see what appears to be a small Indian ruin in a shallow cave.

The vegetation along the trail is agreeable, a forest of sycamores, cypress, juniper and shrubbery.

At 0.41 miles *0.66 km* you reach another fork. You are almost at the end of the trail here. To your left you will see an abandoned stone building and some rock walls and a flat area. This is an old campground. The building was a public toilet. If you take the left fork, you will go uphill and join Highway 89A at the **Casner Canyon** trailhead. If you go right, you will end at a nice scenic place on the creek.

We prefer the back country but every trail has its charm and its contribution to make. This is a pretty trail that is accessible any time of year, and is one of the few that goes right along the creek bank.

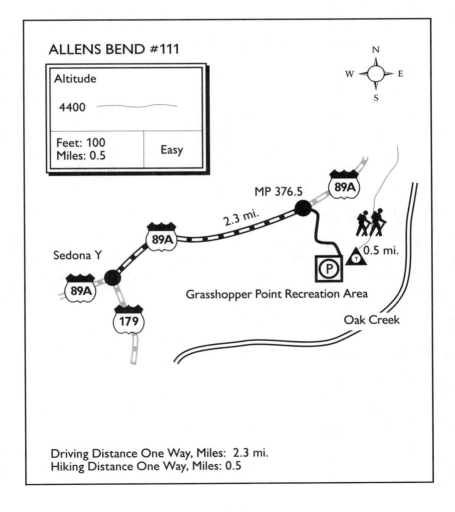

ALLENS BEND #111

Altitude

4400

Feet: 100
Miles: 0.5

Easy

MP 376.5

89A

2.3 mi.

89A

Sedona Y

89A

179

0.5 mi.

P

Grasshopper Point Recreation Area

Oak Creek

Driving Distance One Way, Miles: 2.3 mi.
Hiking Distance One Way, Miles: 0.5

ANGEL FALLS

General Information
Location Map D4
Wilson Mountain USGS Map
Coconino Forest Service Map

Driving Distance One Way: 1.6 miles *2.56 km* (Time 10 minutes)
Access Road: All cars, Last 0.3 miles *0.48 km* fair dirt road
Hiking Distance One Way: 2.5 miles *4.0 km* (Time 90 minutes)
How Strenuous: Moderate—for experienced hikers
Features: Waterfall, Remote area

NUTSHELL: You start this hike on a maintained trail then bushwhack along a streambed to reach a box canyon where two waterfalls pour into a scenic basin (when they are running—which is not often).

DIRECTIONS:
From the Sedona Y Go:
   North on Highway on 89A (toward Flagstaff) for 0.30 miles *0.48 km* to Jordan Road, which is in the middle of uptown Sedona. Turn left (N) and take Jordan Road to its end, at 1.1 miles *1.76 km.* Turn left at the stop sign, onto West Park Ridge, a paved road, which ends at 1.3 miles *2.08 km.* Keep going on the unpaved road. You will reach the old Shooting Range gate at 1.6 miles *2.56 km.* Park outside.

TRAILHEAD: Start this hike at the Brins Mesa Trailhead.

DESCRIPTION: On the other side of the gate you will find a rusty sign reading **Brins Mesa #119**. Follow the Brins Mesa trail. The first 1.25 miles *2.0 km* of the trail follow a closed jeep road, where the way is wide and easy, taking you to the foot of Brins Mesa. The Brins Mesa trail takes off uphill (N) here, looking like a secondary trail.
   Stay at the bottom of the mesa on the old road, going east. It disappears in about 0.2 miles *0.32 km.* From there a footpath is marked by cairns, following along the base of Brins Mesa. The trail goes onto a redrock knoll (good views here). From here you need to follow the cairns carefully as they take you down off the knoll into heavy brush.
   The trail goes into a small steep wash that runs parallel to Mormon Canyon. You must turn right, walking along the bottom, then turn left emerging from the wash to move across country for about 0.1 mile *0.16 km,* where you enter Mormon Canyon, which is much bigger. Turn left.
   From that point, you work your way upstream. There is an irony here: if

there is water in the streambed, you may not be able to hike it. If there is no water, you can hike it, but there will be no water coming over Angel Falls.

Walking the stream requires boulder hopping and you may have to negotiate your way around chokepoints. You will come to a fork at 1.9 miles *3.04 km* where you turn right. Your payoff comes when you get to the end of the canyon. It stops in a spectacular box against the flank of Wilson Mountain, where Angel Falls is located. This place feels truly remote and is fun to explore. You can climb ledges around the box, enjoying fascinating redrock sculptures.

Wilson Mountain is the tallest mountain in the Sedona area with a huge land mass. There are two good hikes to the top of Wilson: **Wilson Mountain North** and **Wilson Mountain South**, but this is one of the rare hikes that takes you to the base of the mountain. The **Old Jim Thompson Road** is another, although it is at a higher level than the Angel Falls hike.

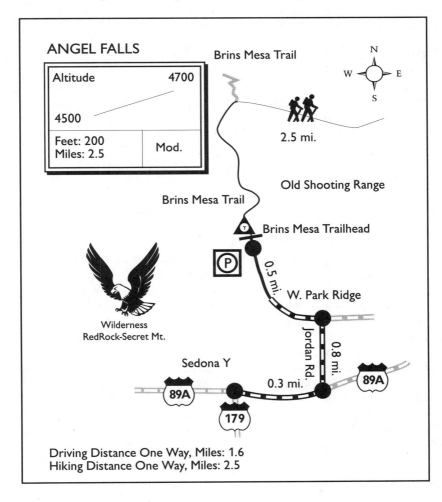

ANGEL FALLS

Altitude	4700
4500	
Feet: 200 Miles: 2.5	Mod.

Brins Mesa Trail

2.5 mi.

Old Shooting Range

Brins Mesa Trail

Brins Mesa Trailhead

W. Park Ridge

0.5 mi.

Jordan Rd.

0.8 mi.

0.3 mi.

Wilderness RedRock-Secret Mt.

Sedona Y

89A

89A

179

Driving Distance One Way, Miles: 1.6
Hiking Distance One Way, Miles: 2.5

APACHE MAID TRAIL #15

General Information
Location Map G6
Casner Butte and Apache Maid USGS Maps
Coconino Forest Service Map

Driving Distance One Way: 17.2 miles *27.6 km* (Time 30 minutes)
Access Road: All cars, Last 0.3 miles *0.48 km* gravel, in good condition
Hiking Distance One Way: 3.75 miles *6.0 km* (Time 2 hours)
How Strenuous: Hard
Features: Views of Wet Beaver Creek Country, Rock Art

NUTSHELL: You hike the Bell Trail for two miles, then branch off to climb Casner Butte, 17 miles south of Sedona.

DIRECTIONS:
From the Sedona Y Go:
   South on Highway 179 (toward Phoenix) for 14.7 Miles *23.5 km* (MP 298.9), to the I-17 intersection. Go straight here rather than getting on I-17. Follow paved road FR 618 until you see a sign for Beaver Creek Ranger Station and trailheads at 16.9 miles *27.1 km*. Turn left. Parking is at 17.2 miles *27.6 km*.

TRAILHEAD: Signed and marked at the parking lot.

DESCRIPTION: From the trailhead, you take the Bell Trail. It goes upcanyon along Wet Beaver Creek, sometimes near it, sometimes away from it, but always following its path. Even when you are not near the creek, you can hear water running, a pleasant sound in desert country. The waterway is lined with tall sycamores and cottonwoods.
   As you look up the canyon, you see a flank of the Mogollon Rim, a giant uplift running across Arizona and New Mexico. The rim marks the southern boundary of the Colorado Plateau. Its base is the northern boundary of the Sonoran Desert; so it is a highly significant land feature.
   The trail is an old jeep road, broad and easy to walk. As you go along the trail, note the canyon walls: they contain the same redrock as in Sedona in the lower layers but the top is covered with a thick cap of lava. If it weren't for that top layer of hard rock, this country would be just as eroded and colorful as Sedona.
   At about 0.6 miles *1.0 km*, look for a large boulder on the left side of the trail. On the side facing away from you is some rock art.
   At the 2.0 mile *3.2 km* point you will hit a fork where the Apache Maid

Trail, #15, branches to the left and climbs Casner Butte. This is a steep climb, rising about 1000 feet in 1.75 miles *2.8 km*. You will be rewarded by good views at the top, but the trail itself is uninteresting. We suggest stopping at the top.

The trail goes on to the head of Wet Beaver Creek, and is the point of departure for the rugged types who hike Wet Beaver Creek from top to bottom, a multi-day trip, definitely not an undertaking for day hikers.

The Apache Maid Trail was built as a cattle trail, not as a scenic path. Sedona ranchers would graze their animals in the lower warm country in winter and then take them to the high county on top of the rim for summer. Apache Maid is the name of a mountain on top of the rim where one of the largest ranches of its day was located. There is a lookout tower on top of Apache Maid that you can drive to by taking the Stoneman Lake Exit off I-17, then FRs 213, 229 and 602.

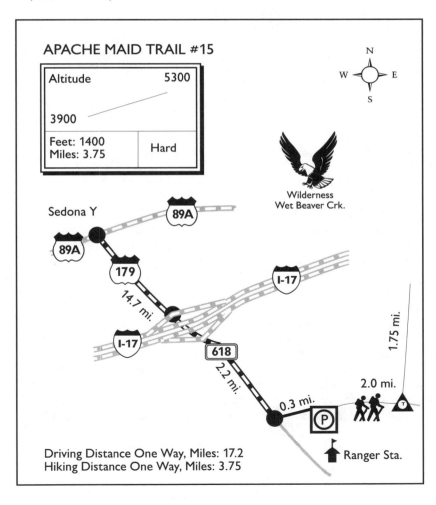

BATTLEMENT MESA

General Information
Location Map E5
Sedona USGS Map
Coconino Forest Service Map

Driving Distance One Way: 2.1 miles *3.36 km* (Time 10 minutes)
Access Road: All cars, Last 0.1 mile *0.16 km* good dirt road
Hiking Distance One Way: 1.5 Miles *2.4 km* (Time 60 minutes)
How Strenuous: Moderate
Features: Redrocks, Views

NUTSHELL: This trail is located in Sedona's "backyard" at the south end of Marg's Draw. It requires a moderate climb among interesting rocks to reach a superb viewpoint.

DIRECTIONS:
From the Sedona Y Go:
    South on Highway 179 (toward Phoenix) for 1.4 miles *2.3 km* (MP 312.1) to Morgan Road in the Broken Arrow Subdivision. Turn left (E) on Morgan Road and follow it to its end, at 2.0 miles *3.2 km*, then go another 0.1 miles *0.16 km* on a dirt road to the parking area.

TRAILHEAD: At the parking lot: use the Broken Arrow Trail.

DESCRIPTION: The Forest Service has changed this area since the previous editions of our book, by creating a nice large parking lot and the **Broken Arrow Trail**. You no longer approach this hike by walking down the road; instead, you begin it by hiking the Broken Arrow Trail.
    From the parking lot, walk southwest across the road and follow the markers and cairns for the Broken Arrow Trail, to the west and south. The trail soon moves over near the redrock cliffs of Battlement Mesa, and the trail then curves around its base.
    At 0.5 miles *0.8 km* you will come down a steep hill to a sinkhole surrounded by a barbed wire fence. The sinkhole is called the Devil's Dining Room and is a local landmark. From this point you continue on the Broken Arrow Trail for another 0.13 miles *0.2 km*. Look carefully, because the trail you are seeking is sometimes camouflaged. You need to leave the Broken Arrow Trail and take a distinct well-worn trail to the right, going uphill, the first such trail you will encounter after leaving Devil's Dining Room. Once you locate the trail you will have no trouble following it because it is distinct. The trail will take you up a canyon toward a saddle between

Battlement Mesa and Twin Buttes, winding its way through a pleasant forest. On the route you will enjoy looking from numerous viewpoints.

Climb the trail to the saddle, where you will have great views to the north toward Sedona and to the southwest toward Poco Diablo. The **Twin Buttes Trail** takes off to the left from the saddle, but you want to go up to the right, toward the "castle" rock formation on top of Battlement Mesa, staying on the main trail.

Battlement Mesa is one of those sites that has a deceptive appearance. From the ground you have the impression that it is flat and bare on top and that you would be able to walk around it as if you were on a football field. Not so. The top is rugged and broken by fissures and declivities, but reaching the tower on top of Battlement Mesa is pretty easy. You will really enjoy the views from its base.

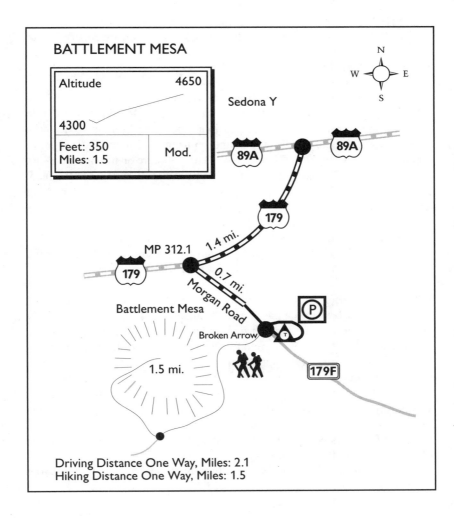

BATTLEMENT MESA

Altitude	4650
4300	
Feet: 350 Miles: 1.5	Mod.

Sedona Y

89A   89A

179

1.4 mi.

MP 312.1

179

0.7 mi.

Morgan Road

Battlement Mesa

Broken Arrow

1.5 mi.

179F

Driving Distance One Way, Miles: 2.1
Hiking Distance One Way, Miles: 1.5

BEAR MOUNTAIN #54

General Information
Location Map C2
Wilson Mountain USGS Map
Coconino Forest Service Map

Driving Distance One Way: 8.9 miles *14.3 km* (Time 20 minutes)
Access Road: All cars, Last 1.2 miles *2.0 km* dirt, in good condition
Hiking Distance One Way: 2.2 miles *3.5 km* (Time 90 minutes)
How Strenuous: Hard, Very steep
Features: View

NUTSHELL: Climbing this prominent mountain 8.9 miles *14.3 km* northwest of Sedona is a challenge, but the views from the top are superb.

DIRECTIONS:
From the Sedona Y Go:
    Southwest on Highway 89A (toward Cottonwood) for 3.2 miles *5.2 km* (MP 371) to Dry Creek Road. Go right on Dry Creek Road to the 6.1 mile *9.8 km* point, where Dry Creek Road joins the Long Canyon Road, both paved. Turn left here, on FR 152C, and go to the 7.7 mile *12.4 km point*, where it joins the Boynton Canyon Road. Turn left here on the Boynton Pass Road, FR 152C. The paving soon ends, to be replaced by a good dirt road. Stop at the 8.9 mile *14.3 km* point, just before a cattle guard. The parking area is on the right.

TRAILHEAD: The Bear Mt. Trail shares its parking space with the **Doe Mt. Trail**, and you will see signs for both trails there. Crawl through the "window frame" in the fence to begin the Bear Mt. Trail, #54.

DESCRIPTION: The first 0.25 miles *0.4 km* of the hike are across what seems to be flat land to the base of the mountain. In fact, the land is badly eroded and there are many gulches. You have to cross three of them. The trail is marked by cairns. Be sure to follow them, because this is cattle country, and wherever the cattle wander in this dry soil they leave what appears to be a trail but is really an aimless meander.
    Bear Mountain will surprise you. As you climb, you keep thinking that you have reached the top. Actually, you will encounter five steppes or terraces. You are climbing steeply almost all the way. The good news is that the beautiful views begin with the first steppe. The higher you go, the more of a panorama you get and the better the views are.
    At 2.2 miles *3.5 km*, you reach the base of steppe number five, the true

top. It's a good stopping place. We quit here, but the trail goes on, making what appears to be a hard climb over slickrock.

The bulk of the mountain is on steppe four. The surface here is eroded along crossbedding lines and a tiny amount of soil has formed in the cracks. Sparse vegetation grows in this soil, making the grasses and other plants form lines and rows that match the seams in the stone. In the right light, this causes fascinating patterns.

The top could well be called *Bare* Mountain rather than Bear Mountain, for there is precious little growing on it.

Friends tell us that from **Capitol Butte** you are supposed to be able to see a bear in the contours of the top of Bear Mountain. We have tried this from several viewpoints but were never able to see the bear. That's the way it is with these figures: sometimes you can see them and sometimes you can't, no matter how hard you try. According to our sources, the bear is lying down and it is his round ears that really make the formation.

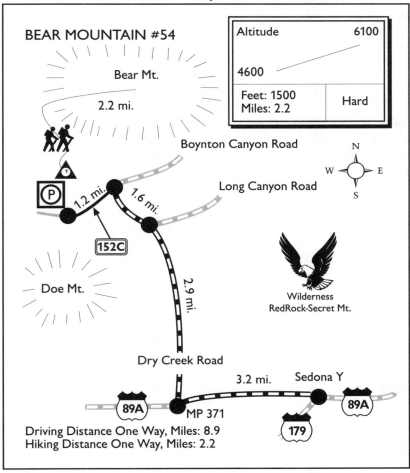

BEAR MOUNTAIN #54

Bear Mt.
2.2 mi.

Altitude	6100
4600	
Feet: 1500 Miles: 2.2	Hard

Boynton Canyon Road

Long Canyon Road

N
W — E
S

P

1.2 mi.   1.6 mi.

152C

Doe Mt.

2.9 mi.

Wilderness
RedRock-Secret Mt.

Dry Creek Road

3.2 mi.   Sedona Y

89A   MP 371   179   89A

Driving Distance One Way, Miles: 8.9
Hiking Distance One Way, Miles: 2.2

BEAR SIGN TRAIL #59

General Information
Location Map C4
Loy Butte and Wilson Mountain USGS Maps
Coconino Forest Service Map

Driving Distance One Way: 9.6 miles *15.4 km* (Time 45 minutes)
Access Road: Last 4.4 miles *7.0 km* bumpy unpaved road
Hiking Distance One Way: 3.25 miles *5.2 km* (Time 90 minutes)
How Strenuous: Moderate
Features: Secluded canyon, Beautiful redrocks

NUTSHELL: Located 9.6 miles *15.4 km* north of Sedona, this is a wilderness hike that follows a streambed to the base of the Mogollon Rim.

DIRECTIONS:
From the Sedona Y Go:
　　Southwest on Highway 89A (toward Cottonwood) for 3.2 miles *5.2 km* (MP 371) to Dry Creek Road. Turn right on Dry Creek Road and proceed to the 5.2 mile *8.4 km* point. Turn right on FR 152, the Vultee Arch Road, and follow it to the 9.6 mile *15.4 km* point. Here there is a parking loop, with the **Vultee Arch** Trailhead at the tip. Curve around and head back, and you will see the parking for the Bear Sign and **Dry Creek** trails to your right, just a few yards beyond the Vultee parking area.

TRAILHEAD: At the parking area. There is a rusty sign: Dry Creek #52.

DESCRIPTION: You will walk across a little arroyo and around the toe of a hill for about 0.1 miles *0.16 km*, where you will encounter Dry Creek. At the entry point, the canyon cut by Dry Creek is rather shallow and wide. Turn right (N) and follow the trail up the creek—which usually *is* dry—northerly. If any appreciable amount of water is running in the creek, you might want to postpone this hike until the creek is dry, for the trail crosses the creek at least a dozen times.

　　As you walk, the trail climbs, but this is gradual and you are barely conscious of it.

　　At 0.63 miles *1.0 km*, you reach a point where the creek forks at a reef. The left-hand channel is the Bear Sign Trail, and the right fork is the **Dry Creek Trail**. There is a rusty sign in the left channel marked "Bear Sign #59."

　　From this point, the canyon deepens and you are treated to the sight of giant redrock buttes on both sides of the creek. As you proceed, you will notice a change in the flora, as the rise in altitude changes the life zones.

The trail ends where it intersects a channel running east and west. We are informed that this channel can be hiked. To the east, it would connect with Dry Creek Trail. Maps indicate that you could do a loop, going up the Bear Sign Trail and coming back via the Dry Creek Pack Trail, but we have not tried this.

Both the Bear Sign Trail and its neighboring Dry Creek Trail take you far away from habitation, and are nice if you want to get away into pristine country. Both trails head toward the Mogollon Rim and bump right against the base of it. The beauty of such trails is that even though they take you into wild and primitive country they are not dangerous. Stay in the canyons that define these trails and you won't get lost.

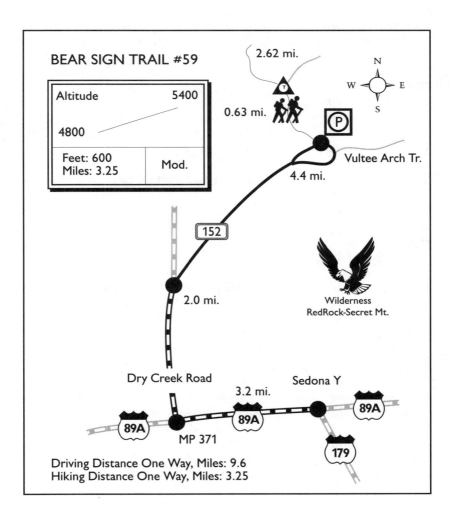

BEAR SIGN TRAIL #59

Altitude	5400
4800	
Feet: 600 Miles: 3.25	Mod.

2.62 mi.

0.63 mi.

4.4 mi.

Vultee Arch Tr.

152

2.0 mi.

Wilderness
RedRock-Secret Mt.

Dry Creek Road

Sedona Y

3.2 mi.

89A

89A

89A

MP 371

179

Driving Distance One Way, Miles: 9.6
Hiking Distance One Way, Miles: 3.25

BEAVERHEAD

General Information
Location Map G5
Casner Butte and Lake Montezuma USGS Maps
Coconino Forest Service Map

Driving Distance One Way: 11.2 miles *18.0 km* (Time 20 minutes)
Access Road: All paved
Hiking Distance One Way: 1.1 miles *1.8 km* (Time 45 minutes)
How Strenuous: Moderate
Features: Historic road, Views

NUTSHELL: Located 11.2 miles *18.0 km* south of Sedona, this hike climbs 1,000 feet to the top of the Mogollon Rim along an ancient Hopi trail that was converted into a wagon road in the 1870s.

DIRECTIONS:
From the Sedona Y Go:
    South on Highway 179 (toward Phoenix) for a distance of 11.2 miles *18.0 km* (MP 302.2) where you will see a gravel driveway to your left. Turn in on it, go left and park by the gate in the barbed wire fence.

TRAILHEAD: You will follow the old road from the gate.

DESCRIPTION: From the unlocked gate where you parked, walk up the dirt road a distance of 0.1 miles *0.16 km*. There you will see a road to your right that has been blocked by a dirt berm. Walk over the berm and you will pick up the old road, which you follow uphill.
    At the start of the hike, take a moment to look at your objective. High above, you will see a ridge with a long section of jagged cliffs. This is not an isolated ridge but a part of the Mogollon Rim. You are about to walk a short stretch of The Palatkwapi Trail, used by the Hopi Indians for more than 1,200 years. The trail starts at the Hopi mesas and ends at Camp Verde (with a branch to Jerome). The challenge to the pathfinders as they came off the high country was to find a gentle way down from the top of the Mogollon Rim to the Verde Valley. The route went from the Hopi mesas via Sunset Crossing (Winslow), Chavez Pass, Stoneman Lake, and Rattlesnake Canyon to the top of the Rim. As you walk along this trail, you can admire the choice that the ancients made. Except for being rocky, the route is excellent.
    Spanish explorers followed the trail in the late 1500s, then army scouts in the 1860s and then, when the army undertook to subdue hostile Indians, the old trail was improved as a wagon road linking Fort Apache and Camp

Verde. Once established by the military, private operators became interested in the road and ran a stage line over it between 1876-1882. Until the Schnebly Hill Road was built in Sedona in 1902, the Beaverhead Road was the only road Sedona residents had to get to Flagstaff in a wagon.

The road is easy to follow and the area has a pleasant feel. You soon climb high enough to get good views of the scenic surrounding country. At 0.75 miles *1.2 km* you will reach the beginning of an incredibly rocky passage. Many a wagon wheel must have broken here.

At 0.85 miles *1.4 km* you will reach the first top. In this area the old road looks almost like a trench, as it is deeply lined by the stones that were rolled to the sides. At 1.1 miles *1.8 km* you will be at the true top, where there are great views. The road veers away from the cliffs and continues its long journey northward (it is 145 miles long) from here over drab country.

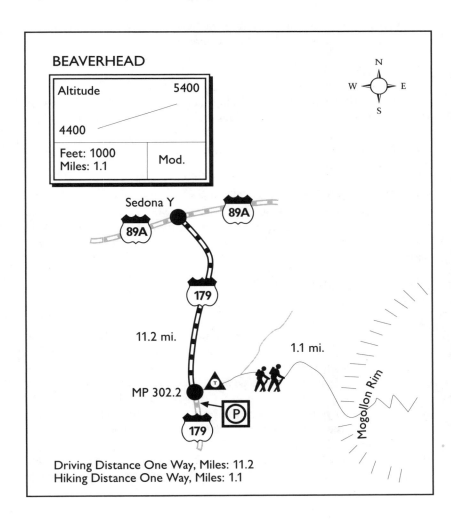

BELL ROCK

VORTEX

General Information
Location Map F5
Sedona USGS Map
Coconino Forest Service Map

Driving Distance One Way: 5.2 miles *8.4 km* (Time 15 minutes)
Access Road: All cars, All paved
Hiking Distance One Way: 1.0 mile *1.6 km* (Time 45 minutes)
How Strenuous: Moderate
Features: Vortex Spot, Views

NUTSHELL: This landmark south of Sedona is one of the famed Vortex Spots. There is no defined trail. You explore as you wish.

DIRECTIONS:
From the Sedona Y Go:
    South on Highway 179 (toward Phoenix) a distance of 5.2 miles *8.4 km* (MP 308.4). You will see parking areas on the opposite side of the road.

TRAILHEAD: Not a marked trail, but hundreds of visitors have worn an easy-to-see path up to the rock. At the rock there are some cairns.

DESCRIPTION: As you near the rock, there are many trails. Don't be concerned about these. Just pick out one that strikes your fancy. All of them go to Bell Rock. Once you are there, you may or may not see cairns marking trails going up onto the rock. If you see none, just pick a likely access and ascend. You are on your own.
    You probably will encounter medicine wheels or other outlines on the rock made by New Agers. We know of no particular spot that is regarded as *the* vortex spot on Bell Rock. Different people get different responses. Other vortex spots covered in this book are shown in the Index, pages 252-254.
    The redrock around Sedona was laid down in layers and has weathered in such a way that it has created ledges that are almost like stairsteps. This is especially true on Bell Rock, with its conical slopes. What you will do on this hike is look for likely ways to go up. Even the timid hiker should be able to get quite close to the top in comfort. Going to the absolute top is dangerous. As you wind your way around the rock, you are treated to great views.
    The early settlers in the area were hard pressed to come up with names for all of the rock formations around Sedona, and there is controversy over the correct names for some of them. Nobody ever disagreed about Bell Rock, however. It *looks* like a bell. This is a very popular place because it is

so well known and easy to reach, and is on the road to Phoenix. So, you won't have a wilderness experience here, but it is a lot of fun, and you may even get a significant experience from the vortex power.

Bell Rock is often a busy site and it doesn't look very big. For those who like solitary places, its aspect is off-putting when you see people of all stripes, including whining infants and disrespectful teenagers assaying its slopes. A funny thing happens when you get to the rock, however. It suddenly seems much bigger than it looked from afar. You can pick out a way that no one else is using and before you know it, you are having an enjoyable peaceful experience in spite of the busy atmosphere. Give it a try in spite of the crowds.

An alternative means of making this hike is to drive 6.2 miles *9.92 km* south from the Y and turn left at the entrance to the Bell Rock Pathway, a new trail created in 1997. You then hike north to Bell Rock, about 0.75 miles *1.2 km.*

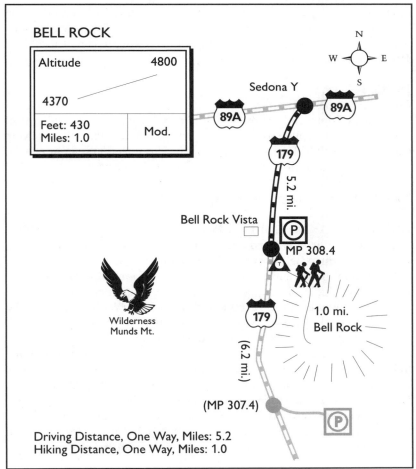

BELL ROCK

Altitude	4800
4370	
Feet: 430 Miles: 1.0	Mod.

N
W — E
S

Sedona Y

89A   89A

179

5.2 mi.

Bell Rock Vista

P

MP 308.4

Wilderness Munds Mt.

179

1.0 mi.
Bell Rock

(6.2 mi.)

(MP 307.4)

P

Driving Distance, One Way, Miles: 5.2
Hiking Distance, One Way, Miles: 1.0

BELL ROCK PATHWAY

General Information
Location Map F5
Sedona USGS Map
Coconino Forest Service Map

Driving Distance One Way: 6.2 miles *9.92 km* (Time 20 minutes)
Access Road: All cars, All paved
Hiking Distance, One Way: 3.5 miles *5.6 km* (Time 2.0 hours)
How Strenuous: Moderate
Features: Views

NUTSHELL: This trail, new in 1997, was designed to connect the Village of Oak Creek with the trail system around Sedona. It starts just north of the Village of Oak Creek and winds its way north parallel to Highway 179, passing **Courthouse Rock** and **Bell Rock** along the way, to end at the **Little Horse** trailhead.

DIRECTIONS:
From the Sedona Y Go:
   South on Highway 179 (toward Phoenix) for a distance of 6.2 miles *9.92 km* (MP 307.4) to a place south of Bell Rock, just short of the Village of Oak Creek, where you will see a road to your left. This road is the entrance to the parking lot for the Bell Rock Pathway. Turn into it and park.

TRAILHEAD: At the parking lot. It is signed.

DESCRIPTION: The Bell Rock Pathway is a new trail for this edition, constructed in 1996-1997, and it is as wide as a road and makes for easy hiking. It runs north to Bell Rock parallel to Highway 179. At a point 0.6 miles *0.96 km* from the beginning, you will be almost to the base of Bell Rock. Here you will find a distinct but much narrower trail running to your right, toward Courthouse Butte. Take the fork to the left (W) here, circling the base of Bell Rock. You will pass very close to Bell Rock, along its shoulder, and will enjoy viewing the famous landmark.
   A short distance beyond Bell Rock you enter the most scenic part of the trail, where you swing away from the highway onto some attractive redrock ledges. The views open up here and you will enjoy looking at Bell Rock, Courthouse Rock, and to the west, Little Park Heights.
   Soon the trail moves over close to the road again, and continues north, toward Twin Buttes. The famous Chapel of the Holy Cross is located on the south face of Twin Buttes, and you can see it as you approach.

The trail ends at the new trailhead for the Little Horse trail.

This is a nice trail and should serve its purpose. It has the earmarks of a trail that will prove to be very popular, so if you want a solitary hiking experience in the wilderness, look elsewhere. We were a bit bothered by its proximity to the busy (and noisy) Highway 179, but the convenience and easy approach made the hike worthwhile.

This would be a good hike after a storm, when the roads into the back country are too wet to travel.

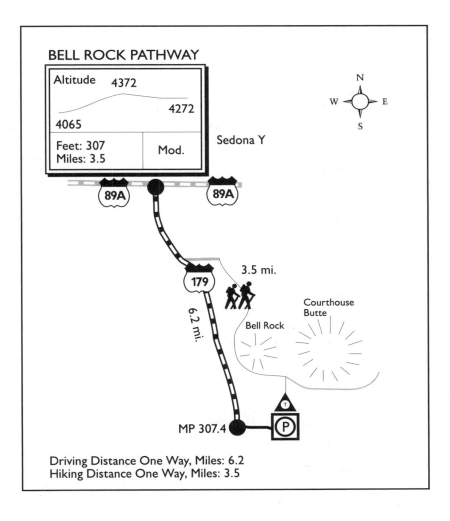

BELL TRAIL #13—WEIR TRAIL #85

General Information
Location Map G6
Apache Maid and Casner Butte USGS Maps
Coconino Forest Service Map

Driving Distance One Way: 17.2 miles *27.6 km* (Time 30 minutes)
Access Road: All cars, Last 0.3 miles *0.48 km* gravel, in good condition
Hiking Distance One Way: Bell 4.0 miles *6.4 km* (Time 2 hours), Weir
2.5 miles *4.0 km* (1.25 hours)
How Strenuous: Moderate
Features: Permanent Stream, Rock Art

NUTSHELL: These trails follow the course of Wet Beaver Creek, 17.2
miles *27.6 km* southwest of Sedona. The trails are broad and easy, with many
attractions.

DIRECTIONS:
From the Sedona Y Go:
   South on Highway 179 (toward Phoenix) for 14.7 Miles *23.5 km* (MP
298.9), to the I-17 intersection. Go straight here rather than getting on I-17.
Follow paved road FR 618 until you see a sign for Beaver Creek Ranger
Station and trailheads at 16.9 miles *27.1 km*. Turn left. Parking is at 17.2
miles *27.6 km*.

TRAILHEAD: Start on the Bell Trail, which is well marked with signs at
the parking area.

DESCRIPTION: From the trailhead, the Bell Trail goes up the canyon
along Wet Beaver Creek. The trail is broad and easy to walk. It was built by
cattle rancher Earl Bell in 1932, as a means for taking his cattle to the top of
the Mogollon Rim in the spring. Earl Bell was a wealthy Easterner who fell
in love with the Beaver Creek area when he was a guest at one of the dude
ranches that flourished there from the 1920s through the 1940s. He bought
a ranch and got into the cattle business.
   At about 0.6 miles *1.0 km*, look for a large boulder on the left side of the
trail. On the side that faces away from you are a number of interesting petroglyphs.
   At 1.5 miles *2.4 km* you will find the **Casner Mt. South Trail** to your
left.
   At the 2.0 mile *3.2 km* point you will hit a fork where the **Apache Maid
Trail, #15** branches to the left and climbs Casner Butte.

Just beyond this fork you will find a signboard containing a map and discussion of the geology, plant and animal life of the area. The life is richer than you might think. Just beyond the billboard is a trail going off to the right, down to the water. This is the **Weir Trail.** It is only 0.5 miles *0.8 km* long and goes down to an attractive pond formed by the weir. A weir is a low dam built to check the flow of water. Water gaging equipment is located here to measure runoff. There is an interesting cable car up the stream a short distance from the weir, and many blackberry bushes.

Bell Crossing is 2.0 miles *3.2 km* up the canyon from the signboard. There the trail narrows and crosses the creek. Along the creekside from the crossing are delightful places for a picnic. We recommend that you go upstream about 100 yards to check out a large pool known as The Crack.

From the crossing, the trail goes 2.5 miles *4.0 km* on up to the top of The Rim. The full hike is scenic, but is much longer and harder. We recommend stopping at the crossing for most day hikers.

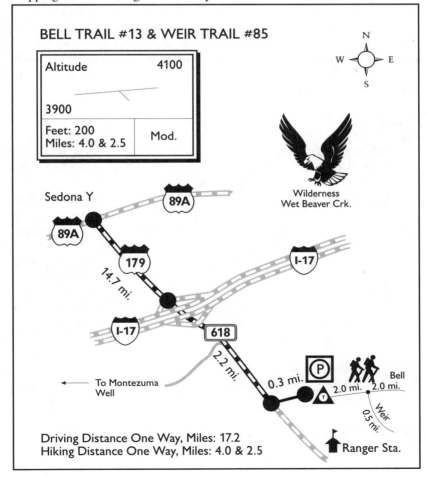

BELL TRAIL #13 & WEIR TRAIL #85

Altitude	4100
3900	
Feet: 200 Miles: 4.0 & 2.5	Mod.

N
W ← → E
S

Wilderness
Wet Beaver Crk.

Sedona Y

89A

89A

179

I-17

14.7 mi.

I-17

618

2.2 mi.

To Montezuma
Well

0.3 mi.

P

2.0 mi. 2.0 mi.

Bell

Weir
0.5 mi.

Driving Distance One Way, Miles: 17.2
Hiking Distance One Way, Miles: 4.0 & 2.5

Ranger Sta.

BLACK MT. & MYSTERY HOUSE

General Information
Location Map C1
Clarkdale, Loy Butte,
Page Springs and Sycamore Basin USGS Maps
Coconino Forest Service Map

Driving Distance One Way: (1) 27.6 mi. *44.2 km* (2) 30.3 mi. *48.5 km*
(Time 60-75 minutes)
Access Road: High clearance vehicles, Last 1.4-4.1 miles *2.2-6.6 km* awful
Hiking Distance One Way: (1) 2.25 mi. *3.6 km* (2) 0.4 miles *0.65 km*
(Time 90 min., 20 min.)
How Strenuous: Moderate for both hikes
Features: Tall mountain, Strange abandoned house in remote area, Views

NUTSHELL: Two hikes here: (1) Black Mountain—You hike a road to the top of Black Mountain, one of the highest points south of Sedona (2) Black Mountain Mystery House—You hike to the ruins of an old house on the northeast side of Black Mountain, to enjoy tremendous views.

DIRECTIONS:
From the Sedona Y Go:

Southwest on Highway 89A (toward Cottonwood) a distance of 16.0 miles *25.6 km* (MP 358) to FR 761, the unpaved Bill Gray Road. Turn right and take FR 761 to the 26.2 miles *42 km* point (passing two forks of the Buckboard Road, FR 258A, on the way) where you will see FR 761A to your left. Take FR 761A. Up to this point, the road has been good, but now it gets quite rough. A high clearance vehicle with sturdy tires is recommended, and only when the road is dry. Go under the power line and turn right. At 27.6 miles *44.2 km*, you reach a Y fork, with FR 761A going right and FR 761C going left. For hike (1) park off the road here and hike FR 761C to the top of Black Mountain. For hike (2) drive FR 761A, to the right. This is a very rough but spectacular road. At the 30.3 mile *48.5 km* point you will reach a locked gate made of steel pipe. There is room for one car to park off the road by the gate.

TRAILHEAD: No marked trails. For hike (1) Black Mountain, you hike FR 761C to the top of the mountain. For hike (2) Black Mountain Mystery House, you hike the old road from the gate up to the house and quarry.

DESCRIPTION: (1) **Black Mountain.** The road up Black Mountain is steep and you will pass some old stone quarries. As you rise higher and higher, views unfold. You reach the top in 1.25 miles *2.0 km.* We hiked along to the 2.0 miles *3.2 km* point, then picked our way north to the edge of the mountain so that we could see the views into Sycamore Canyon.

(2) **Black Mountain Mystery House.** From the parking place you will hike up a steep old road, passing little quarries along the way. When you get to the house site, you will find the ruins of a house, which we estimate was built in the late 40s-early 50s. It was intact when we visited it in February 1996, but had collapsed when we saw it again in April 1997. Even though you can't enjoy exploring the old house anymore, you can enjoy its setting. It is situated uniquely, with a million dollar view.

From the flagstone rubble that is seen all around the premises, it seems that whoever built the house operated a flagstone quarry here—a sizable quarry operation. You can see where almost a whole cliff face was cut away if you walk the road to its end. There was evidence of some kind of renewed activity here on our April 1997 visit.

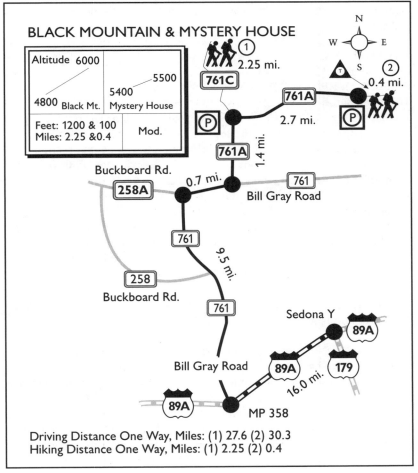

BLODGETT BASIN

General Information
Location Map G6
Walker Mtn. USGS Map
Coconino Forest Service Map

Driving Distance One Way: 28.7 miles *46 km* (Time 1 hour)
Access Road: All cars, Last 14.0 miles *22.4 km* good dirt road
Hiking Distance One Way: 2.0 miles *3.2 km* (Time 1.5 hours)
How Strenuous: Hard
Features: Views

NUTSHELL: This trail runs from a point high on the Mogollon Rim to the bottom of the chasm of West Clear Creek, an 1,800 foot drop in 2.0 miles *3.2 km.*

DIRECTIONS:
From the Sedona Y Go:
    South on Highway 179 (toward Phoenix) for 14.7 miles *23.5 km*, to the I-17 Interchange. Instead of going onto I-17, go underneath it onto the paved road. At 15.2 miles *24.3 km*, you will come to a junction. The right fork goes to Montezuma Castle. Take the left fork (FR 618), toward Beaver Creek Ranger Station. It is paved for a couple of miles. Several minor roads branch off FR 618, but it is always obvious that it is the main one. Follow FR 618 to the 24.5 mile *39.2 km* point, where you will see a dirt road branching left, marked "Cedar Flat." Take this left road, and you will soon see a sign identifying it as FR 214, which takes you to the top of the Mogollon Rim, about a 2,000 foot climb. There are some great views along the way. At the 28.7 mile point *46 km*, high up on the road, you will see the sign for the Blodgett Basin Trail to your right through a fence with tall gate posts. Pull in and park by a number of circular rusty water troughs.

TRAILHEAD: You will see cairns marking the trail as it goes downhill from the parking area.

DESCRIPTION: There is very little shade on this trail and you will be dangerously exposed to the sun. It can get very hot. We recommend that you do not even try this hike in full summer. If you do, please be prepared with lots of water, hats, sunscreen, etc.
    From the place where you park, you can see the huge chasm of West Clear Creek before you. You will wind around the sides of several hills as you work your way down to the bottom, enjoying good views, particularly

of Wingfield Mesa and later the trees lining the bottom of West Clear Creek Canyon. Though the gorge of West Clear Creek is clearly before you, you never come to a lip from where you can look directly down into the main canyon; instead, you will come into it by means of a side canyon.

At the end of the trail, you will intersect the **West Clear Creek Trail #17** (also known as the Bull Pen Trail), on a shelf some distance from the creek. It's about 0.20 miles *0.32 km* down to the water; turn right and you will come to the parking area at the Bull Pen trailhead, from where it's a short hop to the creek.

We definitely recommend using two cars on this hike. Park the first car in the West Clear Creek Campground at the West Clear Creek #17 trailhead. You reach this by following FR 618 south 2.0 miles *3.2 km* from its intersection with FR 214, then turning left (E) on FR 215 and going 3.0 miles *4.8 km* to the campground. Take the second car to the top as described herein.

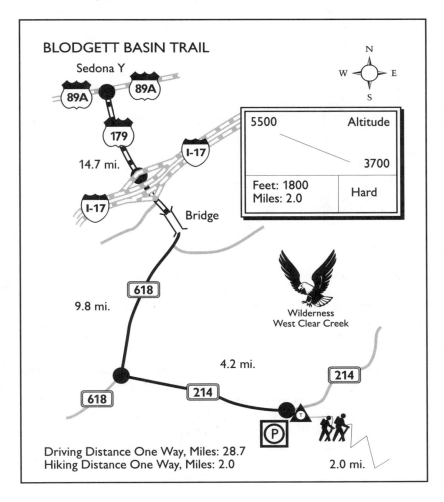

BLODGETT BASIN TRAIL

Sedona Y

89A

89A

179

14.7 mi.

I-17

I-17

Bridge

5500	Altitude
	3700
Feet: 1800 Miles: 2.0	Hard

618

9.8 mi.

Wilderness
West Clear Creek

4.2 mi.

214

618

214

P

2.0 mi.

Driving Distance One Way, Miles: 28.7
Hiking Distance One Way, Miles: 2.0

BOYNTON CANYON #47

VORTEX

General Information
Location Map C3
Wilson Mountain USGS Map
Coconino Forest Service Map

Driving Distance One Way: 8.0 miles *13 km* (Time 20 minutes)
Access Road: All cars, All paved
Hiking Distance One Way: 3.25 miles *5.2 km* (Time 90 minutes)
How Strenuous: Moderate
Features: Indian Ruins, Vortex

NUTSHELL: This wonderful canyon is located just 8.0 miles *13 km* north-west of uptown Sedona, and is easily reached by paved roads. Its beauty is unsurpassed. **A personal favorite.**

DIRECTIONS:
From the Sedona Y Go:
 Southwest on Highway 89A (toward Cottonwood) a distance of 3.2 miles *5.12 km* (MP 371), to Dry Creek Road, where you take a right turn onto Dry Creek Road. Follow it to the 6.1 mile *10.0 km* point, where it joins Long Canyon Road. Take a left here, staying on FR 152C. At the 7.7 mile *12.4 km* point, you reach another junction. Go right. At 8.0 miles *13 km*, just before the gatehouse to the Enchantment Resort, you will see a parking area to the right. Park there. There is also a small parking area on the left side of the road.

TRAILHEAD: It is posted at the parking area.

DESCRIPTION: For the first mile this trail overlooks the Enchantment Resort. The trail winds along the east face of the canyon, hugging the towering ruin-dotted red cliffs so as to skirt the resort property. At the 0.7 mile *1.12 km* point, just as you begin to head downhill toward the fence that marks the end of the Enchantment property, you will see a well worn but unmarked path going off at a sharp angle to your right. This leads uphill to Indian ruins in two caves in an alcove and is well worth a detour. It takes a bit of scrambling and climbing to get up to the ruins, but even if you don't climb to them, it is worth going over to the face of the cliff on which they are located for a look. This is a detour of about 0.25 miles *0.4 km* each way.
 From the Enchantment fence, the trail turns away from the cliffs and follows along the canyon floor. It is much wider and easier to walk from this point on.

At 1.0 miles *1.6 km* you will cross a shallow wash, beyond which the vegetation changes. As you go up canyon, the altitude increases and it is cooler.

At about 3.0 miles *4.8 km*, the trail pinches down suddenly as the canyon narrows. This is a good stopping place. However, you can bushwhack another 0.25 mile *0.4 km* and see the head of Boynton, which is a box canyon against the side of Secret Mountain. The streambed forks here. Take the right fork and you will soon see a primitive path, which is almost a tunnel through the lush growth at stream level. You will emerge into the box, ringed with towering cliffs.

Boynton Canyon is one of the Sedona Vortex spots. We have been to all of them, and this is the only one that really gives us any special feeling. The red cliffs here are really spectacular. We love them at about 4:00 p.m. on a winter's day. There is something about the angle and clarity of the light resonating on the beautiful red rocks that is really special then.

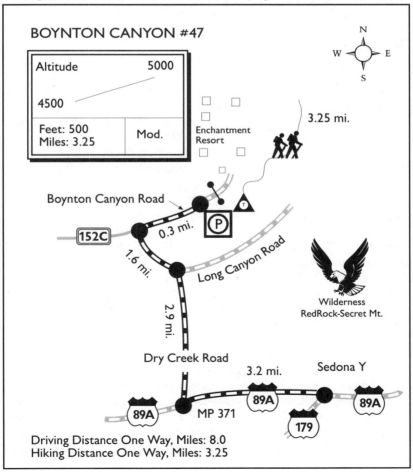

BOYNTON CANYON #47

Altitude	5000
4500	
Feet: 500 Miles: 3.25	Mod.

Enchantment Resort

3.25 mi.

Boynton Canyon Road

152C

0.3 mi.

1.6 mi.

Long Canyon Road

2.9 mi.

Wilderness RedRock-Secret Mt.

Dry Creek Road

3.2 mi.

Sedona Y

89A   MP 371   89A   89A

179

Driving Distance One Way, Miles: 8.0
Hiking Distance One Way, Miles: 3.25

BOYNTON CYN. VISTA TRAIL

VORTEX

General Information
Location Map C3
Wilson Mountain USGS Map
Coconino Forest Service Map

Driving Distance One Way: 8.0 miles *13 km* (Time 20 minutes)
Access Road: All cars, All paved
Hiking Distance One Way: 0.33 miles *0.528 km* (Time 30 minutes)
How Strenuous: Moderate
Features: Vortex site, Views of Boynton Canyon

NUTSHELL: This wonderful canyon is located just 8.0 miles *13 km* north-west of uptown Sedona, and is easily reached by paved roads.

DIRECTIONS:
From the Sedona Y Go:
    Southwest on Highway 89A (toward Cottonwood) a distance of 3.2 miles *5.12 km* (MP 371), to Dry Creek Road, where you take a right turn onto Dry Creek Road. Follow it to the 6.1 mile *10.0 km* point, where it joins Long Canyon Road. Take a left here, staying on FR 152C. At the 7.7 mile *12.4 km* point, you reach another junction. Go right. At 8.0 miles *13 km*, just before the gatehouse to the Enchantment Resort, you will see a parking area to the right. Park there. There is also a small parking area on the left side of the road.

TRAILHEAD: It is posted at the parking area.

DESCRIPTION: We had a hike in the earlier editions of the book called Boynton Spires. Since the book was printed, the Forest Service has laid out the Vista Trail. The **Boynton Canyon Trail** and the Boynton Canyon Vista trail share a common trailhead. Posts painted with diamond markers indicate the trails. The Boynton Canyon Trail is designated by a gray diamond, while the Vista Trail has a green diamond.
    At the trailhead as you begin this hike, look up and to your right and you will see your destination, which is a large redrock formation with two spires that stick up from it. Between the spires is a saddle or gap. You will hike around to the back side of this formation, and up to the saddle.
    As you start the hike, both trails are together. You walk uphill a short distance, then veer off to the right on the Vista Trail, which climbs steadily as it goes to the top of the toe of the rock formation. It then winds around to the back side. On the back it is somewhat difficult to pick out the correct

trail, as there are several maverick trails that meander through the area. Usually these side trails are blocked with a line of stones or brush to show the hiker which trail to take.

If you get confused, it is not a problem, because your objective is always in plain sight. Take the trail that leads to the saddle, and you can't go wrong. Once you reach the top, you can see over into Boynton Canyon, which is mostly filled with the Enchantment Resort. There are views to the other side too, which are very nice. This is an easy little hike.

Some mystic types believe that the two spires are Vortex energy points, one positive and the other negative.

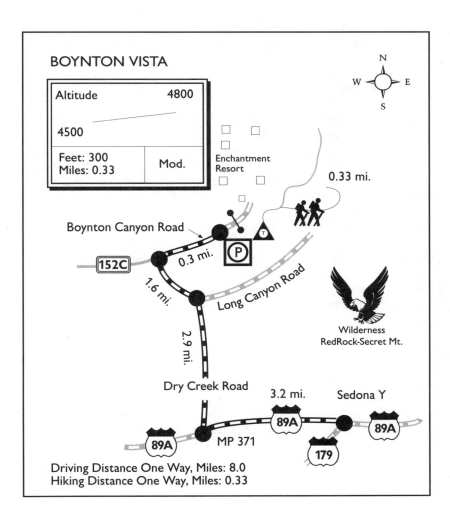

BRINS MESA EAST #119

General Information
Location Map D4
Wilson Mountain USGS Map
Coconino Forest Service Map

Driving Distance One Way: 1.6 miles *2.56 km* (Time 10 minutes)
Access Road: All cars, Last 0.30 miles *0.48 km* rough dirt road
Hiking Distance One Way: 2.75 miles *4.4 km* (Time 1.5 hours)
How Strenuous: Moderate
Features: Easy to reach, Good views

NUTSHELL: You hike a maintained trail to the top of Brins Mesa, then you go across country to a stunning rock formation on the lip of the mesa next to Wilson Mountain.

DIRECTIONS:
From the Y in Sedona, Go:
   North on Highway on 89A (toward Flagstaff) for 0.30 miles *0.48 km* to Jordan Road, which is in the middle of uptown Sedona. Turn left (N) and take Jordan Road to its end, at 1.1 miles *1.76 km*. Turn left at the stop sign, onto West Park Ridge, a paved road, which ends at 1.3 miles *2.08 km*. Keep going on the unpaved road, which is rough but passable. You will reach the old Shooting Range gate at 1.6 miles *2.56 km*. Park outside.

TRAILHEAD: Start this hike at the Brins Mesa Trailhead.

DESCRIPTION: The **Brins Mesa East** Trailhead is on the other side of the gate. Follow this trail, which is wide and crosses over rolling hills on a moderate incline, taking you to the foot of Brins Mesa in 1.25 miles *2.0 km*. The next half mile climbs the mesa. It is fairly steep and moderately strenuous, a 500 foot climb. When you begin the climb, look behind you. As you rise, you will get better and better views.
   When you top out on the mesa, you will be treated to great views. The trail continues across the mesa to the west, where it intersects a trail coming up from the **Soldier Pass Trail** and then goes all the way to the **Brins Mesa West** trailhead on the Vultee Arch Road. However, we are suggesting a different hike. This is to turn right at the mesa top and go north along the rim of the mesa. There is an ill-defined trail there, but it is easy to find your way by just following the rim. You will go 1.0 miles *1.6 km* to the end of the mesa.
   About half way along, there is a great vantage point where a bare redrock

cliff juts out like the prow of a ship. There are beautiful sights from here. But the best is yet to come, at the very end of the mesa, where there is an eroded redrock turret that is easily climbed. The sculptures and carvings in the redrock are a true delight to the eye. There is a deep crevice between the end of the mesa and gigantic Wilson Mountain. This is one of the best sitting and gazing points in all Sedona, one of our all-time favorite spots in the redrock country.

From this point, you will have the best possible place to watch **Angel Falls** and its unnamed neighbor waterfall when they are running. There is a problem with this waterfall viewing, and that is that if it is wet enough for the falls to be running, it probably will be quite muddy on the mesa.

When the mesa is muddy, hiking there is miserable. There is no way to avoid the sticky, heavy mud.

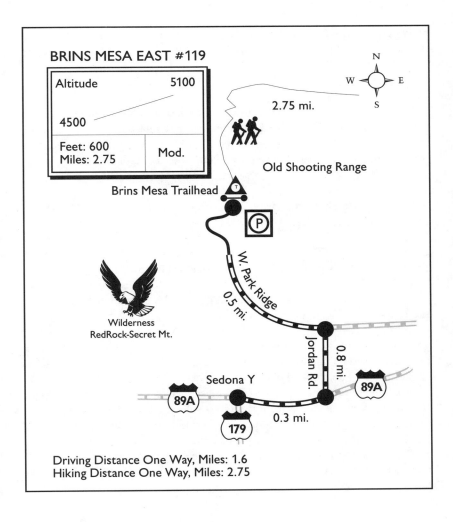

BRINS MESA EAST #119

Altitude	5100
4500	
Feet: 600 Miles: 2.75	Mod.

N
W — E
S

2.75 mi.

Old Shooting Range

Brins Mesa Trailhead

W. Park Ridge

0.5 mi.

Wilderness RedRock-Secret Mt.

Jordan Rd.

0.8 mi.

Sedona Y

89A

89A

179

0.3 mi.

Driving Distance One Way, Miles: 1.6
Hiking Distance One Way, Miles: 2.75

BRINS MESA WEST #119

General Information
Location Map D4
Wilson Mountain USGS Map
Coconino Forest Service Map

Driving Distance One Way: 7.7 miles *12.4 km* (Time 30 minutes)
Access Road: Bumpy dirt road last 2.5 miles *4.0 km*, Any car with reasonable clearance
Hiking Distance One Way: 2.5 miles *4.0 km* (Time 75 minutes)
How Strenuous: Moderate
Features: Views

NUTSHELL: Brins Mesa overlooks uptown Sedona, giving fine views of the south face of Wilson Mountain and the Dry Creek drainage to the west.

DIRECTIONS:
From the Sedona Y Go:
    Southwest on Highway 89A (toward Cottonwood) for 3.2 miles *5.12 km* (MP 371) to Dry Creek Road. Turn right on Dry Creek Road and proceed to the 5.2 mile *8.4 km* point. Turn right on FR 152, the Vultee Arch Road, and follow it to the 7.7 mile *12.4 km* point. Pull off to the right into the big parking area and park.

TRAILHEAD: There is a rusty sign marking the trailhead at the parking area reading, "Brins Mesa #119."

DESCRIPTION: FR 152 is rough, but improvements to the road since the first edition of this book have made the road accessible, though bumpy, to all cars except low riders.
    The trail seems to be a combination of an old jeep road and stock path. It crosses a streambed ten times. Usually this is dry, and is no problem. If it is carrying much water, wait for another day. At the 1.0 mile *1.6 km* point you climb out of the streambed. You then begin to ascend to the top of the mesa. This is on a fairly gradual ramp, because this side (W) of Brins Mesa slopes, forming an inclined plane, which makes for easy access. At 2.0 miles *3.2 km* you are near the top, out on the mesa, where you begin to have some fine views. You can look to your right into Soldier Pass, at **Coffee Pot Rock**. Straight ahead, you look at Sedona. To your left you see Wilson Mountain. Behind you are views of the Dry Creek area.
    The mesa top is quite flat and broad. There are some junipers growing there but in many places the mesa is rather bare. This was good grazing land

for cattle, though it wasn't big enough to support many of them. The mesa itself is not particularly interesting but it makes a fine viewpoint.

You walk all the way east across the mesa and peer down a fairly steep drop into the area of Mormon Canyon and Jordan Road, which is the **Brins Mesa East Trail** access. You can work these two hikes as a two-car shuttle, parking a car at each trailhead. The Brins Mesa West hike has a more gradual climb, is less scenic at the beginning and has more difficult access than the Brins Mesa East hike.

Brins Mesa is a large, interesting place. It forms a low barrier between Sedona and the Dry Creek backcountry. The legend is that in the old ranching days a brindle steer managed to avoid roundup and went wild on the mesa. Cowboys who tried to capture him became so frustrated by his escapes that they finally shot him. Their nickname for the critter was Brins or Brinds because of his brindle coloration, hence the name Brins Mesa.

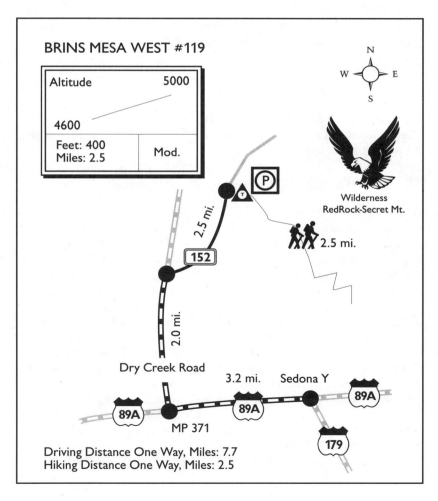

BRINS MESA WEST #119

Altitude	5000
4600	
Feet: 400 Miles: 2.5	Mod.

N
W — E
S

Wilderness
RedRock-Secret Mt.

2.5 mi.

152

2.5 mi.

2.0 mi.

Dry Creek Road

3.2 mi.   Sedona Y

89A   89A   89A

MP 371   179

Driving Distance One Way, Miles: 7.7
Hiking Distance One Way, Miles: 2.5

BROKEN ARROW TRAIL

General Information
Location Map E5
Sedona USGS Map
Coconino Forest Service Map

Driving Distance One Way: 2.1 miles *3.36 km* (Time 10 minutes)
Access Road: All cars, Last 0.1 mile *0.16 km* good dirt road
Hiking Distance One Way: 1.5 Miles *2.4 km* (Time 60 minutes)
How Strenuous: Moderate
Features: Redrocks, Views, Sinkhole

NUTSHELL: This trail is located in Sedona's "backyard" at the south end of Marg's Draw. It winds around redrock cliffs and canyons, ending at Chicken Point, with a stop at Devil's Dining Room along the way.

DIRECTIONS:
From the Sedona Y Go:
   South on Highway 179 (toward Phoenix) for 1.4 miles *2.3 km* (MP 312.1) to Morgan Road in the Broken Arrow Subdivision. Turn left (E) on Morgan Road and follow it to its end, at 2.0 miles *3.2 km*; then go another 0.1 miles *0.16 km* to the parking area.

TRAILHEAD: At the parking lot.

DESCRIPTION: The Forest Service has changed this area since the previous editions of our book, by creating a nice large parking lot and the **Broken Arrow Trail.** Formerly hikers had to walk down the road, dodging tour jeeps. This trail was designed to take you off the road, but it does more than that: it is a great trail in its own right.

   From the parking lot, you walk southwest across the road and follow the markers and cairns west and south. The trail soon moves over near the base of the nice redrock cliffs of Battlement Mesa and climbs up onto a ledge, winding around the base of the mesa.

   At 0.5 miles *0.8 km* you will come downhill to a sinkhole protected by a fence. This is the Devil's Dining Room, a local landmark. At 0.75 miles *1.2 km* you will reach a trail junction. From this point the trail to the left goes down to **Submarine Rock**, while the trail to the right goes to Chicken Point. Take the right fork. You will now do some climbing, but nothing too strenuous. You will come to several very nice viewpoints, one of which looks down on Submarine Rock.

   From this trail junction the Broken Arrow trail winds around the base of

Twin Buttes heading south. The trail moves over near some gorgeous red spires and sculptures that are very fine, and we think you will especially enjoy this last leg of the hike. At 1.45 miles *2.32 km* you come to a gap in the butte, where you have a great view. From here it is a short drop down to Chicken Point, where you can go out onto a red slickrock and enjoy even more views.

The Broken Arrow Trail gets its name from the nearby Broken Arrow Subdivision, which gets its name from a Western movie filmed here, a big-budget film titled *Broken Arrow*, released in 1950. The movie starred Jeff Chandler and Jimmy Stewart. The film was a commercial success and is still available on videotape. Rent it and you will be amazed to see how things have changed around Sedona in the intervening years.

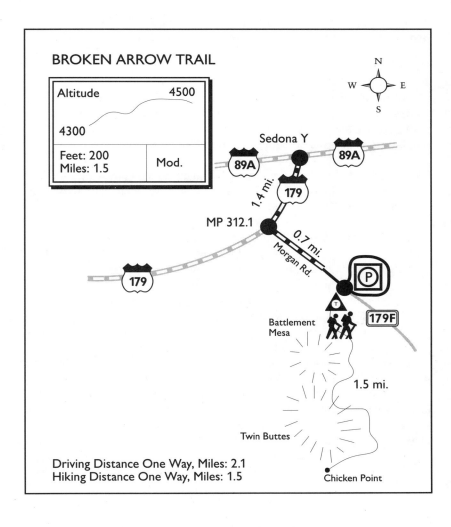

BROWN HOUSE CANYON

General Information
Location Map C5
Wilson Mt. USGS Map
Coconino Forest Service Map

Driving Distance One Way: 6.9 miles *11.1 km* (Time 15 minutes)
Access Road: All cars, All paved
Hiking Distance One Way: 0.3 miles *0.5 km* (Time 20 minutes)
How Strenuous: Moderate
Features: Scenic canyon, Slide Rock State Park

NUTSHELL: While the hordes enjoy the creekside pleasures at Slide Rock
State Park, you can enjoy this little-known scenic canyon hike there.

DIRECTIONS:
From The Y in Sedona Go:
    North on Highway 89A (toward Flagstaff) a distance of 6.9 miles *11.1
km* (MP 381.1) to the entrance to Slide Rock State Park. The park is well
marked and signed and you will have no trouble finding it. Park in the main
parking lot as near the brown house (ticket office) as you can.

TRAILHEAD: This trail is not signed or maintained. You will see the trail
leading west from the picnic tables at the Ponderosa Picnic Area, immediately west of the brown house.

DESCRIPTION: You will have to pay an entrance fee to get into this state
park ($5.00 per car in 1997). The brown house is used by the Park
Department as its headquarters, and is where you buy entrance tickets. This
hike goes up the canyon behind the house. Walk up to the Ponderosa Picnic
Area (signed) and you will see the trail going west of the picnic tables.
    Those who are familiar with the landscape around Sedona are amazed to
find out how different things are in the upper canyon. The altitude at Slide
Rock is about 5100 feet and you are going into a shaded moist canyon. As a
result, you will find a dense alpine forest of pine, oak and maple. Near the
entrance to the canyon blackberry bushes grow profusely.
    The trail is one of those now-you-see-it, now-you-don't affairs, but you
can't go wrong because the canyon is narrow and you just keep following
the main channel to the canyon's end. There is a small streambed in the
canyon and the trail crosses it several times.
    As you begin the hike, your attention is on the trees, but as you go high-
er, you begin to see interesting redrock formations on either side of you. You

get rather mysterious peekaboo glimpses of these through the thick foliage. At about the quarter mile point you come into sight of immense white and gray cliffs.

The canyon ends in a box and you cannot get right to the base of the cliffs without some serious bushwhacking as the place is so overgrown. The trail plays out on a ridge some distance from the cliffs, a remote silent place surrounded by towering cliffs.

This is a good hike for a summer day, cool and delicious.

The area where Slide Rock State Park is located was once an apple orchard owned and operated by the Pendley family. It was the Pendleys who built the long irrigation flume that allowed their orchards to succeed where others had failed. Many apple trees are still on the grounds. One of the main old orchards was cut down in 1991 and new trees were planted, as the old ones had lost their vigor. There are many signs placed around Slide Rock Park showing points of interest.

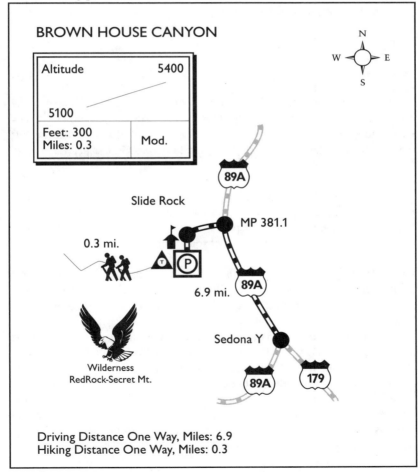

BROWN HOUSE CANYON

Altitude	5400
5100	
Feet: 300 Miles: 0.3	Mod.

N
W — E
S

89A

Slide Rock

MP 381.1

0.3 mi.

89A
6.9 mi.

Sedona Y

Wilderness RedRock-Secret Mt.

89A   179

Driving Distance One Way, Miles: 6.9
Hiking Distance One Way, Miles: 0.3

CAPITOL BUTTE

General Information
Location Map D4
Wilson Mt. USGS Map
Coconino Forest Service Map

Driving Distance One Way: 5.2 miles *8.4 km* (Time 15 minutes)
Access Road: All cars, All paved
Hiking Distance One Way: 0.5 miles *0.8 km* (Time 30 minutes)
How Strenuous: Moderate
Features: Views

NUTSHELL: Capitol Butte is one of the main Sedona landmarks, and the town partly wraps around it on the east. This hike takes you to the top of a ridge radiating from the west face of the butte for fine views out over scenic country.

DIRECTIONS:
From the Sedona Y Go:
    Southwest on Highway 89A (toward Cottonwood) for a distance of 3.2 miles *5.12 km* (MP 371) to the Dry Creek Road. Turn right onto Dry Creek Road and follow it to the 5.2 mile *8.4 km* point, where FR 152 branches off to the right. The road is paved to this point. Pull onto FR 152 just far enough to find a parking place and park.

TRAILHEAD: This trail is not marked, but the trailhead is easily found. From where you park, you will see a large metal sign frame, about 8 feet high. Walk up the road about 75 paces from it and look to your right, where you will see a ditch and a blocked dirt road. This is the trailhead.

DESCRIPTION: Walk up the old road a few yards, where you will meet another trail. Go right (S). At 0.15 miles *0.24 km*, the trail forks. The left fork is an old jeep road. Take the right fork instead. It will lead you down into a little wash and then back up the other side.
    At 0.18 miles *0.3 km*, you will have partly climbed a ridge. Here the main trail, a horse path leading to stables on Dry Creek Road, goes straight ahead, at the same level. You will find a fainter trail going uphill, toward the top of the ridge. This is the trail you want.
    After a short, stiff climb, you will find yourself on the ridge top at 0.4 miles *0.66 km*. Though the top is covered with vegetation, it is not dense and it is easy to walk through it. Go to your right (W), to the bare edge of the ridge, where you can see down onto Dry Creek Road. This is a nice view,

though you are looking down at a lot of homes in subdivisions.

After this, work your way east toward the cliffs that top the butte. High above you is the formation called Lizard Head. Seen from the right angle, it fully lives up to its name. Look to your left (N) in the middle distance and you will see an urn-shaped balanced rock on the skyline.

We bushwhacked around this ridge, did a bit of climbing up the redrock, and felt that we had had a nice outing. While we were there we noticed a hiker coming down from a saddle at the top. He might have even been able to get to the base of Lizard Head from the saddle. As it was late, we were unable to see whether this adventurer had a trail or was just picking his way. You might want to do some exploring here if steep climbing is your fancy.

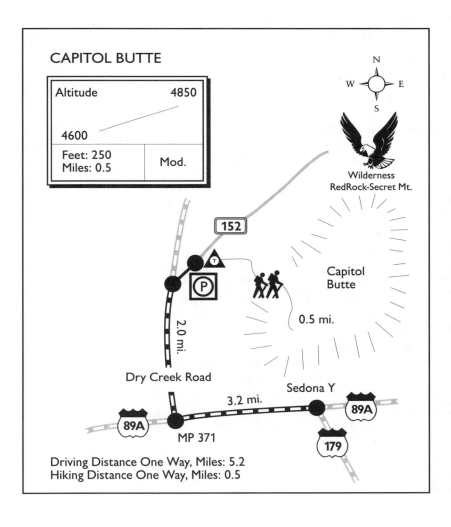

CAPITOL BUTTE

Altitude	4850
4600	
Feet: 250 Miles: 0.5	Mod.

N
W · E
S

Wilderness
RedRock-Secret Mt.

152

P

Capitol
Butte

0.5 mi.

2.0 mi.

Dry Creek Road

Sedona Y

3.2 mi.

89A

89A

179

MP 371

Driving Distance One Way, Miles: 5.2
Hiking Distance One Way, Miles: 0.5

CARROLL CANYON

General Information
Location Map E4
Sedona USGS Map
Coconino Forest Service Map

Driving Distance One Way: 6.2 miles *10.0 km* (Time 20 minutes)
Access Road: All cars, All paved
Hiking Distance One Way: 1.25 miles *2.0 km* (Time 40 minutes)
How Strenuous: Easy
Features: Arch

NUTSHELL: This canyon, located 6.2 miles *10.0 km* southwest of Sedona, runs just south of Airport Hill. An easy walk, it features a "pocket-sized" arch.

DIRECTIONS:
From the Sedona Y Go:
   Southwest on Highway 89A (toward Cottonwood) a distance of 4.2 miles *6.7 km* (MP 368.9) to the Upper Red Rock Loop Road. Turn left and follow the Loop to the 6.0 mile *9.6 km* point, where you turn left, heading toward Red Rock Crossing. At 6.2 miles *10.0 km*, you will come to a small bridge. Park on the shoulder near the bridge.

TRAILHEAD: No marked trail. You walk up the floor of the canyon.

DESCRIPTION: The bridge that you reach at the 6.2 mile point *10.0 km* spans Carroll Canyon, so park anywhere near it.
   Get out and walk into the wash and hike upstream (N). There are many places where the stream has cut down to a redrock shelf, where it is almost like walking on pavement. In other places, you must do a bit of boulder hopping. In about 0.25 miles *0.4 km*, you will be out of sight of habitation, although you will hear lots of airplane activity because the big hill to your right is Airport Hill.
   As you go, the canyon gets deeper and more interesting. At about 0.6 miles *1.0 km*, you reach an area where the canyon rises steeply and has carved out a series of terraces. You can keep climbing upstream over these ledges.
   Many pools have formed in declivities in the rock and some appear to be deep enough to hold water year around.
   At 0.9 miles *1.5 km*, you reach a place where the words "Arch Spring" have been carved into a rock near a pool. The lettering looks old fashioned

and may have been carved there many years ago when the spring was active. It seems inactive now, or perhaps it is active only during the time of snow melt. The arch is at ground level—just about big enough for your cocker spaniel to squeeze through.

Although the canyon goes all the way to Sedona (it crosses under Highway 89-A at Coffee Pot Rock Road), the scenic part of the canyon ends at 1.25 miles *2.0 km*. Beyond there, the channel flattens and due to the nearness of "civilization" becomes littered with trash.

Carroll Canyon is named after the Tom Carroll family, which homesteaded in Sedona in its early days. The Carrolls occupied a tract of land on what is now the Red Rock Loop Road. Exhausted by their hardscrabble existence, they sold the land to Henry Schuerman, a hard working German immigrant of many talents. Schuerman was able to develop the property successfully and his descendants lived there for many years.

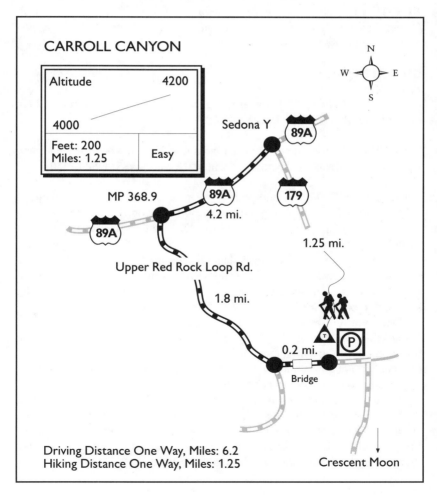

CARROLL CANYON

Altitude	4200
4000	
Feet: 200 Miles: 1.25	Easy

N
W E
S

Sedona Y
89A

MP 368.9
89A
4.2 mi.

89A

179

1.25 mi.

Upper Red Rock Loop Rd.

1.8 mi.

0.2 mi.

P

Bridge

Driving Distance One Way, Miles: 6.2
Hiking Distance One Way, Miles: 1.25

Crescent Moon

CASNER CANYON NORTH #11

General Information
Location Map D5
Munds Park USGS Map
Coconino Forest Service Map

Driving Distance One Way: 2.6 miles *4.2 km* (Time 10 minutes)
Access Road: All cars, All paved
Hiking Distance One Way: 2.0 miles *3.2 km* (Time 75 minutes)
How Strenuous: Hard
Features: Views

NUTSHELL: Located just north of Sedona, this trail takes you across Oak Creek, then up Casner Canyon to a point on the Schnebly Hill Road just north of Schnebly Hill Vista.

DIRECTIONS:
From the Sedona Y Go:
   North on Highway 89A (toward Flagstaff) a distance of 2.6 miles *4.2 km* (MP 376.8) where you park at the mouth of a closed road.

TRAILHEAD: Walk down the old road a few feet and you will see a rusty sign reading, "Casner Canyon #11" where the trail goes downhill left.

DESCRIPTION: Follow the path down to Oak Creek, where you must wade across. We like to bring a towel along to dry our feet when we get to the other side. This is not a hike you would want to do while wearing wet tennies. A good method is to pack a pair of Tevas or other sandals, as walking the creek is tricky. Use the sandals for crossing the creek, then dry your feet and switch back to your hiking shoes on the other shore. You don't want to fall in. Count on wading, because even though there may be stepping stones, our experience is that they are unreliable.
   Once you are across the water and have dry shoes on, you will see Casner Canyon. You head right up the canyon on its right (S) side. Soon the trail lifts out of the canyon and climbs the north wall of the canyon, meaning that you are on a southern exposure. There is no shade and you are fully exposed to sun. Don't do this hike on a hot day.
   From the point where you rise above the crowns of the trees that grow in the bottom of the canyon, the trail goes to the top in a very businesslike way, cutting a straight diagonal line from the bottom of the canyon to the top of Schnebly Hill. There is no scenery along the trail. In fact, it is quite drab, though you do climb high enough to get sweeping views.

You reach the top at a place that is close to the Schnebly Hill Vista, going through a gate in a barbed wire fence; so one way to do this hike is to use the two-car switch, parking one at Schnebly Hill Vista and the other at the Casner Canyon Trailhead. The easy way to do the hike is to start at the top, from Schnebly Hill. It is easy to recognize the start of the trail there by looking for the gate in the fence.

When you stand at the Schnebly Hill Vista you can see the Casner Canyon Trail. Sometimes, when the light is just right, it looks like a road and you wonder what on earth it can be, because no car could drive straight up the mountain as the trail goes. The trail was built by the Casner ranching operation as a livestock trail in the late 1890s.

The Casner family left its name in several areas: **Casner Mountain,** NW of Sedona, the **Casner Canyon South** Trail in the Wet Beaver Creek Country, Casner Canyon Draw near Woody Mountain and others.

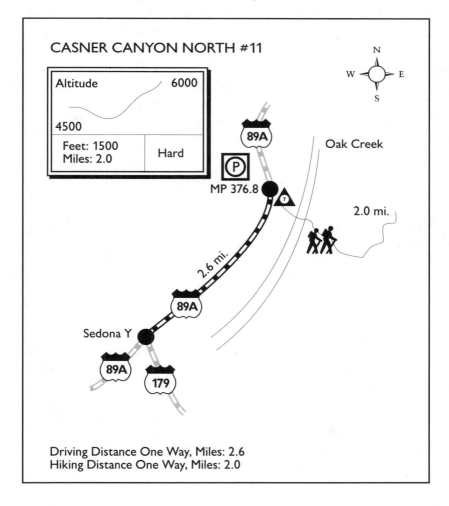

CASNER CANYON NORTH #11

Altitude		6000
4500		
Feet: 1500 Miles: 2.0	Hard	

Oak Creek

89A

MP 376.8

2.0 mi.

2.6 mi.

89A

Sedona Y

89A

179

Driving Distance One Way, Miles: 2.6
Hiking Distance One Way, Miles: 2.0

CASNER CANYON SOUTH

General Information
Location Map G6
Casner Butte USGS Map
Coconino Forest Service Map

Driving Distance One Way: 17.2 miles *27.6 km* (Time 30 minutes)
Access Road: All cars, Last 0.3 miles *0.48 km* gravel, in good condition
Hiking Distance One Way: 2.2 miles *3.52 km* (Time 1.25 hours)
How Strenuous: Moderate
Features: Permanent Stream, Rock Art, Views

NUTSHELL: This trail follows the Bell Trail along the banks of Wet Beaver Creek and then branches off to climb to the top of a mesa.

DIRECTIONS:
From the Sedona Y Go:
South on Highway 179 (toward Phoenix) for 14.7 miles *23.5 km* (MP 298.9), to the I-17 intersection. Go straight here rather than getting on I-17. Follow paved road FR 618 until you see a sign for Beaver Creek Ranger Station and trailheads at 16.9 miles *27.1 km*. Turn left. Parking is at 17.2 miles *27.6 km*.

TRAILHEAD: Several hiking trails here share a common trailhead that is well marked with signs at the parking area.

DESCRIPTION: From the trailhead, the **Bell Trail** goes up canyon along Wet Beaver Creek. The trail is an old road, broad and easy to walk. It was built by cattle rancher Earl Bell in 1932, as a means for taking his cattle to the top of the Mogollon Rim in the spring.

At about 0.6 miles *1.0 km*, look for a large boulder on the left side of the trail. On the side that faces away from you are a number of interesting petroglyphs.

The Forest Service's parking lot sign indicates that the Casner Canyon Trail is 1.5 miles *2.4 km* from the trailhead. When you make the hike, you will see a small sign for the trail to your left just before the Bell Trail dips down into a gully.

The trail goes up the south wall of Casner Canyon in a straight line, not zigzagging as many trails do. It is not terribly strenuous, though it does climb 1,000 feet in 0.70 miles *1.2 km*. Along the way you are treated to some good views and some shows of colorful redrock.

The top of the mesa is covered by a hundred foot thick layer of lava, which is typical of all the mesas in this area. In most places there are sheer cliffs at these mesa rims. This trail takes advantage of a gap in the caprock and emerges at the top without requiring any rock climbing. On the top the trail just ends at a cairn at a point 2.2 miles *3.52 km* from the beginning.

We suggest that you turn left and walk to the edge of the mesa overlooking Beaver Creek (about 0.20 miles *0.32 km*) for some excellent views of the creek and the Verde Valley. Hikers along the Bell Trail will wonder how you got there.

The Casner family was very active in the livestock business and left its name in several locations. In this book you will find the **Casner Mountain South** and **Casner Canyon North** hikes in addition to this hike.

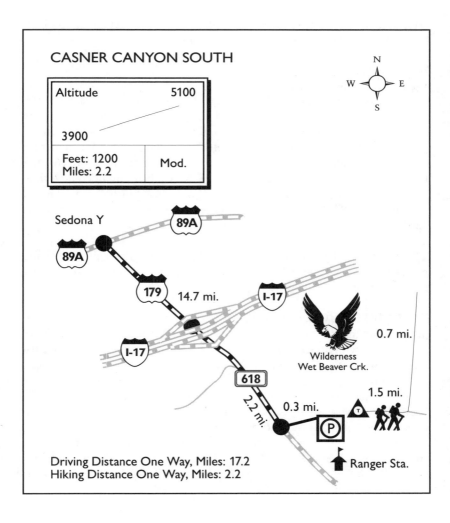

CASNER CANYON SOUTH

N
W — E
S

Altitude	5100
3900	
Feet: 1200 Miles: 2.2	Mod.

Sedona Y

89A

89A

179 14.7 mi.

I-17

I-17

0.7 mi.

Wilderness Wet Beaver Crk.

618

1.5 mi.

2.2 mi.

0.3 mi.

T

P

Ranger Sta.

Driving Distance One Way, Miles: 17.2
Hiking Distance One Way, Miles: 2.2

CASNER MOUNTAIN SOUTH #8

General Information
Location Map C1
Loy Butte and Clarkdale USGS Maps
Coconino Forest Service Map

Driving Distance One Way: 19.6 miles *31.4 km* (Time 30 minutes)
Access Road: All cars, Last 10.0 miles *16 km* good dirt road
Hiking Distance One Way: 2.0 miles *3.2 km* (Time 1.5 hours)
How Strenuous: Hard
Features: Views

NUTSHELL: This hike takes you to the top of a mountain overlooking Sycamore Canyon and the Sedona back country.

DIRECTIONS:
From The Y in Sedona Go:
Southwest on Highway 89A˙ (toward Cottonwood) a distance of 9.6 miles *15.4 km* (MP 364.5) to the Red Canyon Road. Turn right on Red Canyon Road, also known as FR 525, and follow it to the 12.4 mile *20 km* point where FR 525C branches to the left. Turn left on FR 525C and stay on it to the 15.6 mile *25 km* point, the next major junction. Here FR 761, the Bill Gray Road, goes to the left. Stay on FR 525C, the right fork, and follow it to the 19.6 mile *31.4 km* point, where you will see a trail sign marked "Casner Mtn. #8." There is a parking spot big enough for one car at the trailhead.

TRAILHEAD: The trailhead is marked with a sign. The trail follows the power line up the south face of Casner Mountain, and you can see clearly from the start of the hike where the trail goes.

DESCRIPTION: Casner Mountain is bare of shade trees except for a few junipers and the trail takes you up its south face. Because of that, you are in full sunlight with no shade, so take a hat and plenty of water and don't try this hike on a hot day. The trail follows along a jeep road created for the construction of the power line. You will climb about 0.4 miles *0.65 km* to join the power line, then hike across a gradually rising shelf. From there you will begin the steepest ascent. Look over to your right (E) and you will see the rounded red butte known as **Robber's Roost.**

The payoff for this hike is the viewing. Casner is a tall mountain and is situated so that you can see into some beautiful country. To the south you see the Black Hills and Jerome. To the east you will see many Sedona landmarks and parts of the town. As you climb higher you will begin to see the red towers of Sycamore Pass to your left (W).

From the end of the shelf, the trail goes straight up the mountain to about the halfway point, where the pitch becomes quite steep, and from there the trail serpentines. At the 1.6 mile *2.6 km* point you come to a sharp switchback at the west edge of the mountain where you break over a shoulder so that you can suddenly see into the whole of Sycamore Canyon. It is a vast and soul-stirring view, worth the trip all by itself.

From this point you will make the final push and stop at the top, at the highest point. Though Casner Mountain looks like a free-standing mountain when you start the hike, it is attached to the Mogollon Rim by Buck Ridge. The power line runs across this ridge and you can continue hiking the power line road for 4.0 miles *6.4 km* to the rim. We describe the hike from Casner's summit to the rim in *Flagstaff Hikes*, as Casner Mountain North

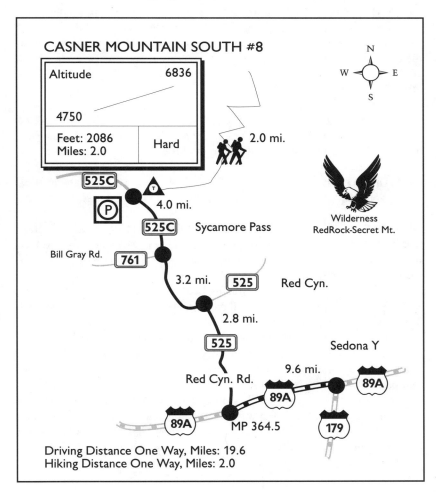

CATHEDRAL RIDGE

General Information
Location Map F4
Sedona USGS Map
Coconino Forest Service Map

Driving Distance One Way: 4.1 miles *6.6 km* (Time 15 minutes)
Access Road: All cars, All paved
Hiking Distance One Way: 1.5 miles *2.4 km* (Time 60 minutes)
How Strenuous: Moderate
Features: Views

NUTSHELL: Located 4.1 miles *6.6 km* south of Sedona, this interesting ridge connects Cathedral Rock and Little Park Heights. You hike a closed road to the base of the ridge and then make a moderately strenuous climb to the top, from where you have interesting exploring and great views.

DIRECTIONS:
From the Sedona Y Go
   South on Highway 179 a distance of 4.1 miles *6.6 km* (MP 309.4) to a point where a dirt road to the left (east) is visible at the city limits sign. Turn left onto the dirt road and park there on the little loop.

TRAILHEAD: This is not a marked trail. You walk across Highway 179, where you will find an old closed road. Then you walk the road.

DESCRIPTION: You will see a marker at the start of this road indicating that it has been closed. Here and there you will see places where the roadbed has been torn up to discourage vehicles from using it. Because it was once a road, it is wide and makes for easy walking.
   The first leg of the hike is confusing because there are a number of false trails. You will walk over a little hill crest and then go down into a creekbed. The road is a bit hard to follow as you come down the hill to the streambed, as there is a berm of dirt across the road, and a false road takes off to the left, where it ends in an old materials pit. If you have any doubt about the trail, head for the creek bottom. There is only one road on the other side, and from that point the way is obvious—just follow the bike tracks.
   The trail takes you over gently rolling land, climbing gradually until you come into a basin at the foot of Cathedral Ridge. Behind you are fine views of the Chapel of the Holy Cross. Near the base of Cathedral Rock, where a bike could not go up on a ledge, the bike tracks curve to your right. Look for a footpath going uphill here and take it.

The trail climbs up the ridge, gradually at first and then becoming steeper. It is less than a half mile to the top. You will first come out onto a redrock ledge over one hundred feet thick, forming some beautiful cliffs. It is fun to explore along this ledge, enjoying the many interesting eroded rock sculptures and formations.

Once you have had your fill of the ledge, you hike up to the next level. This requires another short steep climb. Then there is a final push to the top level, where you have your choice of going either north toward **Cathedral Rock** or south toward **Little Park Heights**, or both. If you do any exploring, then you can add another half mile or more to the 1.5 miles *2.4 km* we have shown as the mileage for this hike.

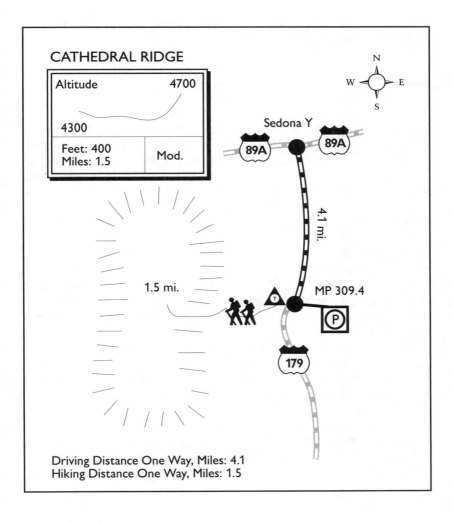

CATHEDRAL RIDGE

Altitude	4700
4300	
Feet: 400 Miles: 1.5	Mod.

Sedona Y

89A 89A

4.1 mi.

1.5 mi.

MP 309.4

P

179

Driving Distance One Way, Miles: 4.1
Hiking Distance One Way, Miles: 1.5

CATHEDRAL ROCK

VORTEX

General Information
Location Map E4
Sedona USGS Map
Coconino Forest Service Map

Driving Distance One Way: 7.1 miles *11.4 km* (Time 20 minutes)
Access Road: All cars, All paved
Hiking Distance One Way: 1.5 miles *2.4 km* (Time 40 minutes)
How Strenuous: Hard
Features: Views, Vortex Site

NUTSHELL: You drive to Crescent Moon Ranch, a state park, then walk across Oak Creek to hike to the base of Cathedral Rock's west face, from where you can climb to its high cliffs.

DIRECTIONS:
From the Sedona Y Go:
   Southwest on Highway 89A (toward Cottonwood) a distance of 4.2 miles *6.8 km* (MP 368.9) to the Upper Red Rock Loop Road. Turn left and follow the Loop to the 6.1 mile *9.8 km* point, where you turn left, heading toward Red Rock Crossing on a paved road. Follow the paved road to Crescent Moon Ranch State Park, a total of 7.1 miles *11.4 km*. You must pay an entry fee. Park inside.

TRAILHEAD: No marked trailhead.

DESCRIPTION: From the parking area, walk south, toward Oak Creek. As you near its bank you will see a trail to your left (E). It is a concrete walk for a short distance. When the sidewalk curves to your left, away from the creek, continue walking upstream along the creek bank. You will notice the Chavez Ranch, established by early Sedona pioneers, to your left, with its a water wheel, an unusual sight in dry Arizona.
   When you come to the irrigation control box, which is built out of concrete block, it is time to go across the creek. The box sticks out into the stream and creates a narrow place where there is sometimes a line of rocks that you can hop. Just above the box is a wide shallow redrock ledge, a good place to wade.
   Once you are across, keep working your way south, away from the water. You will hit a small side stream which you must also cross. Once you have crossed the side stream, keep going south until you run up against a low redrock cliff. Here you will find the main hiking path. It is wide and sandy

and unmistakable.

Turn left (E). As you walk along here, you will see Cathedral Rock ahead of you, in a V-shape, with two smaller spires flanked by much bigger ones. At two-thirds of a mile from the beginning, you will find a gate. Go through the gate.

From the gate, you will walk along the bank and then the bottom of a wash for a short distance. The trail you want to follow soon lifts out of the wash to your left and climbs up the far side of the valley going up to the V in Cathedral Rock. Look carefully here, because you may be confused by a horse trail that follows the wash all the way out and goes to the Verde Valley School Road. There are cairns marking the true way.

From the point where you leave the wash, you climb to the top of some slickrock knobs, along a path that is fairly steep but not too hard. From that point the trail continues, but requires some scrambling and climbing to get to the base of the highest cliffs. There are wonderful views.

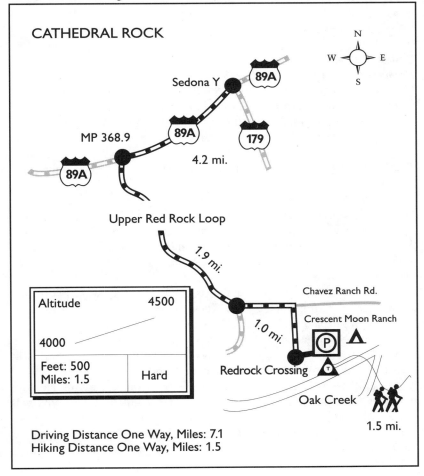

CATHEDRAL ROCK

N
W ←◯→ E
S

Sedona Y   89A

MP 368.9   89A   179

89A   4.2 mi.

Upper Red Rock Loop

1.9 mi.

Chavez Ranch Rd.

Altitude	4500
4000	
Feet: 500 Miles: 1.5	Hard

1.0 mi.

Crescent Moon Ranch

Ⓟ ⛺

Redrock Crossing Ⓣ

Oak Creek

1.5 mi.

Driving Distance One Way, Miles: 7.1
Hiking Distance One Way, Miles: 1.5

CATHEDRAL ROCK, BACK O' BEYOND

VORTEX

General Information
Location Map F4
Sedona USGS Map
Coconino Forest Service Map

Driving Distance One Way: 4.1 miles *6.6 km* (Time 15 minutes)
Access Road: All cars, Last 0.7 miles *1.2 km* good dirt road
Hiking Distance One Way: 1.0 miles *1.6 km* (Time 30 minutes)
How Strenuous: Easy
Features: Views, Vortex spot

NUTSHELL: Cathedral Rock, a prominent Sedona landmark, is accessible from several points. This is the easiest and one of the most satisfying routes, featuring a marvelous natural walkway partly around the butte.

DIRECTIONS:
From the Sedona Y Go
   South on Highway 179 a distance of 3.4 miles *5.5 km* (MP 310.2) to a point where you see a road to the right into an area signed Back O' Beyond. Turn right onto this road and follow it to the 4.1 mile *6.6 km* point, where you will see a marked and fenced parking area to your left.

TRAILHEAD: This is not a marked trail. It starts at the fence at the parking lot.

DESCRIPTION: At the parking area you are quite close to Cathedral Rock, and it dominates the skyline to your right. Enjoy the views of it before starting on the hike. You will see one of its outstanding features on the left end, a spire called The Mace, which is a large column that is larger at the top than the bottom.
   The butte consists of two major parts, the upper sheer-walled cliffs and a lower platform with sloping sides. These slopes make it possible to climb to the top of the platform with relative ease.
   Go through the gap in the fence and you will see several trails. The main trail is easy to see because of its heavy use, and usually is marked with cairns. It goes downhill into a wash and up the other side.
   Once across you will find another network of trails. Stay on the main one, which heads uphill toward the butte. At 0.2 miles *0.32 km* you will come to the top of a red slickrock ledge. Keep going up toward the central mass and in a short distance you will find a wide lip that makes a natural walkway to your left. From here the trail goes to your left and to the right.

Go left, marking your entry point with a cairn, and hike the lip around to the south, hugging the butte all the way. This natural path is an unusual and delightful feature.

The views of the butte are eye-pleasing at every turn and you will also have some great views in the distance. This is a very restful and quieting kind of hike. Stop at the 1.0 mile *1.6 km* point, where the trail turns away from the butte and goes downhill into the junipers, a place where you encounter the remains of an old barbed wire fence. The trail continues but is not very interesting beyond the fence. On the way back, do not overshoot your entry point, as the trail goes beyond it to the north, then west for another 1.5 miles *2.4 km* down to Oak Creek.

We have not found a particular point that seems to be *the* Vortex spot on Cathedral Rock: no medicine wheels or other markers; but the place does have a nice restorative feeling of silent energy to both of us.

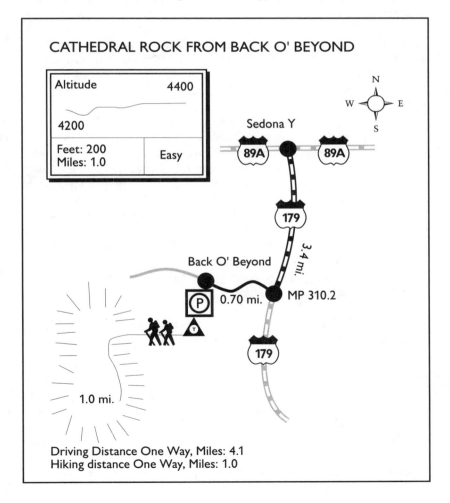

CATHEDRAL ROCK FROM BACK O' BEYOND

Altitude	4400
4200	
Feet: 200 Miles: 1.0	Easy

Sedona Y

89A — 89A

179

3.4 mi.

Back O' Beyond

P 0.70 mi. MP 310.2

179

1.0 mi.

Driving Distance One Way, Miles: 4.1
Hiking distance One Way, Miles: 1.0

CHASM CREEK TRAIL #164

General Information
Location Map G6
Arnold Mesa, Camp Verde and Horner Mt. USGS Maps
Coconino, Prescott and Tonto Forest Service Maps

Driving Distance One Way: 41.6 miles *66.56 km* (Time 1.2 hours)
Access Road: All cars, 6.4 miles *10.24 km* good dirt road, Last 0.2 miles *0.32 km* rough
Hiking Distance One Way: 6.1 miles *9.76 km* (Time 4 Hours)
How Strenuous: Strenuous due to steepness and distance
Features: Scenic rugged back country trail going west over the Black Hills from the Verde River, Cedar Bench Wilderness.

NUTSHELL: This long trail goes from the Verde River side of the Black Hills to the Dugas side, rising and falling over 2,000 feet in rugged terrain.

DIRECTIONS:
From the Sedona Y Go:
    South on Highway 179 (toward Phoenix) for 14.7 miles *23.6 km*, to the I-17 Interchange. Turn south on I-17 and go to the 26.0 miles *41.6 km* point, where you take Exit 287 to Camp Verde. You will reach a stop light at the 26.4 mile *42.24 km* point At the stop light turn left and go through Camp Verde, staying on Highway 260. At the 29.5 mile *47.2 km* point, turn right on the Salt Mine Road, which is paved up to the 35.0 mile *56.0 km* point where dirt road FR 574 begins. Follow this good dirt road to the 41.4 mile 66.24 km point, where you will see a primitive dirt road to your right. There is a lath marker there identifying the road only as 164, with symbols for horses and hikers. This is a short road (0.2 miles *0.32 km*) going to the trailhead, but is very rough and requires high clearance. You may not want to drive it. If you do, it ends at a loop at a gate.

TRAILHEAD: The trailhead is at the parking place. Go through the gate in the barbed wire fence. The trail forks immediately. Take the left fork.

DESCRIPTION: The trail almost immediately descends into the bottom of Chasm Creek. You will walk along the creek bottom for a short distance to reach a spring, an unexpected pleasure in this dry terrain. Cross to the south bank at the spring, staying in the bottom. Just beyond the spring the canyon bends and beyond the bend you will see a trail sign showing the place where you begin to climb.
    From this point until the trail reaches its crest (the 3.5 mile *5.6 km* point)

you will be almost constantly climbing on grades that can be quite steep. At the 1.0 mile *1.6 km* point the trail reaches a little shelf where you can turn around to enjoy fine views, including the sight of the San Francisco Peaks rearing above the red cliffs of Sedona. We thought that this was the best part of the trail and is the place to stop for a good short day hike. Beyond this point you approach Table Mountain and begin to work your way around it, a difficult and not very interesting part of the trail. It was so drab that we quit at the 2.25 mile *3.6 km* point.

Although the Cedar Bench Wilderness was created in 1984 it is unknown. We would like to encourage people to enjoy it, so we include the best of the three trails it contains. The others are the Gap Creek #163 and Cold Water #27 trails, which share a common trailhead at the end of FR 574, another 10.1 miles of rough road beyond the turnoff for the Chasm Creek Trail. These trails were poorly marked and hard to follow.

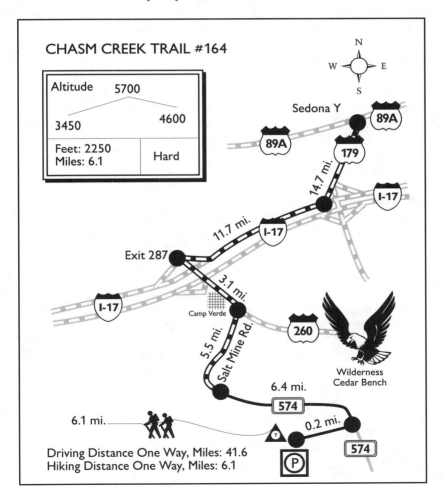

CHASM CREEK TRAIL #164

Altitude	5700	
3450		4600
Feet: 2250 Miles: 6.1		Hard

Driving Distance One Way, Miles: 41.6
Hiking Distance One Way, Miles: 6.1

CHIMNEY ROCK

General Information
Location Map D4
Sedona USGS Map
Coconino Forest Service Map

Driving Distance One Way: 3.6 miles *5.8 km* (Time 10 minutes)
Access Road: All cars, All paved
Hiking Distance One Way: 0.65 miles *1.0 km* (Time 30 minutes)
How Strenuous: Moderate
Features: Rock formations, Views

NUTSHELL: This landmark located 3.6 miles *5.8 km* southwest of uptown Sedona can be climbed with moderate effort for great views.

DIRECTIONS:
From the Sedona Y Go:
   Southwest on Highway 89A (toward Cottonwood) for a distance of 2.5 miles *4.0 km* (MP 371.7), to Andante Drive. Turn right onto Andante Drive. Follow it to the 3.6 mile point *5.8 km* where it intersects Skyview. Drive just across Skyview onto a parking area in the dirt near the water tank.

TRAILHEAD: No signs posted. This is a hiker-made trail.

DESCRIPTION:
   As you begin the hike, there are not many clues to the presence of the trail, but you will see signs that people have parked just outside the fence surrounding the water tank. Walk along the fence to your left from where you parked and you will spot the trail heading down into a gully. Chimney Rock is in plain sight here, so you know which way you must walk.
   After going down into the wash, go upstream about 12 paces and you will find the trail going up the other side. In a couple of hundred feet, the path will intersect a major trail. Take the fork to the right, going uphill.
   At 0.5 miles *0.8 km* you will reach the top of a saddle between Chimney Rock and a ridge running over toward Capitol Butte. Take some time to explore around the interesting features around this ridgetop if you like. There are some great views.
   After you have explored the ridge, get back on the trail, following it for a short distance, looking for a faint trail to your left, which heads toward Chimney Rock.
   The trail up to the Chimney is not well developed, but this doesn't matter much, as your objective is always in sight so that all you need to do is to

keep working toward it. It is a bit of a scramble. From a distance Chimney Rock looks like a monolith, but when you get up close to it you can see that the formation is composed of three pillars. These probably were a single column thousands of years ago, but weathering has done its work. You can walk right up to the base of these pillars. They are fun to look at and you will have a great platform from which to view the surrounding countryside. You can see in all directions except to the north where Capitol Butte blocks your view.

It is possible to walk all the way around the Chimney. The ground is not level but making the loop is well worth the toil. We found it helpful to build a cairn to mark our starting point when we began the loop so that we would know where to descend. From the main trail up to the Chimney, around the Chimney and back down to the main trail is only 0.3 miles *0.5 km* .

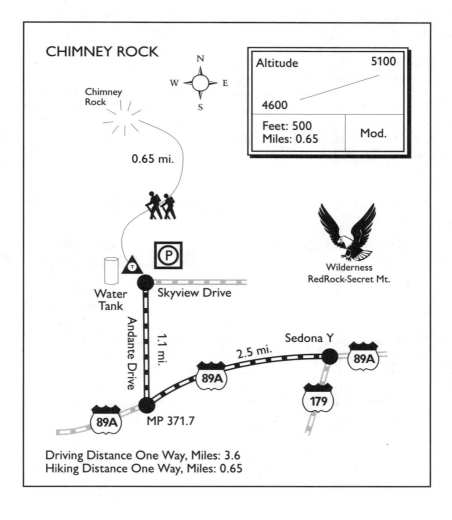

CIBOLA MITTENS

General Information
Location Map D4
Wilson Mt. USGS Maps
Coconino Forest Service Map

Driving Distance One Way: 1.6 miles *2.56km* (Time 10 minutes)
Access Road: All cars, Last 0.3 miles *0.48 km* decent dirt road
Hiking Distance One Way: 1.5 miles *2.4 km* (Time 1 hour)
How Strenuous: Moderate
Features: Rock formations, Views

NUTSHELL: This unmaintained trail takes you to a landmark butte in the Soldier Pass area just 1.6 miles *2.56 km* north of the Sedona Y.

DIRECTIONS:
From the Sedona Y Go:
North on Highway on 89A (toward Flagstaff) for 0.30 miles *0.48 km* to Jordan Road, which is in the middle of uptown Sedona. Turn left (N) and take Jordan Road to its end, at 1.1 miles *1.76 km*. Turn left at the stop sign, onto West Park Ridge, a paved road, which ends at 1.3 miles *2.08 km*. Keep going on the unpaved road. You will reach the old Shooting Range gate at 1.6 miles *2.56 km*. Park outside.

TRAILHEAD: Use the **Brins Mesa East** Trail. Its trailhead is just beyond the gate.

DESCRIPTION: Hike the Brins Mesa East trail for 0.7 miles *1.12 km*, to a point where you find an unmarked but distinct trail to the left marked by cairns.

Follow this left trail. At 0.75 miles *1.2 km,* near the top of the ridge, take a fork to the right.

In a few yards, you will come out on top of the north end of **Shooting Range Ridge**. Take a minute while you are there to enjoy the views. You might even want to explore it a bit, then look for cairns leading right (N), which take you to the end of the slickrock.

Ahead of you, fully in view, is your objective, the gap between Cibola Mittens and Brins Ridge. The trail goes into a brushy area, then climbs, being fairly steep but short. Cairns mark the way.

At the top you will stand on a saddle from which you have outstanding views. To your right (N) is the Mormon Canyon country, bounded to the north by Brins Mesa. To the east is Wilson Mountain. Behind you are good views of uptown Sedona and the country beyond. To your left (W) is the Soldier Pass area. The saddle you are standing on divides Mormon Canyon and Soldier Pass.

You are at the base of one thumb of the mitten at this place. Keep going toward the hand of the mitten. You will find trails there, which seem to be deer trails but work fine for humans.

There is a truly scenic gap between the first thumb and the hand. Just above head level at this gap you will find a rusted piton that was driven into the rock by a climber years ago. You can keep working your way around the hand of the mitten on a narrow but safe ledge to the other thumb, where the trail ends.

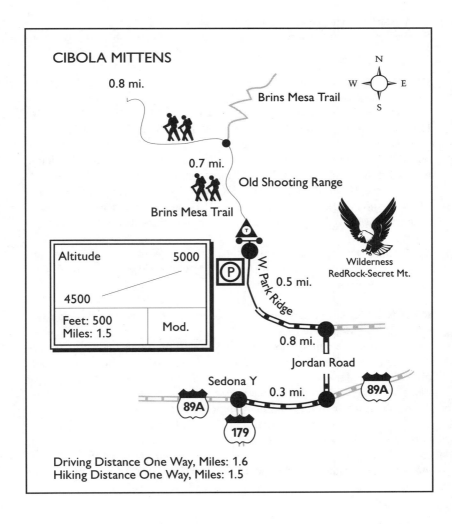

CIBOLA MITTENS

0.8 mi.

Brins Mesa Trail

N
W ← → E
S

0.7 mi.

Old Shooting Range

Brins Mesa Trail

Wilderness
RedRock-Secret Mt.

Altitude	5000
4500	
Feet: 500 Miles: 1.5	Mod.

T

P

W. Park Ridge

0.5 mi.

0.8 mi.

Jordan Road

Sedona Y

0.3 mi.

89A

89A

179

Driving Distance One Way, Miles: 1.6
Hiking Distance One Way, Miles: 1.5

COCKSCOMB, THE

General Information
Location Map D3
Wilson Mountain USGS Map
Coconino Forest Service Map

Driving Distance One Way: 10.7 miles *17.12 km* (Time 20 minutes)
Access Road: All cars, Last 3.0 miles good dirt roads
Hiking Distance One Way: 0.75 miles *1.2 km* (Time 1.0 hour)
How Strenuous: Moderate
Features: Views

NUTSHELL: The Cockscomb is the southernmost redrock butte in the Sedona area. After a short, level approach, you make a 400 foot climb to enjoy exploring the top and take in the wonderful views.

DIRECTIONS:
From the Sedona Y Go:
    Southwest on Highway 89A a distance of 3.2 miles *5.12 km* (MP 371) to Dry Creek Road and turn right onto Dry Creek Road. Follow it to the 6.1 mile *9.8 km* point, where it joins Long Canyon Road. Turn left here, staying on FR 152C. At the 7.7 mile *12.32 km* point, turn left on FR 152C, which is now a dirt road. At the 9.7 mile *15.52 km* point, turn left on FR 9583 and follow it to the 10.7 mile *17.12 km* point, where you will find a locked gate. There are no designated parking spaces. Park on the shoulder of the road in such a way that you do not block access through the gate.

TRAILHEAD: There are no signs or markings. Walk up to the gate, turn right, and follow the barbed wire fence. You will soon see a well worn path that follows around the ranch fence.

DESCRIPTION: We have changed the access for this hike, making this hike much shorter and easier.
    The ranch, the boundaries of which you will follow, is known to Sedona old-timers as the Tree Farm, although the sign inside the gate read Legends of Sedona, the last time we were there. As you walk around the fence, you will see some patches of cultivated trees.
    At about the 0.35 mile *0.56 km* point the trail will move away from the fence, bearing southeast, and heading toward the Cockscomb. You are almost at the foot of the Cockscomb at this point. From the place where you can no longer see the fence, look for a path going to the right (S) and heading uphill. It is usually marked with cairns. We measured this point as being

at 0.43 miles *0.69 km.*

The trail has been level up to here. You will now climb 400 feet to the top. Look carefully. We have never had any trouble following this trail, but you want to keep checking the cairns, because there is only one route to the top. The trail winds up the face and "around the corner" where you will find some natural stairsteps and some hiker-built steps to the top. The top is small, easy to explore, and has many clear areas for excellent views out over the area.

Plans are underway as this is written to develop the former tree farm property into a subdivision. We can only hope that if this occurs, it does not interfere with this good hike.

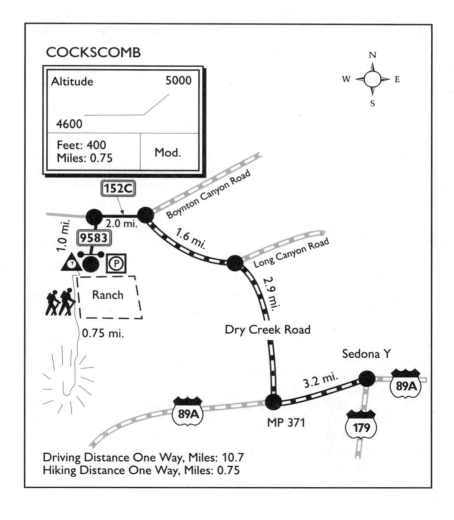

COFFEE POT TRAIL

General Information
Location Map D4
Sedona and Wilson Mt. USGS Maps
Coconino Forest Service Map

Driving Distance One Way: 2.6 miles *4.2 km* (Time 10 minutes)
Access Road: All cars, All paved
Hiking Distance One Way: 1.0 miles *1.6 km* (Time 45 minutes)
How Strenuous: Easy
Features: Rock formations, Views

NUTSHELL: Coffee Pot Rock is one of the most familiar Sedona land-marks. This trail allows you easy access to its base. You walk to a point under the "spout" where you enjoy great views.

DIRECTIONS:
From the Sedona Y Go:
   Southwest on Highway 89A (toward Cottonwood) for a distance of 1.7 miles *2.8 km* (MP 372.5) to Mt. Shadows Street. Turn right onto Mt. Shadows Street. Follow it to the 2.6 mile *4.2 km* point, where it meets Fabulous Texan Way. (The streets in this area are named after movies filmed in Sedona). There you will find a large water storage tank and a microwave tower inside a chain link fence. Drive across the road up onto the dirt apron around the fenced area, where there is parking space for a couple of cars.

TRAILHEAD: At the parking area. No signs posted. Follow the instructions below.

DESCRIPTION: To begin the hike, go through a crawl-through in the fence, a sort of window frame. On the other side you will find several trails, which can be confusing. We found no cairns or other markers, but you can see Coffee Pot Rock ahead of you. Your first objective is to circle to the back of **Sugarloaf**, the hill at the parking place. At every trail fork take the branch that leads toward the back of the Sugarloaf, usually the left fork. The correct path circles the base of Sugarloaf and takes you around to its north side.
   You will pass under a power line. Beyond the line there is a wide cleared place. This is about 0.33 miles *0.5 km* from the beginning. In the clearing you will see a road going up Sugarloaf. The entrance to the road has been blocked by a row of flat red stones. Instead of going up Sugarloaf, look for a jeep road to your right. It heads up a low ridge that connects to the base of

the cliffs where Coffee Pot Rock is located.

Once you get confidently established on this old road, the rest of the hike is easy. Whenever you come to a side path (and there are several of them), just remember where Coffee Pot Rock is and keep moving toward it.

The trail goes to the base of the cliffs and then moves along a ledge toward Coffee Pot. You will enjoy looking at the cliffs here, as they are very colorful and highly sculptured. As the trail nears Coffee Pot it becomes rougher and you have to watch carefully to see where it goes. Eventually the ledge you walk on will reduce down to the point where you can't walk it any further. Here you can look up and see the spout of Coffee Pot towering hundreds of feet above your head. It will seem that you are right under it, though you will be a little west of it.

At this farthest point, about 1.0 mile *1.6 km* from the parking spot, you will have some great views. The views to the north are marred by the plentiful home building that has occurred there.

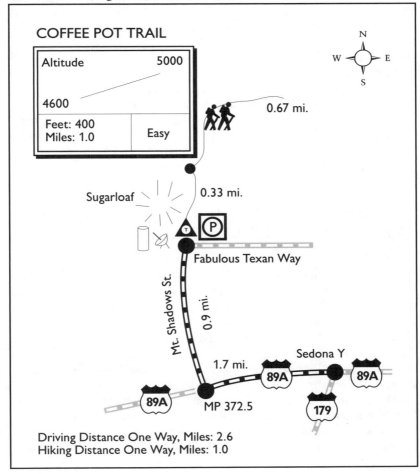

COFFEE POT TRAIL

Altitude	5000
4600	
Feet: 400 Miles: 1.0	Easy

0.67 mi.

Sugarloaf

0.33 mi.

Fabulous Texan Way

Mt. Shadows St.

0.9 mi.

1.7 mi.

Sedona Y

89A

89A

MP 372.5

179

Driving Distance One Way, Miles: 2.6
Hiking Distance One Way, Miles: 1.0

COOKSTOVE TRAIL #143

General Information
Location Map B5
Mountainaire USGS Map
Coconino Forest Service Map

Driving Distance One Way: 12.7 miles *20.4 km* (Time 20 minutes)
Access Road: All cars, All paved
Hiking Distance One Way: 0.75 miles *1.2 km* (Time 45 minutes)
How Strenuous: Hard
Features: Views

NUTSHELL: This is a marked and posted trail located just across Highway 89A from the Pine Flat Campground 12.7 miles *20.4 km* north of Sedona. It climbs the east wall of Oak Creek Canyon.

DIRECTIONS:
From the Sedona Y Go:
   North on Highway 89A (toward Flagstaff) for a distance of 12.7 miles *20.4 km* (MP 386.9) to the Pine Flat Campground. On your left at the upper end of the campground on the shoulder of the highway, you will see a structure about 5 feet high and 4 feet square made of round stones that houses a spring. You will see water flowing out of a pipe that sticks out the back of the structure. Park anywhere near here. There are wide aprons on both shoulders in this area.

TRAILHEAD: On the east side of the road just across Highway 89A from the spring. It is marked by a rusty sign reading, "Cookstove Trail #143."

DESCRIPTION: The water in the spring at Pine Flat is pure, and you will see people filling bottles and jugs there, as we do ourselves. There is a caution about this water, however: even though it is pure, it contains microbes that *your* system may not handle well, whereas local residents can drink it with no trouble.
   The Cookstove Trail is typical of all trails in upper Oak Creek Canyon that climb the east wall of the canyon: namely, it goes virtually straight up with little finesse. Similar trails are **Harding Spring, Purtymun, Thomas Point** and Thompson's Ladder. They are all strenuous hikes.
   The trail starts right by the highway and immediately begins to climb. At first the trail parallels Cookstove Draw. At 0.1 miles *0.16 km* you get a great view down into the draw, where there is a small waterfall during snow melt and after hard rains. Then the trail veers away from Cookstove Draw as it

rises.

The forest through which this trail passes is typical for upper Oak Creek Canyon, with pine at the beginning, changing into mixed pines and firs as you climb and the altitude increases.

The trail does a little zigging and zagging. When you top out, you are in a spot where you get good views of the west wall of Oak Creek Canyon, but the views are not as good as the views you get at the top of the Harding Spring trail.

The altitude at the rim is about 6,600 feet, almost as high as Flagstaff, and the climate is similar to Flagstaff's climate. These hikes can often be pleasant in summer when hiking in Sedona would be too hot.

On the rim the country is flat and not scenic. The old-timers who built these trails would travel to Flagstaff once they got to the top, and did not build trails for the scenery. We like to walk along the rim looking for viewpoints, which are plentiful.

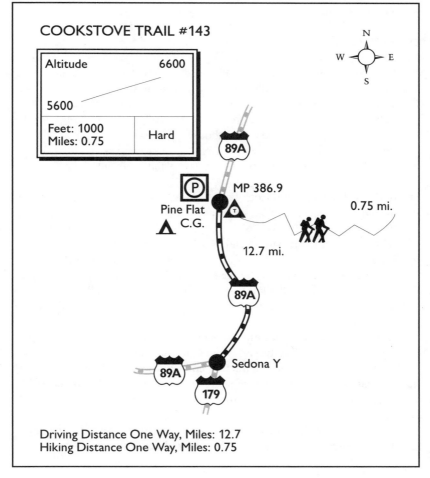

COOKSTOVE TRAIL #143

Altitude	6600
5600	
Feet: 1000 Miles: 0.75	Hard

MP 386.9

Pine Flat
C.G.

0.75 mi.

12.7 mi.

Sedona Y

Driving Distance One Way, Miles: 12.7
Hiking Distance One Way, Miles: 0.75

COURTHOUSE BUTTE BRIDLE TRAIL

General Information
Location Map F5
Sedona and Munds Mt. USGS Maps
Coconino Forest Service Map

Driving Distance One Way: 6.2 miles *9.92 km* (Time 20 minutes)
Access Road: All cars, All paved
Hiking Distance, Complete Loop: 6.0 miles *9.6 km* (Time 3.0 hours)
How Strenuous: Moderate
Features: Views

NUTSHELL: This easy trail features Courthouse Butte, a landmark located south of Sedona.

DIRECTIONS:
From the Sedona Y Go:
     South on Highway 179 (toward Phoenix) for a distance of 6.2 miles *9.92 km* (MP 307.4) to a place south of Bell Rock, just short of the Village of Oak Creek, where you will see a road to your left. This road provides access to the Bell Rock Pathway, a trail created in 1997. There is parking and the Pathway provides access to the Courthouse Butte Trail.

TRAILHEAD: Use the Bell Rock Pathway as the trailhead.

DESCRIPTION: The Bell Rock Pathway is a new trail for this edition, and it is as wide as a road and makes for easy hiking. It runs north to Bell Rock parallel to Highway 179. At a point 0.6 miles *0.96 km* from the beginning, you will be almost to the base of Bell Rock. Here you will find a distinct but much narrower trail running to your right, toward Courthouse Butte. The trail will quickly take you to the base of this Sedona landmark. (The Bell Rock Pathway curves to the left here, circling the base of Bell Rock. It provides an alternative approach to Bell Rock, as the north access is often crowded).
     Unlike many of the rock formations in Sedona that are attached to ridges, mountains or the rim, Courthouse Butte is freestanding.
     Courthouse Butte is very attractive and seems to be "built" on a more human scale than some of the gigantic formations around Sedona. It has weathered into some very interesting carvings and features and has a friendly feel.
     The trail will take you beyond Courthouse Butte to a ridge behind a small subdivision. At 3.0 miles *4.8 km* the trail forks at a fence corner and

turns left toward Lee Mountain. The trail takes you close to Lee Mountain and climbs higher, up a talus slope, as it approaches the mountain. At the trail's highest point you have fine views to the south into the Jack's Canyon and Village of Oak Creek areas. The trail does not go very high against the side of Lee Mountain, just climbing the talus slope and then descending. From this point you follow a wash back to the beginning. If you have doubts about where the trail is, you can generally follow the mountain bike tracks.

What is now called Courthouse Butte was originally called Cathedral Rock and *vice versa*. One of the early government map makers confused the two names and switched them. It doesn't seem to matter much, as either name seems appropriate, but some old-timers were pretty irate about the change.

The country through which this trail passes is cut by several arroyos that carry runoff from Lee Mountain. These arroyos are fun to explore and can make hikes or hikelets in their own right.

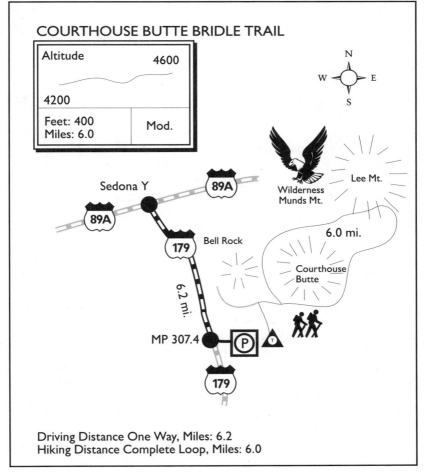

COURTHOUSE BUTTE BRIDLE TRAIL

Altitude	4600
4200	
Feet: 400 Miles: 6.0	Mod.

Sedona Y — 89A

89A

179 — Bell Rock

Lee Mt. — Wilderness Munds Mt.

6.0 mi.

6.2 mi.

Courthouse Butte

MP 307.4 — P — T

179

Driving Distance One Way, Miles: 6.2
Hiking Distance Complete Loop, Miles: 6.0

COW PIES

VORTEX

General Information
Location Map E5
Munds Mt. and Munds Park USGS Maps
Coconino Forest Service Map

Driving Distance One Way: 3.8 miles *6.1 km* (Time 20 minutes)
Access Road: All cars, Last 3.0 miles *4.8 km* bumpy dirt road
Hiking Distance One Way: 1.5 miles *2.4 km* (Time 40 minutes)
How Strenuous: Easy
Features: Views, Fascinating rock formations and sculptures, Vortex

NUTSHELL: An ugly name for a beautiful area. The Cow Pies are redrock formations just off the Schnebly Hill Road, 3.8 miles *6.1 km* east of uptown Sedona. If you like redrocks, you will love the Cow Pies. **A personal favorite**.

DIRECTIONS:
From the Sedona Y Go:
    South on Highway 179 (toward Phoenix) for a distance of 0.3 miles *0.48 km* (MP 313.1) to the Schnebly Hill Road. It is just across the bridge past Tlaquepaque. Turn left onto the Schnebly Hill Road. It is paved for the first 0.5 mile *0.8 km* and then turns into a gravel road that is all right for any car unless the road is muddy. At the 3.8 mile *6.1 km* point, pull over and park.

TRAILHEAD: There are no signs. You will see a trail going over the left side of the road (to the west). Follow it.

DESCRIPTION: What's in a name? Many Sedona landmarks have grand names, such as the Crimson Cliffs. This hike takes place on a formation known by the ugly name, Cow Pies. The name does describe the appearance of the rock forms, but utterly fails to convey a sense of how beautiful and interesting they are. The "pies" look like hardened blobs of soft warm red mud, dropped into Bear Wallow Canyon the way you'd drop cookie dough onto a baking sheet. They are a unique Sedona experience, easy to reach and hike on. We prefer to call these formations "muffins."
    At 0.2 miles *0.32 km* you will come to the first muffin, a redrock shelf that had a very thin crust of volcanic basalt on top. This crust has broken up into small black stones which New Agers have arranged into a giant medicine wheel. This place is one of the fabled Sedona Vortex spots.
    At 0.43 miles *0.7 km* you reach the next muffin. The trail you have been following continues in a straight line (for a hike called **Mitten Ridge**). You

want to quit the trail here and turn to the left. Now you will get a better idea of the muffins. They are mounds of slickrock with many ridges and levels. Walk west, to your left, on the level area to the end of this muffin, where at 0.52 miles *0.84 km* you will find a land bridge linking it to the largest muffins, which sit by themselves in the bottom of the gorge.

You will top out on the Master Muffin at about 0.59 miles *1.0 km*. There is usually a cairn marking this spot. Take note of it, since it will help you find your way down on the return trip. From this point there is no trail. You just walk around and explore. In fact, it is so easy to walk around on these formations that you won't realize how substantial they are until you get to their edges and look down

The farthest extension of these rocks takes you out about 1.5 miles *2.4 km* from the parking place.

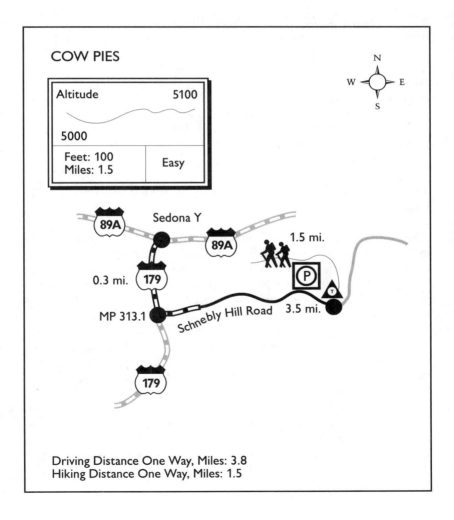

DAMFINO CANYON

General Information
Location Map E5
Munds Mt. and Munds Park USGS Maps
Coconino Forest Service Map

Driving Distance One Way: 1.85 miles *3.0 km* (Time 20 minutes)
Access Road: All cars, Last 1.05 miles *1.68 km* bumpy dirt road
Hiking Distance One Way: 1.0 miles *1.6 km* (Time 45 minutes)
How Strenuous: Moderate
Features: Views, Arches

NUTSHELL: Located off the Schnebly Hill Road, just 1.85 miles *3.0 km* from uptown Sedona, this hike takes you straight up a side canyon in wild and unspoiled country.

DIRECTIONS:
From the Sedona Y Go:
   South on Highway 179 (toward Phoenix) for a distance of 0.30 miles *0.48 km* (MP 313.1) to the Schnebly Hill Road, which is just across the bridge, past Tlaquepaque. Go left on the Schnebly Hill Road (the first half mile is paved) and follow it to the 1.85 mile *3.0 km* point, at a sharp bend.

TRAILHEAD: There are no signs marking this hike. There really is no trail. You work your way up the canyon floor.

DESCRIPTION: The Schnebly Hill Road is very popular and gets a lot of use. Sometimes it is in poor condition, but usually an ordinary passenger car can make it all right. If it is muddy you may need four-wheel drive.
   At 1.85 miles *3.0 km*, at a hairpin turn, you will see Damfino Canyon to your right. There is a clearing at its entrance that is wide enough for four cars. This is the place to park.
   There is an apparent trail on the left bank of the canyon, but do not take it. It vanishes soon, going nowhere. Instead, walk straight up the bottom of the canyon. As you climb, some side canyons will appear. Don't go into these. Stay in the main canyon. At 0.40 miles *0.65 km* you will reach a major fork. Go left there.
   At 0.60 miles *1.0 km* you will see an arch in a redrock cliff ahead of you to your left. At 0.75 miles 1.2 *km* you will see an even bigger arch also on the left. At 1.0 miles *1.6 km* the going gets very rough and steep. This is a good place to stop although if you are hardy and in good shape you might try to struggle farther up the canyon. This is a good hike if you like rock hop-

ping. You get right in amongst the beautiful cliffs which form the walls of this canyon. It has a great remote wilderness feeling.

The original Schnebly Hill Road was built by a coalition of Sedona residents and Coconino County in 1902. Before that time, the only wagon road from Sedona to Flagstaff was along the difficult **Beaverhead** road, which was accessed 11.2 miles *17.92 km* south of Sedona. Damfino Canyon got its name during the 1930s when government officials were surveying the Schnebly Hill Road in order to realign and improve it. The survey party included a pioneer who had participated in the original road construction. When they came to this canyon, the head surveyor asked the old-timer for the name of the canyon. Although the veteran guide had provided the names of many a landmark for the engineer, this particular canyon stumped the old-timer and he replied, "Damn if I know," which came out sounding like "Damfino." The engineer thought he was reciting a name and wrote Damfino Canyon on the official map.

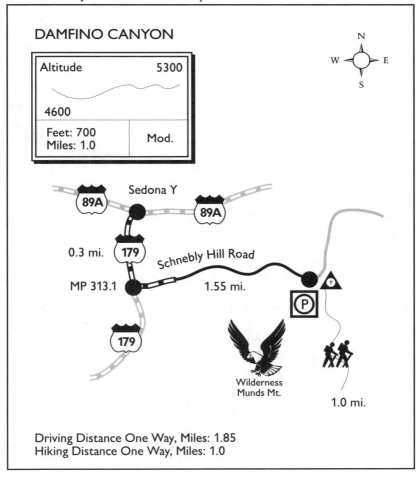

DAMFINO CANYON

Altitude	5300
4600	

Feet: 700 Miles: 1.0	Mod.

N
W — E
S

Sedona Y

89A   89A

0.3 mi.   179

Schnebly Hill Road

MP 313.1   1.55 mi.

179

P

T

Wilderness
Munds Mt.

1.0 mi.

Driving Distance One Way, Miles: 1.85
Hiking Distance One Way, Miles: 1.0

DEER PASS TRAIL

General Information
Location Map G3
Lake Montezuma USGS Map
Coconino Forest Service Map

Driving Distance One Way: 12.0 miles *19.2 km* (Time 25 minutes)
Access Road: Last 1.0 mile *1.6 km* needs high clearance
Hiking Distance One Way: 0.75 miles *1.2 km* (Time 30 minutes)
How Strenuous: Moderate
Features: Interesting canyon, Views

NUTSHELL: A sleeper—you would never know this fine hike is available in the rather drab landscape you see as you drive south on Highway 179. You follow an old cattle trail from a pond up to a pass from which you can see out over the Village of Oak Creek area.

DIRECTIONS:
From the Sedona Y Go:
  Southeast on Highway 179 (toward Phoenix) a distance of 10.4 miles *16.64 km* (MP 303), to FR 120, the Cornville Road, where you take a right turn onto FR 120. Follow FR 120 to the 11.0 mile *17.6 km* point, where you will see the mouth of a shallow wash to your right. There is a lath-type marker here for FR 9501L. Turn right here onto FR 9501L. The wash is a bit difficult to drive across, but most cars should be able to make it. If you have a high clearance vehicle, you can drive all the way to the pond. If you are in a low slung car, park somewhere in the first 0.1 mile *0.16 km* and walk to the pond. It is an easy walk.

TRAILHEAD: There is no marked trail. You walk the jeep road, FR 9501L to a pond, then follow a cattle trail the rest of the way.

DESCRIPTION: There are several small extinct volcanoes in the area you will hike. As you make the approach, one of them stands out, filling the landscape before you. You will walk or drive toward it. At its base the road forks. Take the fork to the left.
  You will head toward a ravine and then follow along its bank to a pond which has been created by damming the ravine. This is a deep dam and the pond holds water in all but the driest years.
  Go past the pond on either side. On the north bank you will see a cattle trail going up the canyon. Although it is not a maintained hiking trail, it is easy to follow and makes a fine path.

From the pond upwards, this hike has a nice remote feeling. You are surrounded by pointy volcanic peaks. There are a few places where some redrock ledges are exposed, adding a welcome touch of color.

As you near the top, you will see that you are heading toward a saddle. At the saddle you will look down on the tremendous development that has taken place in the last few years in the Village of Oak Creek area.

On the northern horizon some area landmarks are well displayed, such as Bell Rock, Courthouse Rock and Cathedral Rock. This is an excellent place to sit and meditate.

For a more adventurous hike, you can climb from the saddle up to the top of Castle Dome, the butte to the east. It is a 500 foot climb in 0.33 miles *0.53 km*.

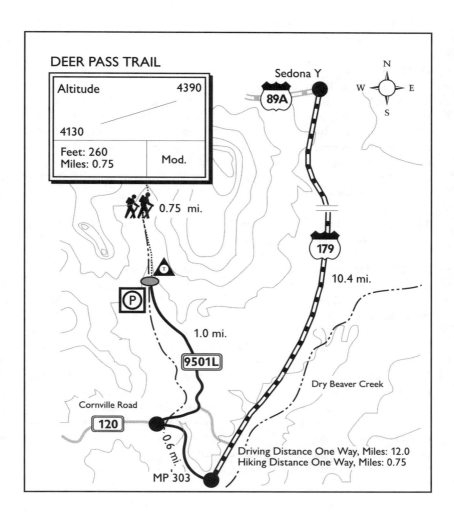

DEVIL'S BRIDGE #120

General Information
Location Map D4
Loy Butte and Wilson Mt. USGS Maps
Coconino Forest Service Map

Driving Distance One Way: 6.5 miles *10.4 km* (Time 30 minutes)
Access Road: All cars, Last 1.3 miles *2.1 km* bumpy dirt road
Hiking Distance One Way: 1.0 miles *1.6 km* (Time 30 minutes)
How Strenuous: Moderate
Features: Views, Arch

NUTSHELL: Located 6.5 miles *10.4 km* northwest of Sedona, this is a short hike to a fascinating arch.

DIRECTIONS:
From the Sedona Y Go:
   Southwest on Highway 89A (toward Cottonwood) for a distance of 3.2 miles *5.12 km* (MP 371) to the Dry Creek Road. Turn right onto Dry Creek Road and follow it to the 5.2 mile *8.4 km* point, where FR 152 branches off to the right. The road is paved to this point. FR 152 is a dirt road that has been improved since the first edition of this book. Ordinary passenger cars can make it, though it can be rough. At 6.5 miles *10.4 km* you will turn right on the signed dirt road to the parking lot.

TRAILHEAD: This is a marked and maintained trail. There is a rusty sign where you park reading "Devil's Bridge #120."

DESCRIPTION: You will walk up an old road for about 0.4 miles *0.7 km*, to a point where the hiking path forks off to your right. You will see that it leads up toward a red ledge on the east face of Capitol Butte. The path is steep but fairly short, being about 0.4 miles *0.7 km* from the fork.
   Halfway up the trail from the fork you will begin to see the arch off to your left in the red ledge. It is hidden from your sight until you get to this point.
   The path itself is very interesting as it begins to climb up the cliff. The Forest Service has used some natural stairsteps made by erosion and has added to these by cementing in some sandstone slabs to form stair steps.
   At the top you have great views into colorful backcountry. You come out behind the arch. You can follow the trail to the end of the arch and loop around to stand on the arch if you are daring. The trail places you in a spot where you are above the arch looking down on it.

To get under the arch, go back down to the bottom of the trail and look for cairns about 100 yards from the bottom, marking a small trail going off to your right. The trail goes down into a wash. You walk up the wash and find yourself under the arch.

This is a fine hike but attracts so many visitors that they may lessen your experience if you like solitude. Devil's Bridge is generally regarded as the largest of the natural arches around Sedona, and is an impressive sight.

If you face across the canyon (N) you will be looking at the last leg of the **Lost Canyon Trail,** which is one of our personal favorites.

After you have reached the top and walk down to the arch, you will see a side trail to your right which is worth a look for the adventurous.

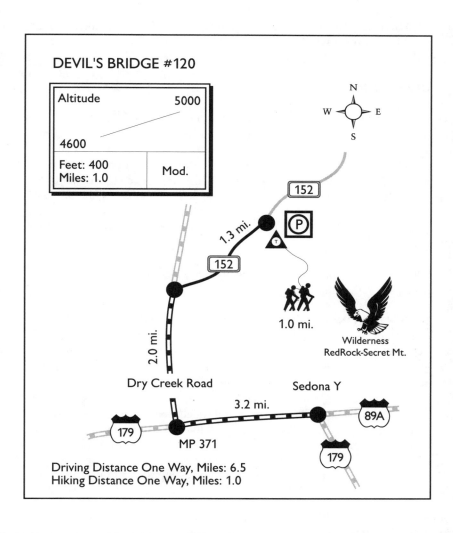

DEVIL'S BRIDGE #120

Altitude	5000
4600	
Feet: 400 Miles: 1.0	Mod.

152

1.3 mi.

152

P

T

2.0 mi.

1.0 mi.

Wilderness
RedRock-Secret Mt.

Dry Creek Road

Sedona Y

3.2 mi.

179

89A

MP 371

179

Driving Distance One Way, Miles: 6.5
Hiking Distance One Way, Miles: 1.0

DOE MOUNTAIN #60

General Information
Location Map D3
Wilson Mt. USGS Map
Coconino Forest Service Map

Driving Distance One Way: 8.9 miles *14.3 km* (Time 20 minutes)
Access Road: All cars, Last 1.2 miles *1.9 km* good dirt road
Hiking Distance One Way: 1.8 miles *2.9 km* (Time 1 hour)
How Strenuous: Moderate
Features: Views

NUTSHELL: This small mesa, 8.9 miles *14.3 km* west of uptown Sedona, is fairly easy to climb. Its weathered cliffs are a delight to explore and it provides great views. **A personal favorite**

DIRECTIONS:
From the Sedona Y Go:
    Southwest on Highway 89A (toward Cottonwood) for 3.2 miles *5.12 km* (MP 371) to Dry Creek Road. Go right on Dry Creek Road to the 6.1 mile *9.8 km* point, where Dry Creek Road joins the Long Canyon Road, both paved. Turn left here, on FR 152C, and go to the 7.7 mile *12.4 km point*, where it joins the Boynton Canyon Road. Turn left here on the Boynton Pass Road, FR 152C. The paving soon ends, to be replaced by a good dirt road. Stop at the 8.9 mile *14.3 km* point, just before a cattle guard. The parking area is on the right. This is also the parking place for the **Bear Mountain** hike.

TRAILHEAD: You will see a rusty sign across the road reading "Doe Mountain #60."

DESCRIPTION: Doe Mountain is a small mesa standing by itself. It is one of the most southerly redrock formations in the west-of-Sedona area. Only the **Cockscomb** is farther south. The trail zigzags to the top of the mesa, climbing steadily. Since our last write-up the trail has been improved. It is now a bit longer, but it climbs up on more gradual grades.
    The top of Doe Mountain is not bare rock as you might think when you see it from a distance. Soil has formed through weathering and low junipers and shrubs grow there. The best part of this hike once on top is to walk around the rim, the edge of which is mostly bare redrock. This means that there are no trees to obstruct your views, so Doe Mountain is a terrific viewpoint and it is situated so that there are interesting things to look at. Views

of Sedona are particularly good from here.

In addition to the views of far off objects, you will see some wonderful things on Doe Mountain itself, where erosion has worked the cliff faces into some really fantastic rock sculptures. The Sedona Westerners report that there are Indian ruins on the top of the mesa but in our trips we have never seen any. The south side of Doe looks down on a tree farm, which is an unexpected and interesting sight. The farm lies between Doe Mountain and the Cockscomb.

The peacefulness and wildness of this hike were spoiled for us twice when helicopter tours touched down here to show tourists the views. If this is progress, spare us.

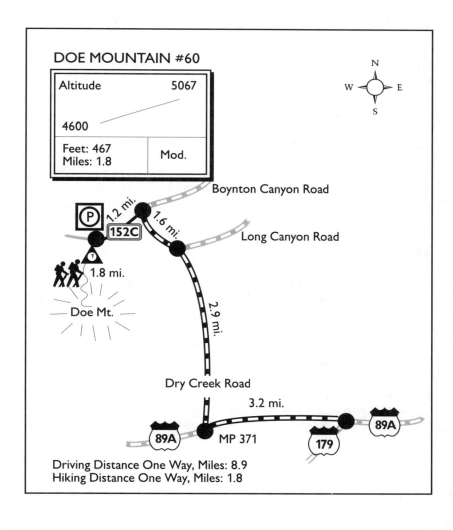

DOE MOUNTAIN #60

Altitude	5067
4600	
Feet: 467 Miles: 1.8	Mod.

Boynton Canyon Road

1.2 mi.

152C

1.6 mi.

Long Canyon Road

1.8 mi.

Doe Mt.

2.9 mi.

Dry Creek Road

3.2 mi.

89A   MP 371   179   89A

Driving Distance One Way, Miles: 8.9
Hiking Distance One Way, Miles: 1.8

DOGIE TRAIL #116

General Information
Location Map C1
Loy Butte and Clarkdale USGS Maps
Coconino Forest Service Map

Driving Distance One Way: 20.7 miles *33 km* (Time 45 minutes)
Access Road: All cars, Last 11.1 miles *17.8 km* good dirt road
Hiking Distance One Way: 4.0 miles *6.4 km* (Time 2.5 hours)
How Strenuous: Moderate
Features: Sycamore Canyon access, Views

NUTSHELL: This hike provides access into Sycamore Canyon at Sycamore Pass, located 20.7 miles *33 km* northwest of Sedona.

DIRECTIONS:
From The Y in Sedona Go:
Southwest on Highway 89A (toward Cottonwood) a distance of 9.6 miles *15.4 km* (MP 364.5) to the Red Canyon Road. Turn right on Red Canyon Road, also known as FR 525, and follow it to the 12.4 mile *19.8 km* point where FR 525C branches to the left. Turn left on FR 525C and stay on it to the 15.6 mile *25 km* point where it meets FR 761, the Bill Gray Road. Your destination is Sycamore Pass. Go right here, staying on FR 525C to the 19.7 mile *31.6 km* point, where it meets FR 9529. Turn left here and go to the 20.7 mile *33 km* point, where the road meets FR 9528. Park near this intersection. Don't try to drive on FR 9528.

TRAILHEAD: At the intersection beyond your parking spot you will see a road sign reading, *"Sycamore Pass, Dogie Trail"* with an arrow pointing to the right. Follow the arrow and walk down the road. You will reach a fork in the road, where you should take the right hand path. From there you will walk down a jeep road to the trailhead. Distance from the parking area to the trailhead is 0.5 miles *0.8 km*.
At the trailhead you will see a sign: *"Sycamore Canyon 5 miles, Sycamore Basin Trail 5.5 miles, Road 525C 0.5 miles, Dogie Trail #116."*

DESCRIPTION: From the beginning, this trail slopes gradually toward Sycamore Canyon. You will walk down an old stock trail that is very rocky, but the grade is gentle. After hiking a few hundred yards, the landscape will open up to some great views ahead of you, where you will see redrock spires and buttes that are just as impressive as those nearer Sedona.
There are two cattle tanks on this trail. To get to the first one, you must

detour to your left. The path goes right around the rim of the second one.

We recommend that you stop at about the 3.0 mile *4.8 km* or 4.0 mile *6.4 km* point rather than going all the way into Sycamore Canyon, for it is a very strenuous hike to go to the bottom. By staying on top you will have a fine hike and enjoy tremendous views. Remember that the return leg of this hike is all uphill.

Sycamore Canyon is a huge wild place. Even experienced hikers should not attempt a multi-day trip through it unless they are thoroughly prepared and know what they are doing. The brief sight of the canyon you get on a day hike like this is misleading and understates the rigors of the place. It is very beautiful and deserves to be better known and visited, as we hope to encourage in this book, but please do not overextend yourself.

DRY CREEK TRAIL #52

General Information
Location Map C4
Loy Butte and Wilson Mt. USGS Maps
Coconino Forest Service Map

Driving Distance One Way: 9.6 miles *15.4 km* (Time 45 minutes)
Access Road: Most cars, Last 4.4 miles *7.0 km* Bumpy unpaved road
Hiking Distance One Way: 2.0 miles *3.2 km* (Time 1 hour)
How Strenuous: Moderate
Features: Scenic canyon

NUTSHELL: Located 9.6 miles *15.4 km* north of Sedona, this is a wilderness hike that follows the course of Dry Creek to its head at the base of the Mogollon Rim.

DIRECTIONS:
From The Y in Sedona Go:
Southwest on Highway 89A (toward Cottonwood) for 3.2 miles *5.12 km* (MP 371) to Dry Creek Road. Turn right on Dry Creek Road and proceed to the 5.2 mile *8.4 km* point. Turn right on FR 152, the Vultee Arch Road, and follow it to its end at the 9.6 mile *15.4 km* point. Here there is a parking loop, with the **Vultee Arch** Trailhead at the tip. Curve around and head back, and you will see the parking for the **Bear Sign** and Dry Creek trails to your right, just a few yards beyond the Vultee Arch parking spot.

TRAILHEAD: The parking area is in a grove of trees. Walk west across a little gully. There you will see a rusty sign marked "Dry Creek #52."

DESCRIPTION: Since the first edition of this book came out, FR 152 has been improved and can now be driven by any car with reasonable clearance if you keep a lookout for rocks and ruts.

From the parking place, walk across a little arroyo and around the toe of a hill for about 0.10 miles *0.16 km* where you will encounter Dry Creek. Where you enter it, the canyon cut by Dry Creek is rather shallow and wide. The trail follows up the creek (which usually is *dry*, living up to its name) in a northerly direction.

If there is any appreciable amount of water in the creek, you might want to postpone this hike for another day when the creek is dry because the trail crosses the creekbed at least a dozen times.

As you walk, the trail gains altitude but this is a gradual climb and you are barely conscious of it. The walking is pretty easy and the trail is a good one.

At 0.63 miles *1.0 km* you reach a point where the creek forks at a reef. The left hand channel is the **Bear Sign Trail** and the right fork is the Dry Creek Trail. There is a rusty sign in the left channel marked "Bear Sign #59." From this point the canyon deepens and you are treated to the sight of giant redrock buttes on both sides of the creek. As you proceed you will notice a change in the vegetation as the increase in altitude causes changes in the life zones.

The trail ends where it intersects a channel running east and west. We are informed that this channel can be hiked but it would be very steep and rugged, for advanced hikers only. To the east, it appears to go all the way to the top of the rim to East Pocket, where the East Pocket fire lookout tower is located.

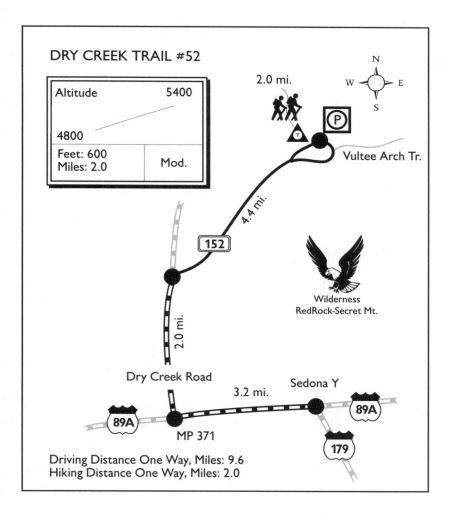

DRY CREEK TRAIL #52

Altitude	5400
4800	
Feet: 600 Miles: 2.0	Mod.

2.0 mi.

Vultee Arch Tr.

4.4 mi.

152

Wilderness
RedRock-Secret Mt.

2.0 mi.

Dry Creek Road

Sedona Y

3.2 mi.

89A

89A

MP 371

179

Driving Distance One Way, Miles: 9.6
Hiking Distance One Way, Miles: 2.0

FAY CANYON #53

General Information
Location Map C3
Wilson Mt. USGS Map
Coconino Forest Service Map

Driving Distance One Way: 8.2 miles *13.2 km* (Time 20 minutes)
Access Road: All cars, Last half mile good dirt road
Hiking Distance One Way: 1.2 miles *2.0 km* (Time 30 minutes)
How Strenuous: Moderate
Features: Views, Arch, Indian ruins

NUTSHELL: This is an easy hike 8.2 miles *13.2 km* northwest of uptown Sedona, featuring a lovely canyon on the side of Bear Mountain with a natural arch and Indian ruins. **A personal favorite.**

DIRECTIONS:
From the Sedona Y Go:
    Southwest on Highway 89A (toward Cottonwood) for a distance of 3.2 miles *5.12 km* (MP 371) to Dry Creek Road. Turn right onto Dry Creek Road and follow it to the 6.1 mile *9.8 km* point, where it intersects the Long Canyon Road, where you turn left on FR 152C. Stay on FR 152C to the 7.7 mile *12.4 km* point, where it intersects the Boynton Canyon Road. Here you will turn left onto the Boynton Pass Road. It is paved for a short distance and then becomes unpaved. At the 8.2 mile *13.2 km* point you will reach the driveway to the parking area, which is off to your right. Pull in and park there.

TRAILHEAD: You will see a rusty sign at the gate: "Fay Canyon #53."

DESCRIPTION: The trail is gentle and wide. You will find a forest of oaks, many of them quite sizable. Though the canyon is short, about one mile long, it is broad and very scenic. There are impressive red cliffs on both sides with buff colored cliffs rimming the back of the canyon.
    At just over 0.50 miles *0.8 km*, a side trail branches off to the right (E) and makes a sharp climb up the east side of the canyon to Fay Arch. This trail is usually marked with cairns. The path to the arch is nothing like the main trail. It seems to have just been scratched out of the side of the canyon haphazardly. It is steep and there are places where the footing is tricky. Aunt Maude would have no trouble with the main trail along the canyon floor but the climb to the arch would be too much for her.
    There is a small Indian ruin just before you reach the arch. This isn't much of a ruin, just knee high walls outlining one room in a low, shallow

cave. There are a few rock art figures on the cliff face above the ruin but we suspect that they are modern. Canyon wrens, tiny birds with a glorious call, live in this cliff face, and if you are lucky you may hear one.

There is a narrow slot between the arch and the wall from which it has broken away. You can stand underneath the gap and look up through it for an interesting view. The clamber up the side of the canyon would be worthwhile for the views even if there were no arch. Spectacular.

After visiting the arch, return to the main trail and continue up the canyon. Near its end it forks around a redrock fin that sticks out like the prow of a ship. You can quit right where you are for a 1.2 mile *2.0 km* hike or you can climb up on the fin. You can go in either direction around the fin, but we recommend the left hand fork. It will take you up and out on a slickrock shelf where you will find a few caves that contain fragmentary Indian ruins.

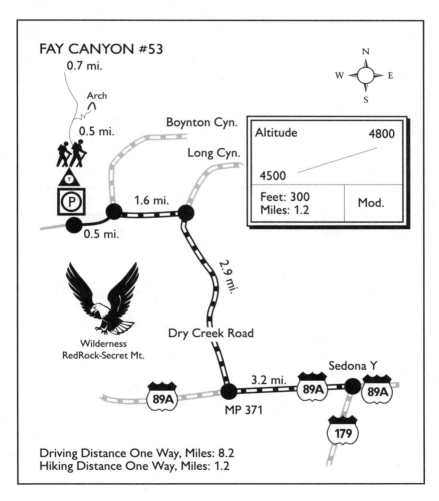

FAY CANYON #53

0.7 mi.

Arch

0.5 mi.

Boynton Cyn.

Long Cyn.

1.6 mi.

0.5 mi.

2.9 mi.

Dry Creek Road

Wilderness
RedRock-Secret Mt.

Altitude	4800
4500	
Feet: 300 Miles: 1.2	Mod.

Sedona Y

89A

89A

89A

MP 371

3.2 mi.

179

Driving Distance One Way, Miles: 8.2
Hiking Distance One Way, Miles: 1.2

FLUME ROAD TRAIL #154

General Information
Location Map G6
Strawberry USGS Map
Coconino Forest Service Map

Driving Distance One Way: 52.2 miles *83.5 km* (Time 1.5 hours)
Access Road: All cars, Last 16.8 miles *26.9 km* good dirt road
Hiking Distance One Way: 4.0 miles *6.4 km* (Time 2.0 hours)
How Strenuous: Moderate, but you have to wade across Fossil Creek
Features: Historic flume, Gorgeous riparian creek, Wide easy trail, Views

NUTSHELL: This adventure is worth making for the sake of the drive alone, but includes wild country, an historic electrical power plant and flume, a spring-fed creek and great natural beauty. NOTE: You must be equipped with wading shoes and shorts to wade across the creek at the beginning.

DIRECTIONS:
From the Sedona Y Go:
    South on Highway 179 (toward Phoenix) for 14.7 miles *23.6 km*, to the I-17 Interchange. Turn south on I-17 and go to the 23.6 miles *37.8 km* point, where you take Exit 289 for Camp Verde. Go into Camp Verde, where you will come to a stop light at 27.3 miles *43.7 km*. Turn left here and go east on Highway 260 to the 35.4 mile *56.6 km* point (MP 228.5), where you turn right (south) on unpaved FR 708. It is signed. Follow this narrow winding mountain road to the 49.5 mile *79.2 km* point, where it meets FR 502. Turn left (east), staying on FR 708 and go just past the Irving power plant. At the 52.2 mile point *83.5 km*, turn left into the trailhead parking. It is signed.

TRAILHEAD: At the parking lot.

DESCRIPTION: The flume you will follow on this hike carries water through two hydroelectric turbines, one at Irving, and the other at Childs. This hike follows the road used when the flume was built in 1916. The road is still used for maintenance.
    Crossing the creek means wading across a swift mountain stream. You will want wading shoes for this and perhaps a stick for balancing. The water will be knee to hip high, so be prepared. Once across, you must turn to your left (west) and hike about twenty yards to pick up the trail. (There is also a path to the right [east], along the creekbank, but it is not the hiking trail). From the creek level, the trail goes up steeply for 0.5 miles *0.8 km* to meet

the road.

Once on the road, you walk east up the canyon for 3.5 miles *5.6 km*, with the flume as your constant companion. The flume construction was quite a project for 1916.

You climb, but the grade is gradual, and this is not a strenuous hike. Along the way, you will enjoy the scenery, from the rich geological diversity to the sweeping views. The canyon is impressive, and so are the surrounding cliffs, whose rocks are multi-hued.

In the last quarter mile, the road dips down to lush riparian creek level, ending at a dam. From the dam, the flume begins its seven mile journey down to the Verde River. The steep fall of the canyon and the copious springs mean that the water develops plenty of power, enough to keep those turbines humming.

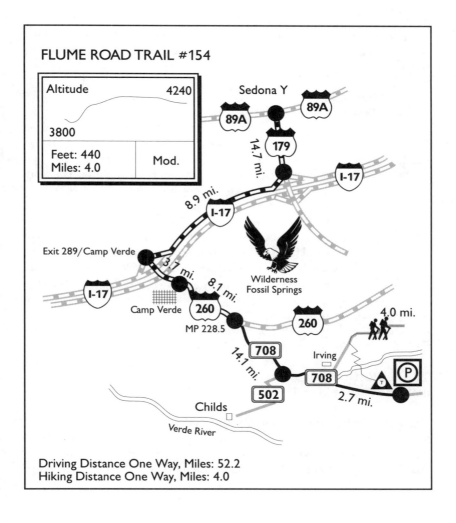

FLUME ROAD TRAIL #154

Altitude	4240
3800	
Feet: 440 Miles: 4.0	Mod.

Sedona Y

89A 89A 179 I-17

14.7 mi.

8.9 mi. I-17

Exit 289/Camp Verde

3.7 mi.

Wilderness Fossil Springs

I-17 Camp Verde 260 MP 228.5

8.1 mi. 260 4.0 mi.

14.1 mi. 708 Irving 708

502 2.7 mi.

Childs

Verde River

Driving Distance One Way, Miles: 52.2
Hiking Distance One Way, Miles: 4.0

GADDES CANYON TRAIL #110

General Information
Location Map G1 (off the map)
Cottonwood, Hickey Mtn. USGS Maps
Prescott Forest Service Map

Driving Distance One Way: 40.1 miles *64.16 km* (Time 1 hour)
Access Road: All vehicles, Last 4.5 miles *7.2 km* good gravel roads
Hiking Distance One Way: 3.0 miles *4.8 km* (Time 2.5 hours)
How Strenuous: Moderate to hard
Features: Jerome, Mountain trail through pine forests, Spring, Pretty canyon

NUTSHELL: You pass through Jerome and go up to Mingus Mountain, where you take one of Mingus's main trails, passing through pleasant pine forests to a point just below the fire lookout tower.

DIRECTIONS:
From the Sedona Y Go:
Southwest on Highway 89A. As you enter Cottonwood, do not turn on Highway 260. Keep going on Highway 89A. At the 23.2 mile *37.12 km* point, you will come to a stoplight where Highway 89A turns left. The sign is marked, "To Prescott." Take this left turn and keep going on Highway 89A and you will soon begin to climb the long hill to Jerome. At 28.0 miles *44.8 km*, you will come to the stop sign in downtown Jerome. Turn right here, staying on Highway 89A. You will immediately begin to climb Mingus Mountain on a very winding road through a scenic canyon, where you will see ruins of old industrial structures. As you near the top of Mingus, you will see signs for the Mingus Recreation Area, which is your goal. The turn for the recreation area is at 35.6 miles *57 km* MP 336.3. Turn left on the gravel road toward Mingus Camp. At 37.1 miles *59.36 km* you will reach a road junction, where you turn right on FR 413, the road to Cherry. Stay on it to the 40.1 mile *64.16 km* point, where you will see the Gaddes Canyon trailhead sign. Pull off to the right and park.

TRAILHEAD: This is a marked and maintained trail, part of a network of trails on Mingus Mountain.

DESCRIPTION: This book is entitled *Sedona Hikes*, and to make that legitimate, we try to confine the hikes to places near Sedona. We have found that many Sedona visitors include a trip to Jerome as part of the things to see and do in Sedona. For Sedona residents, Jerome is a good place to go to escape summer heat. So we include this hike for both groups. Previously, we hesitated to recommend the Mingus Mt. trails, but in 1994 the Forest Service did some major work, and these trails are now well delineated and signed; so that we are happy to recommend them.

We love Jerome. For us, a perfect day is to go to Jerome in the morning, spend a while browsing the shops and sightseeing, have lunch there, and then toodle on up to Mingus for a post-lunch hike.

This trail climbs about 700 feet in the first mile, but the path is good and the forest is shady and pleasant. You then top out on an old road, which is rocky but level, and walk along it for half a mile. After that, you descend to the bottom of Gaddes Canyon and come up out of it walking along its east bank, for the last leg of the trail. Half a mile from the end you will pass by Gaddes Spring, a fenced green area to your right. From the spring you climb out of the canyon to end the trail on the road to the fire lookout, 0.25 miles *0.4 km* below the fire tower.

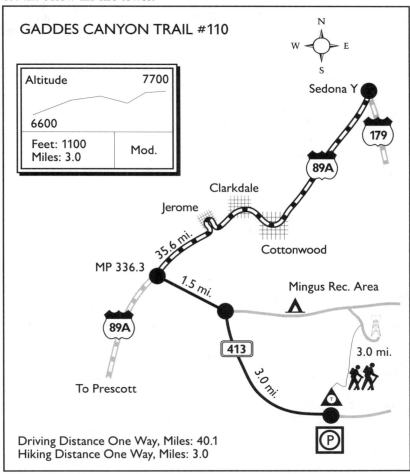

GADDES CANYON TRAIL #110

Altitude   7700

6600

Feet: 1100
Miles: 3.0   Mod.

N
W   E
S

Sedona Y

179

89A

Clarkdale

Jerome

35.6 mi.

Cottonwood

MP 336.3

1.5 mi.

Mingus Rec. Area

89A

413

3.0 mi.

To Prescott

3.0 mi.

P

Driving Distance One Way, Miles: 40.1
Hiking Distance One Way, Miles: 3.0

GENERAL CROOK TRAIL, P 5-7

General Information
Location Map G1
Middle Verde USGS Map
Coconino Forest Service Map

Driving Distance One Way: 35.9 miles *57.44 km* (Time 1 hour)
Access Road: All cars, Last 2.9 miles *4.64 km* good unpaved road
Hiking Distance One Way: 2.25 miles *3.6 km* (Time 1.5 Hours)
How Strenuous: Easy
Features: Famous old trail built in 1871 during the Apache wars, Enchanting riparian ramble

NUTSHELL: We have picked an interesting and scenic segment of this historic trail that is easy to reach and offers something rare in Arizona—a streamside walk.

DIRECTIONS:
From the Sedona Y Go:
   South on Highway 179 (toward Phoenix) for 14.7 miles *23.6 km*, to the I-17 Interchange. Turn south on I-17 and go to the 27.7 miles *44.32 km* point, where you take Exit 285 "Gen. Crook Trail," to Camp Verde. You will reach a stop sign at the 28.2 mile *45.12 km* point. Turn left on Yavapai 35 and go to a road fork at 31.3 miles *50.08 km,* where you turn right on Highway 260. You will immediately come to a stop sign at 31.4 miles *50.24 km.* Turn right here, still on Highway 260. Follow Highway 260 east to the 31.6 mile *50.56 km* point, where you turn right on Salt Mine Road. Follow Salt Mine Road to the 33.0 mile *52.8 km* point, where you turn right on Oasis Road. Take an immediate left on FR 136 and drive it to the 35.9 mile *57.44 km* point, where you see an old corral to your right. Pull off here and park.

TRAILHEAD: FR 136 is the General Crook Trail.

DESCRIPTION: This hike takes you along the Prescott leg of the General Crook Trail. Although the trail was built 1871-1874, well before the days of modern engineering, using nothing but mule power and a little black powder, our forefathers knew the terrain intimately and found the line of least resistance on which to locate their roads and trails. General Crook's people picked Copper Canyon as a natural land route by means of which they could lift out of the Verde Valley and get into the high country. There was a bonus to this route: it contained water (in the stretch you will hike), and the Apaches—for some unexplained reason—would not go into the canyon.

Modern engineers could do no better than to locate later roads right on top of Crook's road here.

As you drive into the canyon, you will see typical bare high desert landscape, little suspecting that there is a hidden Shangri-La awaiting you. From the point where we have you park, which was Mile 5 on the classic road, you will soon cross a little stream. From this point onward you will have the stream at your side, accompanied by lush growth. The stream meanders across the road several times, shoe-top high, so you may want to being a towel, so you can wade across and dry your feet. We think you will love this two-mile portion of the trail, as you move quietly through this enchanted place, thinking of an earlier time, while high overhead, a jillion cars roar back and forth on I-17.

Look for a little waterfall in a side canyon to your left. The hike ends at a green metal gate. Just beyond it, the stream disappears. You can go on, though stopping at the gate makes a lovely and relaxing day hike.

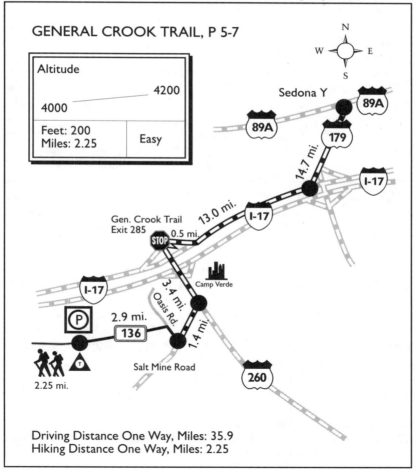

GENERAL CROOK TRAIL, P 5-7

Altitude
4200
4000
Feet: 200
Miles: 2.25
Easy

Sedona Y
89A
89A
179
I-17
14.7 mi.
13.0 mi.
I-17
Gen. Crook Trail
Exit 285
STOP 0.5 mi.
Camp Verde
I-17
3.4 mi.
Oasis Rd.
2.9 mi.
136
1.4 mi.
Salt Mine Road
260
2.25 mi.

Driving Distance One Way, Miles: 35.9
Hiking Distance One Way, Miles: 2.25

GENERAL CROOK TRAIL, V 13-14

General Information
Location Map G6
Hackberry Mtn., Walker Mtn. USGS Maps
Coconino Forest Service Map

Driving Distance One Way: 44.7 miles *71.52 km* (Time 1.2 hours)
Access Road: All cars, Last 0.05 miles *0.08 km* medium unpaved
Hiking Distance One Way: 1.8 miles *2.88 km* (Time 1.5 Hours)
How Strenuous: Hard due to steepness
Features: Famous old trail built in 1871 during the Apache wars, Views

NUTSHELL: We have picked an interesting and scenic segment of this historic trail that is easy to reach and offers a satisfying loop hike.

DIRECTIONS:
From the Sedona Y Go:
   South on Highway 179 (toward Phoenix) for 14.7 miles *23.6 km,* to the I-17 Interchange. Turn south on I-17 and go to the 27.7 miles *44.32 km* point, where you take Exit 285 "Gen. Crook Trail," to Camp Verde. You will reach a stop sign at the 28.2 mile *45.12 km* point. Turn left on Yavapai 35 and go to a road fork at 31.3 miles *50.08 km,* where you turn right on Highway 260. You will immediately come to a stop sign at 31.4 miles *50.24 km.* Turn right here, still on Highway 260. Follow Highway 260 east. The road will begin to climb to the rim. At the 44.65 mile *71.44 km* point (MP 234.1), you will see a dirt road going uphill to your left. Take this road through the gate in the barbed wire fence and drive a couple of hundred yards to the top of a saddle. Park there, at 44.7 miles *71.52 km.*

TRAILHEAD: The Gen. Crook Trail comes across the saddle where you park. Markers are posts planted in cairns. Take the trail to your right (NE).

DESCRIPTION: At the point where you pick up the trail and begin hiking, 13-Mile Rock Butte fills the sky before you. This was a well-known landmark on the old military road, and a welcome one, as it told travelers they were near 13-Mile Spring.
   The General Crook Trail was built by the army in 1871, as a means of connecting Fort Whipple, at Prescott, with Camp Apache on the Mogollon Rim, with an intermediate stop in Camp Verde. The trail was 200 miles *320 km* long and was used until 1928, but was eventually abandoned. In 1975, 133 miles *212.8 km* of the trail was located, cleared and marked for recreational use by Boy Scouts. In the old days, the trail between Camp Verde

and Camp Apache was marked every mile by a V. Modern V markers follow this practice.

The first part of this hike is not on the old trail, which is covered by Highway 260. It is a hiker trail located above and parallel to the old trail. At about 0.5 miles *0.8 km* you will look down to your right onto the 13-Mile Rock monument at a roadside pullout.

You will reach the V-13 milepost at 0.7 miles *1.12 km.* Go left here. Soon you will reach a strange long row of stones. Here you get back on the real wagon road to the end of the hike. At 1.0 miles *1.6 km* you will reach a trail fork where a sign gives the choice of taking the original rough route or a later reroute. Take the lower, newer road here. You will climb gradually to the top of a ridge near the V-14 marker, where the old and new trails merge again at 1.8 miles *2.88 km.* Turn around and go back on the old road and enjoy great views.

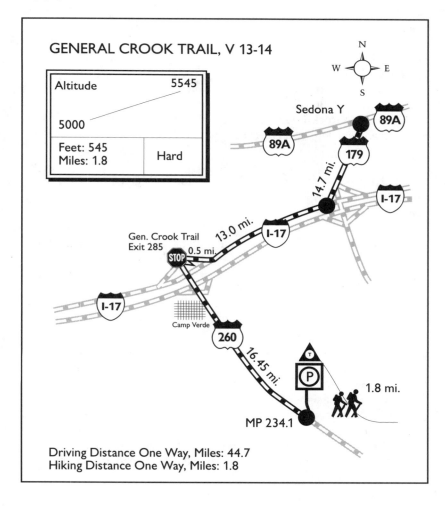

GENERAL CROOK TRAIL, V 13-14

Altitude	5545
5000	
Feet: 545 Miles: 1.8	Hard

Sedona Y

89A

89A

179

I-17

14.7 mi.

13.0 mi.

I-17

Gen. Crook Trail Exit 285

STOP 0.5 mi.

I-17

Camp Verde

260

16.45 mi.

P

1.8 mi.

MP 234.1

Driving Distance One Way, Miles: 44.7
Hiking Distance One Way, Miles: 1.8

GOOSENECKS

General Information
Location Map F3
Sedona USGS Map
Coconino Forest Service Map

Driving Distance One Way: 7.3 miles *11.68 km* (Time 15 minutes)
Access Road: All vehicles, All paved
Hiking Distance One Way: 1.8 miles *2.88 km* (Time 1.0 hours)
How Strenuous: Moderate
Features: Views, Picnic site on the banks of Oak Creek, Easy to reach

NUTSHELL: This hike follows a horse trail from the Lower Red Rock Loop Road to the Goosenecks of Oak Creek through pretty back country.

DIRECTIONS:
From the Sedona Y Go:
   Southwest on Highway 89 (toward Cottonwood) for a distance of 5.5 miles *8.8 km* (MP 368.6) to the Lower Red Rock Loop Road. Turn left on the Lower Red Rock Loop Road and follow it to the 7.3 miles *11.68 km* point, where you will see a gravel parking apron to your right big enough for about four cars.

TRAILHEAD: Walk back the way you came for about 170 paces, where you will see a trail to your left (W). It is marked with a lath bearing a horse symbol.

DESCRIPTION: This is a horse trail and you may encounter some riders coming over from the stables to the west. If you look at the lath marking the trail you will see that the letter S has been added to it. You will first follow Trail S.
   Hike the horse trail up and down some low red hills until at 0.6 miles *0.96 km*, you come to a red dirt road, FR 9845. Keep walking straight ahead, where you will see horse Trail S take up again after crossing the road. At this point you will walk for a time behind a subdivision, just outside the fence that encloses it. At the 1.0 mile *1.6 km* point you will reach a trail junction. Go left here (S), turning away from the fence. You will go over a rise and soon will be out of sight of the works of man.
   From now on you will be in a terrain that is scenic with hills and cliffs; so there is a bit of going up and down, but nothing strenuous. At the 1.3 mile *2.08 km* point you will meet a jeep road. In a few steps the trail veers away from the road only to join it again a short distance beyond, then move away

from it and join it again. Hike on the horse trail wherever you meet the road—don't follow the road. The horse trail switches numbers in this area and becomes Trail A.

At the 1.5 mile *2.4 km* point you will come to a viewpoint where you can see down into Oak Creek, where the stream makes a couple of recurving goosenecks against a high wall of red cliffs. The trail forks here, with one branch going down to the creek and the other going up over a hill. Take the left fork, going downhill.

You will now encounter the most strenuous part of this trail, which drops 250 feet in 0.3 miles *0.48 km*, but it is well worth the effort. When you reach the bottom you will find that you have come to a secluded bend in the river where the creek forms a long pool against red cliffs. This is a very pretty, quiet spot, perfect for a picnic.

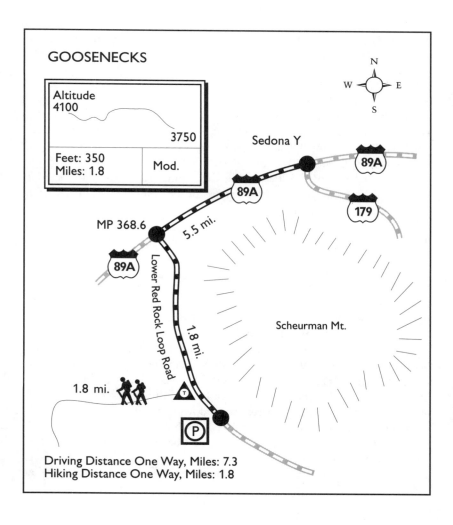

GRIEF HILL

General Information
Location Map G1
Middle Verde USGS Map
Prescott Forest Service Map

Driving Distance One Way: 31.1 miles *49.76 km* (Time 45 Minutes)
Access Road: All cars, Last 1.1 miles *1.76 km* good dirt road
Hiking Distance Complete Loop: 7.0 miles *11.2 km* (Time 5 Hours)
How Strenuous: Strenuous, steep. Pathfinding required. *For experienced hikers*
Features: Historic old road, Views

NUTSHELL: You will hike a portion of one of the oldest roads in northern Arizona, of 1864 vintage, enjoying grand views.

DIRECTIONS:
From the Sedona Y Go:
   South on Highway 179 (toward Phoenix) for 14.7 miles *23.6 km*, to the I-17 Interchange. Drive I-17 south to the 26.4 miles *42.24 km* point, where you take Exit 287. At the stop sign, go right (W), toward Cottonwood on Highway 260. At the 29.0 mile *46.4 km* point (MP 215.8), turn left on the Cherry Road, Yavapai 75. Paving ends in a mile. Keep going to the 31.1 mile *49.76 km* point, where you see signs for the Grief Hill Trailhead, with a parking area and toilet to your left.

TRAILHEAD: As you pull into the parking lot, you will see a track heading south, FR 9650C. This is the trail.

DESCRIPTION: Read the interpretive signs by the toilet, but be advised that they give a very misleading impression of the hike. The hiking trail does not go up Grief Hill. Instead, it circles Hull Hill, which is the big hill you see. You can't see Grief Hill from the lot.
   For the first mile you hike FR 9650C along the flat. Do not turn right on 9650B, up the hill. FR 9650C moves SE-S along the base of Hull Hill, ending at Hull Hill Tank. Here the road ends and the next leg is a footpath. Look SE, above the tank, where the trail is a bare dirt trail going uphill. Climb about 100 feet, then level off across a meadow, where the trail is hard to see. Keep angling SE at about the same level, climbing to the right only enough to avoid the arroyo on the far side. The trail becomes visible again a few yards above the arroyo.
   At 2.3 miles *3.68 km,* you will come to the top of a narrow ridge. You

drop down the other side onto a good dirt road. Turn right and follow the road along Grief Hill Wash into a scenic fold among three hills where water tanks and corrals are located, at the 3.0 mile *4.8 km* point. As you stand at the corral, Grief Hill is the long, high crescent shaped hill to the SW. You do not climb it. Walk straight through the corrals and on the far side, still at creek level, you will find the trail.

From the corrals, the trail follows the banks of the main channel, between Hull Hill and Grief Hill, crossing the streambed several times, making a 400 foot climb to a saddle, the 4.0 mile *6.4 km* point, where there is a gate. From here you make a mile-long 720 foot descent into a wash. This leg has poor footing and must be taken slowly.

In the wash, turn right and walk up the wide sandy bottom to a fence, where you take a road to the left. It brings you up onto the Cherry Road. From here it is another 1.0 mile *1.6 km* walking Cherry Road back to the parking lot.

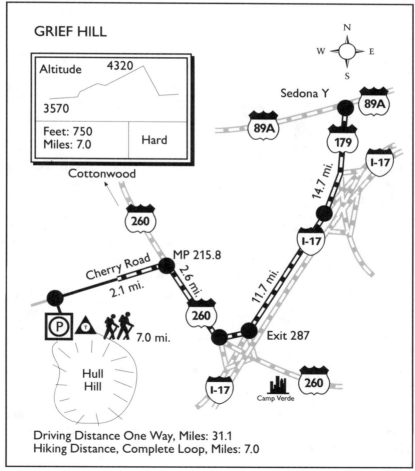

GRIEF HILL

Altitude 4320
3570
Feet: 750
Miles: 7.0
Hard

Cottonwood

Sedona Y

89A

89A

179

I-17

14.7 mi.

260

I-17

Cherry Road   MP 215.8

2.1 mi.   2.6 mi.   11.7 mi.

260

P   7.0 mi.

Exit 287

Hull
Hill

I-17   Camp Verde   260

Driving Distance One Way, Miles: 31.1
Hiking Distance, Complete Loop, Miles: 7.0

HARDING SPRING TRAIL #51

General Information
Location Map B5
Mountainaire and Munds Park USGS Maps
Coconino Forest Service Map

Driving Distance One Way: 11.4 miles *18.3 km* (Time 20 minutes)
Access Road: All cars, All paved
Hiking Distance One Way: 0.80 miles *1.3 km* (Time 45 minutes)
How Strenuous: Hard
Features: Views

NUTSHELL: This is a marked and posted trail located just across Highway 89A from the Cave Spring Campground 11.4 miles *18.3 km* north of Sedona. It climbs the east wall of Oak Creek Canyon.

DIRECTIONS:
From the Sedona Y Go:
   North on Highway 89A (toward Flagstaff) for a distance of 11.4 miles *18.3 km* (MP 385.6) to the entrance to the Cave Spring Campground, which is on your left (west). Park anywhere around here on the shoulder of the road.

TRAILHEAD: On the east side of Highway 89A just across from the Cave Spring Campground entrance. It is marked by a rusty sign reading, "Harding Spring Trail #51."

DESCRIPTION: There is no official parking area for this hike. Cars park all along the shoulders of the road wherever there is a wide spot. If you are lucky you might find a parking spot in the Cave Spring Campground but don't count on it. Camping in the campground requires the payment of a fee.
   Since you will be so near the Cave Spring Campground after you park, you might as well walk into the campground and take a look at Cave Spring, as it is an interesting place.
   Like the other trails going up the east wall of upper Oak Creek Canyon the Harding Spring trail goes virtually straight up with little finesse. You start in a pine and spruce forest and then reach a more open area as you climb above tree line. Then you get into a region of pine forest again at the top.
   The trail zigzags in such a way that it isn't a killer, like the **Purtymun Trail** or Thompson's Ladder. It is more like the **Cookstove Trail** or the **Thomas Point Trail.**

The trail was built about in the 1890s to provide access to the canyon rim by O. P. Harding, who lived in the Cave Spring area, so that he could get to the top and go to Flagstaff. Harding came to Flagstaff in 1884 and worked as a contractor, building some of the historic buildings in downtown. He was very secretive about his past and would never talk about it. In those days there were many people who had come West for reasons of which they were not proud, and it was considered impolite to pry. In 1893 Harding moved to an Oak Creek homestead and took up fruit ranching, planting some 600 trees on the flat shelf of land around today's Troutdale. He was quite a hiker himself, and in 1910—for a lark—walked from Cave Spring to Flagstaff at the age of 76. Only after he died in June 1915 did Harding's family reveal his secret: he had been a distinguished Brigadier General in the Union Army during the Civil War, leading Pennsylvania troops in several battles. He was so horrified by the experience that he came to Arizona to get as far away as possible from the battlefields and the reminders of his past.

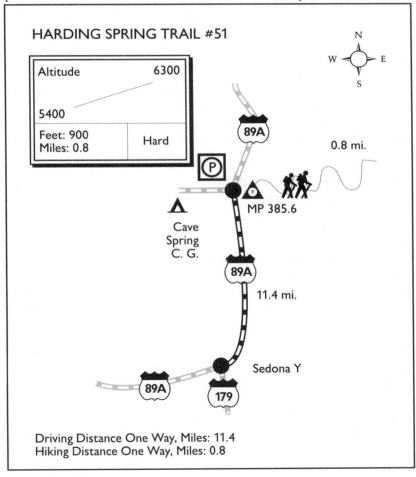

HARDING SPRING TRAIL #51

Altitude	6300
5400	
Feet: 900 Miles: 0.8	Hard

N
W — E
S

89A

0.8 mi.

P

MP 385.6

Cave
Spring
C. G.

89A

11.4 mi.

Sedona Y

89A

179

Driving Distance One Way, Miles: 11.4
Hiking Distance One Way, Miles: 0.8

HERMIT RIDGE

General Information
Location Map D5
Munds Mt. and Munds Park USGS Map
Coconino Forest Service Map

Driving Distance One Way: 2.6 miles *4.2 km* (Time 10 minutes)
Access Road: All cars, All paved
Hiking Distance One Way: 1.4 miles *2.3 km* (Time 1.5 hours)
How Strenuous: Moderate
Features: Views

NUTSHELL: This hike is located 2.6 miles *4.2 km* north of Sedona. There is no marked trail, but for those who enjoy bushwhacking and steep climbs, it is very rewarding.

DIRECTIONS:
From the Sedona Y Go:
    North on Highway 89A (toward Flagstaff) a distance of 2.6 miles *4.2 km* (MP 376.8) where you park at the mouth of a closed road.

TRAILHEAD: Walk down the closed road a few feet beyond a pole gate to a place where you will see a sign, "Casner Canyon #11."

DESCRIPTION: Follow the **Casner Canyon Trail** down to Oak Creek. When you get to the floor of the gorge, you will find it strewn with boulders. You will see a canyon on the other side. Head for it. When you get to the creek, you will have to wade it or rock hop over it, depending on the depth of the water.
    Once across, hike into Casner Canyon, its entrance marked by a high jutting ledge. Keep jumping boulders to get to the right hand (south) side, where you will soon pick up the Casner Canyon Trail. At 0.33 miles *0.53 km*, the trail goes up a knob and then starts down at the base of an undercut cliff. At the top of this knob you will see a faint trail going steeply uphill by a barbed wire fence. Take it.
    You will come out onto a shoulder of Hermit Ridge near a power line. The highest point of the ridge is just above your head here. You can make reaching the top easier by walking southwest along the shoulder for about 0.1 mile *0.16 km*, then going up. There are no marked paths, but there are game trails. Look for a likely spot to make the short, steep climb to the top.
    Hermit Ridge is quite narrow, covered with manzanita and other scrub through which there are many open lanes made by cattle. Your destination

is to the south, toward Sedona, where you will see the towering cliffs of Mitten Ridge. Bushwhack, following open alleys through the growth.

We picked up a deer trail that follows along the west side of the ridge, overlooking the creek and the highway. Great views from here. On the east side of the ridge you have equally fine views. Near the 1.0 mile *1.6 km* point you will be directly opposite the popular Grasshopper Point Picnic Ground. The creek makes a pretty picture here.

As you get closer to the buttes you will climb again, then reach an area where wide eroded ledges on the face of the ridge are almost like roadways. As you approach the cliffs, these paths turn into bare redrock ledges. At this point you can move upward or hike the ledges on the lower levels. We recommend the low ones. Finally the ledges pinch out in a scenic bowl, where it is dangerous to try to go any farther.

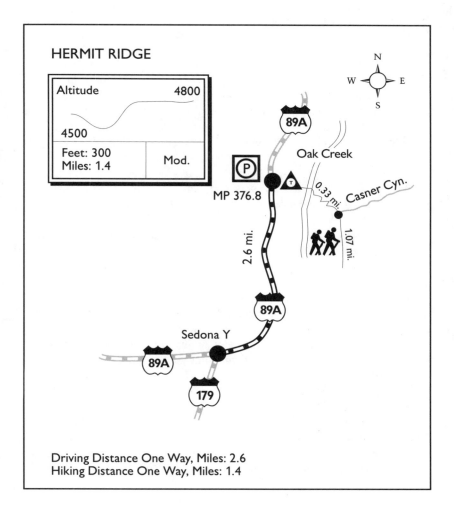

HERMIT RIDGE

Altitude	4800
4500	
Feet: 300 Miles: 1.4	Mod.

Oak Creek

Casner Cyn.

0.33 mi.

1.07 mi.

2.6 mi.

MP 376.8

Sedona Y

Driving Distance One Way, Miles: 2.6
Hiking Distance One Way, Miles: 1.4

HIDDEN CABIN

General Information
Location Map F3
Sedona USGS Map
Coconino Forest Service Map

Driving Distance One Way: 7.3 miles *11.68 km* (Time 15 minutes)
Access Road: All vehicles, All paved
Hiking Distance One Way: 2.5 miles *4.0 km* (Time 1.5 hours)
How Strenuous: Moderate
Features: Views, Picnic site on the banks of Oak Creek, Cabin ruins

NUTSHELL: This hike follows a horse trail from the Lower Red Rock Loop Road to the hidden ruins of a cabin beside the banks of Oak Creek.

DIRECTIONS:
From the Sedona Y Go:
   Southwest on Highway 89 (toward Cottonwood) for a distance of 5.5 miles *8.8 km* (MP 368.6) to the Lower Red Rock Loop Road. Turn left on the Lower Red Rock Loop Road and follow it to the 7.3 miles *11.68 km* point, where you will see a gravel parking apron to your right big enough for about four cars.

TRAILHEAD: Walk back the way you came for about 170 paces, where you will see a trail to your left (W). It is marked with a horse symbol.

DESCRIPTION: You will follow a series of horse trails on this hike and you may encounter some riders coming over from the stables to the west. Laths mark the trails and you will see trails S and A on this adventure. You will first follow Trail S.
   Hike the horse trail up and down some low red hills until at 0.6 miles *0.96 km*, you come to a red dirt road, FR 9845. Keep walking straight ahead, where you will see horse Trail S take up again after crossing the road. At this point you will walk for a time behind a subdivision, just outside the fence that encloses it. At the 1.0 mile *1.6 km* point you will reach a trail junction. Go left here (S), turning away from the fence. You will go over a rise and soon will be out of sight of the works of man.
   From now on you will be in a terrain that is scenic with hills and cliffs; so there is a bit of going up and down, but nothing strenuous. At the 1.3 mile *2.08 km* point you will meet a jeep road. In a few steps the trail veers away from the road only to join it again a short distance beyond, then move away from it and join it again. Hike on the horse trail wherever you meet the

road—don't follow the road: go on horse trail A.

At the 1.5 mile *2.4 km* point you will come to a viewpoint where you can see down into Oak Creek, where the stream makes a couple of recurving goosenecks against a high wall of red cliffs. The trail forks here, with the **Gooseneck Trail** going down to the creek. You want to take the other fork, the one going straight up over a hill.

The trail climbs steeply for a while, to the high point, then follows hilltops and ridges until it turns down toward the creek. You will come to a "major" road, where you turn left (E) on the road itself. In a few yards Horse Trail A forks, going downhill. Stay on the horse trail, going left from the road. Soon you will see how the trail meets the road again and goes downhill to Oak Creek, following an old ranch road. When you come to a gate in the barbed wire fence, go on through. At the end of the road you will find the ruins of the cabin. The trail makes a short turn to the left to the water. The road runs on another 0.2 miles *0.32 km*, then ends.

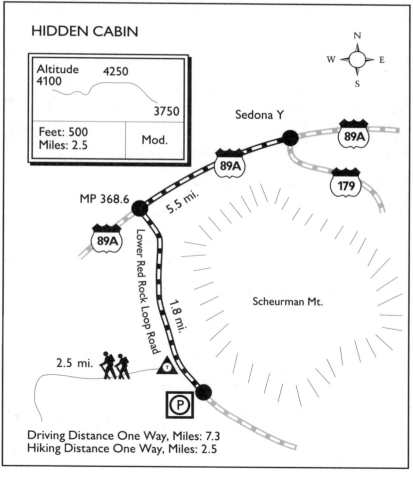

HIDDEN CABIN

Altitude 4100   4250   3750

Feet: 500
Miles: 2.5   Mod.

Sedona Y

89A   89A   179

MP 368.6   5.5 mi.   Lower Red Rock Loop Road   1.8 mi.

89A

Scheurman Mt.

2.5 mi.   T   P

Driving Distance One Way, Miles: 7.3
Hiking Distance One Way, Miles: 2.5

HOT LOOP TRAIL #94

General Information
Location Map F5
Munds Mountain USGS Map
Coconino Forest Service Map

Driving Distance One Way: 9.55 miles *15.28 km* (Time 15 minutes)
Access Road: All cars, Last 0.25 miles *0.4 km* good dirt road
Hiking Distance One Way: 3.0 miles *4.8 km* (Time 2 hours)
How Strenuous: Hard
Features: Views

NUTSHELL: This trail starts at a corral on the Jack's Canyon Road, skirts a subdivision, climbs over a low saddle, then rises to the top of Wild Horse Mesa.

DIRECTIONS:
From the Sedona Y Go:
South on Highway 179 (toward Phoenix) for a distance of 7.2 miles *11.5 km* (MP 306.2) to Jack's Canyon Road (stoplight). Turn left (E) onto Jack's Canyon Road and follow it to the 9.3 miles *15 km* point, where there is a road to your right going to a corral. Go through the gate and drive an additional 0.25 miles *0.4 km* and park by the trailhead sign.

TRAILHEAD: Rusty sign at the end of the access road.

DESCRIPTION: For the first 0.6 miles *1.0 km*, the trail moves around a subdivision. Do not take any of the branch trails to your right, as they lead to private corrals. Keep moving uphill, toward the mountain.

As the trail passes the last house, it begins to rise significantly. You can see a low saddle on the ridge ahead of you, your first target. Look behind you as you climb, for good views.

You will reach the top of the saddle in about 1.1 miles *1.76 km*. From this vantage point you will have excellent views to the north, into the Village of Oak Creek area and its surroundings. A particularly nice feature about this hike is that just over the other side of the ridge, the landscape changes entirely—going from urban to wild in just a few steps.

The trail dips down below the ridge and moves east. You will pass through some nice redrocks, with thrilling views. The big canyon you can see here is Woods Canyon. Your trail winds down and comes to a side canyon where you cross a slickrock face. On the other side of this you will intersect a larger trail, at 1.75 miles *2.8 km*. To the right is the old (now bypassed) part of the Hot Loop Trail, coming up from the **Woods Canyon Trail**. From this point you turn left and climb to the top of Wild Horse Mesa. The trail to the top is difficult, where it goes over loose lava stones, and is a steep climb of 700' in about 0.75 miles *1.2 km*.

When you finally struggle to the top of Wild Horse Mesa, the trail improves, with more soil and fewer rocks. At the 3.0 mile point *4.8 km* it is obvious that the rim of the mesa is to your left. Walk over to it and enjoy the view—a great vantage point from which to see Pine Valley, Jacks Canyon and Lee Mountain. For a day hike, this is a good stopping point, though the trail continues some 7.0 miles *11.2 km* to Jack's Point.

When the first homesteaders came into the Sedona area in 1876 (after the Apaches had been subdued by troops from Camp Verde) they found many wild horses. Some men made money trapping and selling these horses. Wild Horse Mesa was the location for a sizable horse herd and that is how it got its name. It is also called Horse Mesa. A Hot Loop was a branding iron.

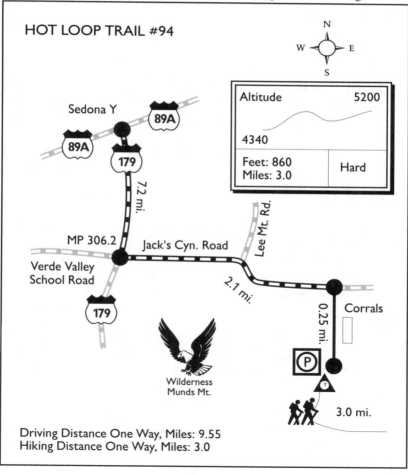

HOT LOOP TRAIL #94

Altitude 5200
4340
Feet: 860
Miles: 3.0
Hard

Sedona Y

89A
89A
179

7.2 mi.

MP 306.2
Jack's Cyn. Road
Lee Mt. Rd.
Verde Valley School Road
179

2.1 mi.

0.25 mi.
Corrals

P

Wilderness Munds Mt.

3.0 mi.

Driving Distance One Way, Miles: 9.55
Hiking Distance One Way, Miles: 3.0

HOUSE MOUNTAIN

General Information
Location Map G3
Sedona and Lake Montezuma USGS Maps
Coconino Forest Service Map

Driving Distance One Way: 14.4 miles *23.04 km* (Time 40 minutes)
Access Road: High clearance vehicles, last 4.0 miles *6.4 km* poor dirt road
Hiking Distance One Way: 2.25 miles *3.6 km* (Time 70 minutes)
How Strenuous: Easy
Features: Views

NUTSHELL: This sprawling mountain located 14.4 miles *23.04 km* south of Sedona is rather drab but is a platform for great views.

DIRECTIONS:
From the Sedona Y Go:
    South on Highway 179 (toward Phoenix) for a distance of 10.4 miles *16.64 km* (MP 303) to unpaved road FR 120. Turn right on FR 120 and follow it to the 12.2 miles *19.52 km* point, where FR 9120A intersects it. Turn right onto FR 9120A. The road up to this point has been good, but from here to the end it is rough, with deep ruts, rocks and other hazards. At the 14.4 mile *23.04 km* point you will be on top of House Mountain. The road here becomes too rough to drive farther. Pull off the road and park in this area.

TRAILHEAD: No trail markings. Walk the road, FR 9120A.

DESCRIPTION: House Mountain is a shield volcano so it is more rounded than conical on top. A shield volcano doesn't erupt with a big upthrusting bang. It sort of rises like a pimple and then oozes lava. As a result it can create a sprawling low mountain, which is exactly what House Mountain is.
    The driving instructions take you to the top of House Mountain and along the top to a point where the road gets extremely rough. Using a truck with high clearance, or a bike, you could go two miles more on the road, almost to the north face of the mountain, the face that looks at Sedona.
    The top of the mountain is uninteresting. There has been some livestock activity there and some wood cutting: the purposes for which the road was built. As you walk along the road you are not close enough to the rim of the mountain to get any views. You must walk across the top to the north edge to get to a viewpoint.
    Once you are at the north edge, the location of the rim will be obvious to you. Just leave the road and bushwhack your way along to the rim, where

there are tremendous views. You will find some places where lava has formed bare columns where no trees grow. These spots are excellent viewpoints.

There is another hike in the book that goes to the top of House Mountain. This is The **Turkey Creek Trail** that climbs the northwest face, with access from the Verde Valley School Road. Though the Turkey Creek Trail is a steep climb, it is much more scenic and enjoyable than the hike described in this article.

The top of House Mountain shows signs of considerable ranching activity. When we first began to hike around Sedona, we were surprised to find signs of cattle grazing (and sometimes the cattle themselves) on mountain tops, including some that must be hard for cattle to climb, such as **Doe Mountain**. House Mountain would be fairly easy to climb from the south approach used on this hike. So, if you hear a large animal crashing through the brush, it is much more likely to be a Guernsey than a Grizzly.

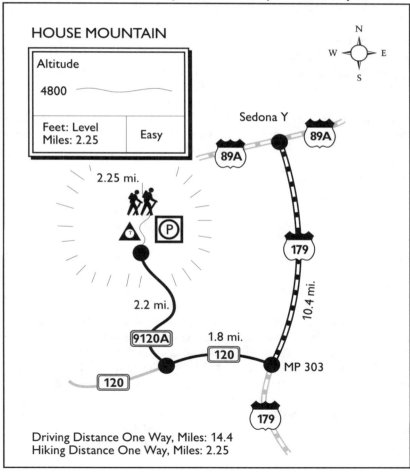

HOUSE MOUNTAIN

Altitude

4800

Feet: Level   Easy
Miles: 2.25

2.25 mi.

2.2 mi.

1.8 mi.

10.4 mi.

Sedona Y

89A

89A

179

9120A

120

120

MP 303

179

Driving Distance One Way, Miles: 14.4
Hiking Distance One Way, Miles: 2.25

HS CANYON #50

General Information
Location Map C4
Loy Butte and Wilson Mt. USGS Maps
Coconino Forest Service Map

Driving Distance One Way: 8.6 miles *13.8 km* (Time 30 minutes)
Access Road: Last 3.4 miles *5.5 km* rough dirt
Hiking Distance One Way: 2.0 miles *3.2 km* (Time 70 minutes)
How Strenuous: Moderate
Features: Views, Remote side canyon

NUTSHELL: This beautiful canyon, 8.6 miles *13.8 km* northwest of uptown Sedona, provides a delightful hike.

DIRECTIONS:
From the Sedona Y Go:
   Southwest on Highway 89A (toward Cottonwood) for 3.2 miles *5.12 km* (MP 371) to Dry Creek Road. Turn right on Dry Creek Road and proceed to the 5.2 mile *8.4 km* point. Turn right on FR 152, the Vultee Arch Road, and follow it to the 8.6 mile *13.8 km* point. You will see a road sign pointing to the Secret Canyon trail turnoff. Make a sharp turn to your left into the parking area.

TRAILHEAD: Hike the Secret Canyon Trail, which starts at the parking area, for 0.6 miles *1.0 km* to reach the HS Canyon trailhead.

DESCRIPTION: The access road, FR 152, road is often rough. but it has been improved since we came out with the first edition of this book. Unless there has been a recent washout, we think most ordinary passenger cars, unless they are very low slung, can make it.
   Once you get to the trailhead, you hike the **Secret Canyon Trail**. It goes immediately over to Dry Creek and then proceeds along the Dry Creek drainage. If water is running in Dry Creek you may not be able to make this hike because the trail winds across the creekbed several times.
   At 0.6 miles *1.0 km* you will see a trail going off to the left marked with a rusty sign reading, "H S Canyon #50." Take this trail. H S Canyon is narrow. It goes mostly to the west toward the north face of Maroon Mountain, and you can see a huge fin of Maroon Mountain in the distance. H S Canyon is a pretty little canyon and not very well known. We have never encountered any other hikers on this trail, but usually find them on the better known Secret Canyon Trail.

An easy walk, the trail is mostly shaded by a pleasant forest. It climbs but the climb is so gradual that it is not exhausting. There are great views. The canyon walls here are lower than those flanking some of the other hikes in this book. As a result they seem to be on a more human scale, and consequently the canyon has a nice friendly feeling.

The trail takes you to the base of Maroon Mountain where it ends in a box canyon surrounded by thousand foot high white cliffs—truly an impressive place. The end of the trail gives a false appearance of climbing out of the canyon but that is an illusion, for it plays out against the mountain.

The old cowboys who named many of the Sedona landmarks were an earthy bunch. They called this place Horse Shit Canyon, but that was too salty for the map makers, who have sanitized it to HS Canyon.

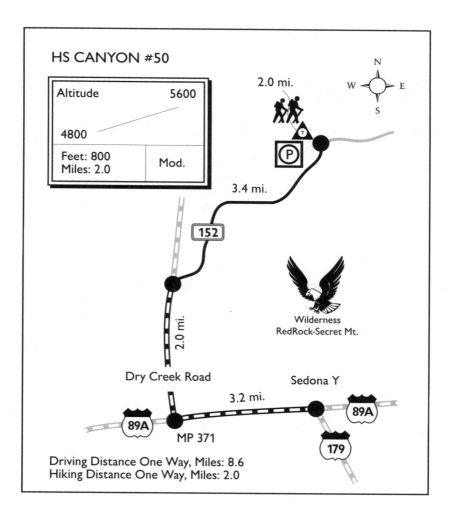

HS CANYON #50

Altitude	5600
4800	
Feet: 800 Miles: 2.0	Mod.

2.0 mi.

N
W — E
S

3.4 mi.

152

Wilderness
RedRock-Secret Mt.

2.0 mi.

Dry Creek Road

Sedona Y

3.2 mi.

89A

89A

MP 371

179

Driving Distance One Way, Miles: 8.6
Hiking Distance One Way, Miles: 2.0

JACK'S CANYON TRAIL #55

General Information
Location Map F5
Munds Mountain and Sedona USGS Maps
Coconino Forest Service Map

Driving Distance One Way: 9.4 miles *15.04 km* (Time 15 minutes)
Access Road: All cars, Last 0.1 mile *0.16 km* good dirt road
Hiking Distance One Way: 5.0 miles *8.0 km* (Time 2.5 hours)
How Strenuous: Moderate
Features: Old cattle trail, Views

NUTSHELL: Located 9.4 miles *15.04 km* south of the Sedona Y, this old cattle trail starts in an inhabited area. It then proceeds into some remote back country.

DIRECTIONS:
From the Sedona Y Go:
   South on Highway 179 (toward Phoenix) for a distance of 7.2 miles *11.5 km* (MP 306.2) to Jack's Canyon Road (stoplight). Turn left (E) onto Jack's Canyon Road and follow it to the 9.3 miles *14.88 km* point, where you turn right onto an unpaved road into a corral area. Go through the fence and park at the 9.4 mile *15.04 km* point, next to a brown metal gate.

TRAILHEAD: You will see a pole gate and rusty sign reading, "Jack's Canyon #55."

DESCRIPTION: The trailhead has been changed since the previous edition of this book. You now must walk an additional mile on a new leg of the trail parallel to the paved road to get to the Pine Valley subdivision. The first 1.5 miles *2.4 km* of the hike are not very attractive because you are always in sight of the houses. For a time you will feel as if you are walking through people's backyards.
   Jack's Canyon runs between Lee Mountain on your left (W) and the lower (Wild) Horse Mesa on your right and curves around Lee Mountain going to the north. Eventually it climbs up to the top of the Mogollon Rim at Jack's Point, where it meets the **Munds Mt. Trail**. The rim in that location is quite flat and open and makes a good grazing area for cattle. This trail provided a means of taking cattle herds up to the top of the rim in the summer and bringing the critters back to the low country in the winter.
   The trail follows an eastward course for about 2.5 miles *4.0 km* to Jack's Tank. Just beyond the tank the jeep road ends and your route turns into a foot

path that branches off to the right, down into the canyon floor. The canyon curves at the tank and begins a northerly course from there. (The jeep road continues about 0.50 miles *0.8 km* from Jack's Tank parallel to the canyon but up on the shoulder of the hill. It terminates at a pasture—not worth hiking).

The hiking trail is more interesting from Jack's Tank onward, especially if there is water running in the canyon. You don't want a lot of water, just a bit, since you will be walking across the canyon bottom.

Over many centuries the intermittent flow of water has worn the soil in the channel down to redrock and in many places the water has carved interesting sculptures in the soft stone. The canyon is narrow and scenic.

We recommend stopping at the 5.0 mile *8.0 km* point, which is where the trail leaves the canyon bottom and begins its steep ascent to the rim, which requires a climb of over 1200 feet in 2.0 miles *3.2 km*. The trail tops out on Munds Ridge, near the **Munds Mt.** Trailhead.

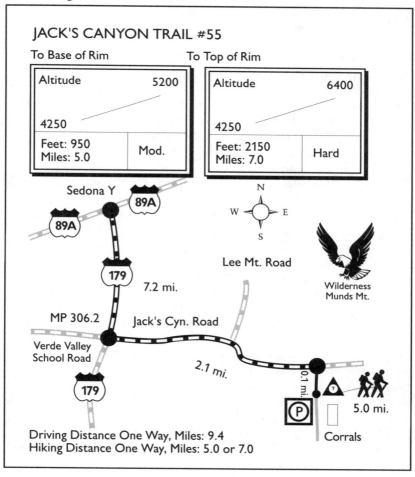

JACK'S CANYON TRAIL #55

To Base of Rim

Altitude	5200
4250	
Feet: 950 Miles: 5.0	Mod.

To Top of Rim

Altitude	6400
4250	
Feet: 2150 Miles: 7.0	Hard

Sedona Y

89A

89A

179

7.2 mi.

MP 306.2

Jack's Cyn. Road

Verde Valley School Road

179

Lee Mt. Road

N
W ← → E
S

Wilderness Munds Mt.

2.1 mi.

0.1 mi.

5.0 mi.

Corrals

Driving Distance One Way, Miles: 9.4
Hiking Distance One Way, Miles: 5.0 or 7.0

LITTLE HORSE TRAIL #61

General Information
Location Map E5
Munds Mt. and Sedona USGS Maps
Coconino Forest Service Map

Driving Distance One Way: 3.55 miles *5.68 km* (Time 10 minutes)
Access Road: All cars, All paved
Hiking Distance One Way: 3.25 miles *5.2 km* (Time 1.5 hours)
How Strenuous: Moderate
Features: Views, Redrocks, Secluded canyon

NUTSHELL: Located near downtown Sedona, this hike takes you across relatively flat land to the beautiful redrocks below Chicken Point, then on to Briant Canyon, a hidden gem.

DIRECTIONS:
From the Sedona Y Go:
    South on Highway 179 (toward Phoenix) for a distance of 3.55 miles *5.68 km* (MP 310).Turn left into the trailhead parking lot. This was constructed in the fall of 1996 and spring of 1997 to serve as the parking lot for both the Little Horse Trail and the **Bell Rock Pathway.** It is a nice improvement over the old access to Little Horse, which was a bit tricky.

TRAILHEAD: Where you park. You will start the hike on the Bell Rock Pathway, then veer off.

DESCRIPTION: From the parking area you hike south, parallel to the highway, for about 0.25 miles *0.4 km* down to the old trailhead, where the trail picks up an old road that has been worked for the new Bell Rock Pathway. Soon the Little Horse Trail will branch off to the left.
    You will come to a streambed at the base of a small red cliff, where you go left (N) and walk along the bed for a few yards. The next marker is a power line. From here you can see the top of the Chapel of the Holy Cross in the distance. It helps to know what your destination is from here, since there are many paths in the area, which can cause confusion. You want to go to the Madonna and Nuns redrock formation, two pyramidal spires at the east end of Twin Buttes—that is to say, the far end of the buttes against which the Chapel is built. The correct trail will always head in this direction, which is northeast.
    The trail will bring you to the base of the redrocks of Twin Buttes, where you turn right. Soon you will come to a gate. Go through the gate. Just

beyond the gate you will be at the foot of Chicken Point, which is at the top of the redrocks to your left, a slickrock saddle between red buttes. The jeep tours drive there frequently, so don't be surprised if you hear people on top, towering above you. Mountain bikers come down from the top just beyond this. From Chicken Point the trail heads on easterly through a lovely cypress forest to the head of Briant Canyon, a hidden fold on the side of Lee Mountain.

The trail turns southeast, dips to the canyon bottom, then climbs out of the bottom and goes up on a ledge, where you hike to the end of the trail. Briant Canyon has a nice secluded feeling, away from all signs of people, and yet it is quite close to town.

The trail's end seems rather mysterious, as the trail just stops without reaching any apparent destination.

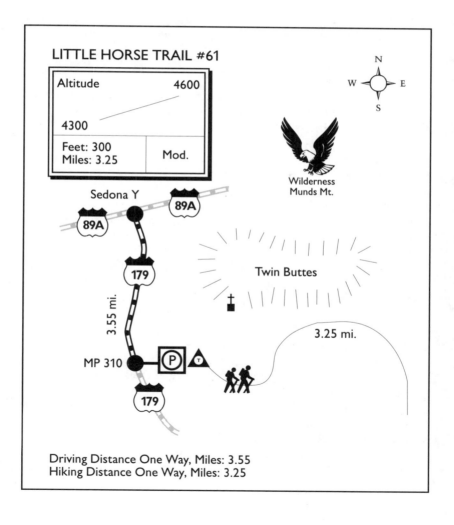

LITTLE HORSE TRAIL #61

Altitude	4600
4300	

Feet: 300 Miles: 3.25	Mod.

Wilderness Munds Mt.

N
W — E
S

Sedona Y
89A
89A
179

Twin Buttes

3.55 mi.

3.25 mi.

MP 310 Ⓟ

179

Driving Distance One Way, Miles: 3.55
Hiking Distance One Way, Miles: 3.25

LITTLE PARK HEIGHTS

General Information
Location Map F4
Sedona USGS Map
Coconino Forest Service Map

Driving Distance One Way: 5.1 miles *8.2 km* (Time 15 minutes)
Access Road: All cars, All paved
Hiking Distance One Way: 1.0 miles *1.6 km* (Time 40 minutes)
How Strenuous: Hard
Features: Views

NUTSHELL: Located across the highway from Bell Rock, just south of Sedona, this tall butte rewards your steep climb with great views.

DIRECTIONS:
From the Sedona Y Go:
   South on Highway 179 (toward Phoenix) for a distance of 5.1 miles *8.2 km* (MP 308.3) to Bell Rock Vista, on your right. There is a parking place for several cars at the vista. Pull in and park.

TRAILHEAD: There are no signs. A trail marked with cairns starts just south of the outhouse at Bell Rock Vista.

DESCRIPTION: On the south end of the parking area at Bell Rock Vista there is a public toilet. This is set back from the highway. Just south of this you will find the trail. Begin counting your paces at the side of the toilet. In 25 paces, the trail dips down into a little wash. Turn right here, walking 7 or 8 paces along the floor of the wash. The trail then goes up. Look carefully for cairns from this point. Many false trails meander through this area as a result of cattle grazing so it is important to use the cairns for guides. If in doubt, keep heading toward the butte.
   You will climb constantly on this hike. The climb is gradual for the first quarter of a mile, to the base of the butte, then becomes steep.
   Your destination will be obvious from the beginning. It is the saddle in the high butte located west of Bell Rock Vista. **Bell Rock** merits its fame, as it is an interesting place. It is listed in this book and makes for a fine hike. Its neighbor across the highway, the subject of this hike, is not well known but deserves to be. When you begin the hike it will seem as if it is an impossible task, that, "You can't get there from here." Then you will see how the trail makes use of the terrain and will realize that it is not only possible but that you are going to do it.

Earth Angel Spire from Brins Mesa

Reflection of Mitten Ridge

Soldier Pass Arches

Bear Mountain from Doe Mountain

Bear Mountain

Steamboat Rock and Spires

Sinagua Cliff Dwelling

Red Canyon

Silhouette of Kushman's Cone

Sinagua Petroglyphs

Sunset on Schnebly Hill

As you climb up to the saddle you will reach two major benches before you come to the top. Each of these benches becomes a natural resting place and a good observation point. From the benches you can see Bell Rock, Courthouse Butte and the colorful country between them and the Chapel of the Holy Cross.

Above the second bench you will have a hard steep haul and then you will reach the saddle. The saddle is at 1.0 miles *1.6 km*. From there you can go to knobs on either the north or south ends of the butte. There is also an extension to the west where the main trail leads you onto a bare finger of rock from which you get excellent views. Depending on how much you roam around on the top, you can easily add another mile to this hike.

Once you are on top you can see to the west, where you will have views down on the Verde Valley School and the Red Rock Loop Road areas.

Some hikers report finding fossils on top of this butte.

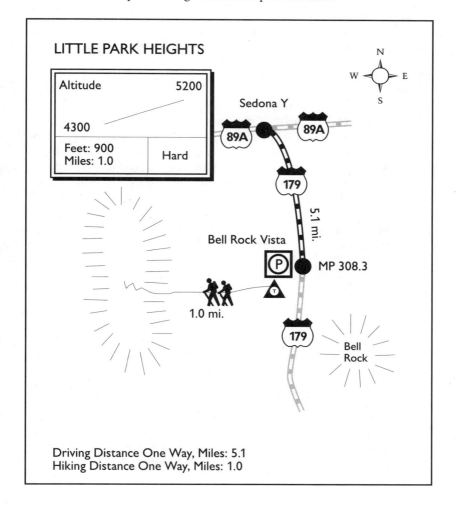

LONG CANYON #122

General Information
Location Map C3
Wilson Mt. USGS Map
Coconino Forest Service Map

Driving Distance One Way: 6.7 miles *10.7 km* (Time 15 minutes)
Access Road: All cars, All paved
Hiking Distance One Way: 3.0 miles *4.8 km* (Time 2 hours)
How Strenuous: Moderate
Features: Views, Great cliffs

NUTSHELL: Located 6.7 miles *10.7 km* northwest of uptown Sedona, this trail takes you right up against the base of gorgeous red cliffs. This is one of the best trails for viewing rock formations. **A personal favorite.**

DIRECTIONS:
From the Sedona Y Go:
Southwest on Highway 89A (toward Cottonwood) for a distance of 3.2 miles *5.12 km* (MP 371) to the Dry Creek Road. Turn right onto Dry Creek Road and follow it to the 6.1 mile *9.8 km* point, where there is a stop sign. The paved road to your right is the Long Canyon Road. Take it to the 6.7 miles *10.7 km* point, where you will see an unpaved road to your left. The entrance to the road is blocked with boulders. There is a parking area in front of the boulders. Park there.

TRAILHEAD: This is a marked and maintained trail. There is a rusty sign where you park reading, "Long Canyon #122."

DESCRIPTION: The trail begins as a wide jeep road. In fact, the Forest Service has moved several boulders across the road at its entrance to keep vehicles from using it.

At 0.30 miles *0.48 km* you will come to a 3-pronged fork. Take the left fork. At 0.60 miles *1.0 km* you will come to a big gate. This marks the entrance to the Redrock-Secret Mt. Wilderness Area. Go through the gate. The trail is a footpath from this point. At 1.0 miles *1.6 km* you will reach another fork. Here one trail goes left parallel to a power line and the other trail goes right. Take the right fork. The left fork goes to Boynton Canyon.

For the first 1.5 miles *2.4 km* on this trail you will be walking in open country with almost no shade. This part of the trail isn't much fun in hot weather. After that you will enter a cypress forest where there is shade. By then you will have moved fairly close to Maroon Mountain which is to your right (north). You will catch glimpses through the trees of the magnificent red and white sculptured cliffs of Maroon Mountain as you hike.

Beyond the 2.5 mile *4.0 km* point the vegetation becomes more alpine and less desert-like. Here you will encounter many oaks and huge alligator bark junipers. Some of the junipers are many centuries old.

At 3.0 miles *4.8 km* the trail, which has been generally following a north-west course parallel to the base of the mountain, turns and goes straight north, climbing steeply. This is the stopping point for this hike. Here you will find genuine alpine conditions with pines and firs and a carpet of green on the forest floor. The canyon walls are nearer to you now and you get tremendous views.

The trail continues but becomes difficult. It plays out completely at 4.0 miles *6.4 km* in a side canyon, in a place that is one of the wildest in the Sedona area. It really feels remote. The path narrows there to a barely discernible game trail where you are totally out of sight of the works of man.

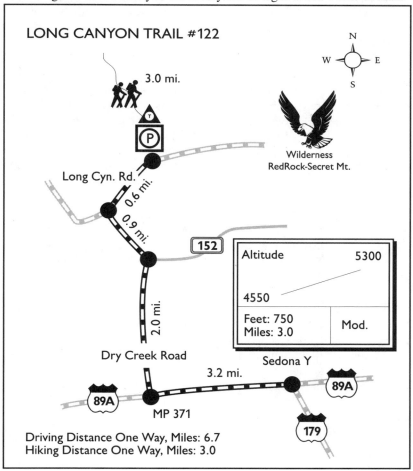

LONG CANYON TRAIL #63

General Information
Location Map G6
Casner Butte, Buckhorn Mtn. USGS Maps
Coconino Forest Service Map

Driving Distance One Way: 18.0 miles *28.8 km* (Time 30 minutes)
Access Road: All cars, Last 0.80 miles *1.28 km* good dirt road
Hiking Distance One Way: 2.5 miles *4.0 km* (Time 2 hours 30 minutes)
How Strenuous: Hard due to steep climb on first leg
Features: Views

NUTSHELL: Starting on the east bank of Wet Beaver Creek, this hike takes you along an old cattle trail, as you climb over one thousand feet.

DIRECTIONS:
From the Sedona Y Go:
    South on Highway 179 (toward Phoenix) for 14.7 miles *23.52 km,* to the I-17 Interchange. Instead of going onto I-17, go underneath it and get onto the paved country road FR 618. You will pass the Beaver Creek Ranger Station and the bridge over Beaver Creek, where the paving ends. Just after the paving ends, you will reach a three-way fork at 17.4 miles *27.8 km.* Turn left here, where you see a sign for Southwest Academy. At 18.0 miles *28.8 km,* look to your right. You will see the trail sign uphill just beyond a fence. There is almost no parking. We found a pullout big enough for one car.

TRAILHEAD: The trailhead is uphill to your right, where you will see a couple of vertical railroad ties used as fence supports. There is a wire gate with a hiker symbol on a fence post. On the other side is a sign that says, "Long Canyon Trail #63. Bell Trail #13—10 miles. Trail difficult to find after 2 miles." [We had no trouble finding the trail].

DESCRIPTION: This is an old cattle trail, like several others in the area, such as the **Bell Trail**. The Long Canyon Trail climbs steeply, rising 700 feet in the first 0.4 miles *0.64 km.*
    As you rise, you begin to enjoy views. At first these views are of the nearby creek. You can see a ranch to the south and some of the buildings of the academy to the north of your starting point. Climbing even higher, you begin to see over the banks of Beaver Creek. The climb is steep, but the trail zigzags and is well maintained.
    You climb to a ridge that is more level, and walk east along it. You can walk over to the rim of the ridge anywhere and have views of the Verde

Valley. You can also see some of the colored cliffs of the Sedona country. At the 1.0 miles *1.6 km* point you make another climb, but this one is not as steep or as long as the first climb.

When you finish the second climb, you emerge onto the top of a mesa, where it is fairly flat and the walking is easy—except for the fact that the ground is strewn with rocks everywhere, making for hard footing.

You will find the trail marked by wire-cage cairns. In spite of the warning sign at the trailhead, we had no trouble seeing the trail.

On top, we found the hike disappointing, as it passes through flat and uninteresting county. The trail moves east, parallel to the south side of Long Canyon. Maps indicate that the trail nears the edge of the canyon at about the 4.0 mile *6.4 km* point, and meets the Bell Trail, which skirts along the north side of Long Canyon, at the canyon's mouth. We stopped at the 2.5 mile point.

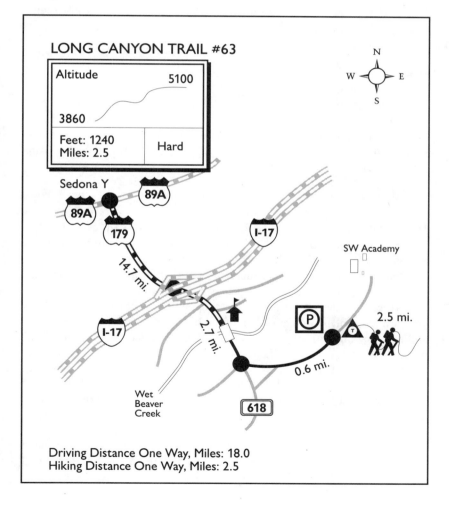

LOST CANYON

General Information
Location Map C4
Wilson Mt. USGS Map
Coconino Forest Service Map

Driving Distance One Way: 7.7 miles *12.4 km* (Time 25 minutes)
Access Road: Most cars, Last 2.5 miles *4.0 km*, bumpy dirt road
Hiking Distance One Way: 2.2 miles 3.6 km (Time 80 minutes)
How Strenuous: Moderate, one short stretch is strenuous
Features: Scenic canyons, Indian ruins, Cave

NUTSHELL: You climb onto a ledge, which you follow into two scenic canyons, enjoying Indian ruins and spectacular scenery on the way. **A personal favorite.**

DIRECTIONS:
From The Y in Sedona Go:
Southwest on Highway 89A (toward Cottonwood) for 3.2 miles *5.12 km* (MP 371) to Dry Creek Road. Turn right on Dry Creek Road and proceed to the 5.2 mile *8.4 km* point. Turn right on FR 152, the Vultee Arch Road, and follow it to the 7.7 mile *12.4 km* point. Pull off to the right into the big Brins Mesa Trail parking area and park.

TRAILHEAD: Use the "Brins Mesa #119" trailhead.

DESCRIPTION: Start this hike by taking the **Brins Mesa West** trail. From the rusty sign walk up the trail 210 feet. At this point you must take a minor trail going off to the right (S) marked by a cairn.
Once you successfully find the path, it is easy to follow and is marked with cairns. You will immediately cross a wash strewn with gray boulders and go across country to an arroyo that empties across a redrock ledge. Here you turn left (E) and hike up this redrock lined arroyo. You are now facing a climb of about 450 feet. The trail becomes very steep on this short segment. At its steepest point, the trail veers off to the right (S), still climbing.
At the apex, you will meet a ledge about 15 feet high, but have no fear, it is easy to climb. On top of the ledge, you have finished the climb and will have spectacular views. Keep hiking south on level ground, moving toward a giant red reef that marks the northern toe of Lost Canyon. The trail goes around the reef and into the canyon.
In Lost Canyon the walls are tall and sheer, a visual delight. At times the trail comes breathtakingly close to the edge of the rim. It you aren't bothered

by heights, this is a very rewarding canyon hike. The ledge you walk on is made of stone that is harder than the layers of rock above it. The upper layers have weathered and receded leaving a sort of balcony all around the canyon. Above you are beautiful red cliffs topped with cream stone. Below are sheer drops.

At 0.75 miles *1.2 km* you will see upstairs to your left (N) a long shallow cave half way up the cliff. There is a ruin in the cave. Cairns mark the place where you turn to clamber up to the ruin (optional).

From the ruin the trail follows the ledge to the head, or Vee of the canyon. Look down into the bottom at the Vee and you will see another ruin. You can reach it by taking the **Lost Canyon Ruin** hike.

The Vee is a good place to stop but the trail goes on. It follows back out to the canyon mouth and then curves south around another toe and goes into the canyon on the south wall of which the natural arch called **Devil's Bridge** is located. You can keep going to the 2.2 mile *3.6 km* point.

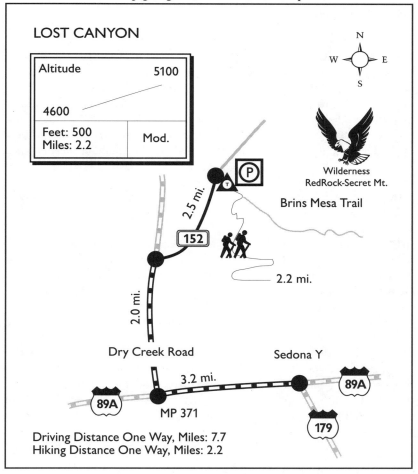

LOST CANYON RUINS

General Information
Location Map C4
Wilson Mt. USGS Map
Coconino Forest Service Map

Driving Distance One Way: 7.1 miles *11.4 km* (Time 25 minutes)
Access Road: Most cars, Last 1.9 miles *3.0 km* bumpy dirt road
Hiking Distance One Way: 0.60 miles *0.96 km* (Time 30 minutes)
How Strenuous: Easy
Features: Indian ruins

NUTSHELL: On this easy hike you bushwhack up a canyon bottom to a hidden Indian ruin.

DIRECTIONS:
From The Y in Sedona Go:
Southwest on Highway 89A (toward Cottonwood) a distance of 3.2 miles *5.12 km* (MP 371) to the Dry Creek Road. Turn right on Dry Creek Road, and follow it to the 5.2 mile point *8.32 km* where unpaved FR 152 branches to the right. Take FR 152. Follow the road to the 7.1 miles point *11.4 km*, where you will see a canyon that comes from your right and cuts under the road. It is marked with four reflecting signs. Find a parking place nearby.

TRAILHEAD: There is no marked trail. You walk SE along the canyon bottom to the head of the canyon.

DESCRIPTION: The Sedona area has so many remarkable land features—monuments, spires, buttes, etc.—that naming them all was impossible. We have never been able to find a name for this charming little canyon with its gem of an Indian ruin, so we decided to bestow a name upon it and have called it Lost Canyon.

We have taken many hikes in the Sedona area that require hiking a streambed in the bottom of a canyon. Some of these are quite difficult because of brush and obstacles that choke the watercourse. This hike is one of the nicest, easiest streambed hikes, because the actual floor of the canyon is redrock, with most of the soil washed off, so nothing grows in its middle, leaving it clear for walking. There are a couple of places where the channel is blocked, one by a boulder and the other by fallen trees. Both are easy to detour.

The canyon is forested with Arizona cypresses, one of the prettiest groves in the region. They are of all ages and sizes, making for an interesting mixture. We love cypress forests, as they're quiet and pleasant. The trees often take fantastic shapes. Some are twisted while neighbor trees of the same age are straight as an arrow.

The canyon climbs gently. At the start, as you begin the hike, look high up to your left and you will see a cave. This contains the Indian ruin you can visit on the **Lost Canyon** hike. Some smaller caves not so high up show signs of rock work too and are probably Indian ruins.

As you go farther up the canyon, the middle cliffs block the horizon so you can't see the tallest cliffs. At the end of the canyon, you enter a box. The ruin is under an overhang to your right, and you have an easy climb of about 20 feet to get to it. It has been pothunted but is fairly intact. Enjoy it and then walk up to the very end of the canyon and look up. The water has undercut the cliff so that it projects over you. This would be a terrific sight when a gentle waterfall was running.

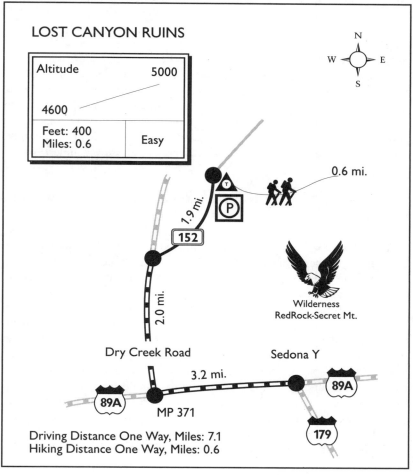

LOST WILSON MOUNTAIN

General Information
Location Map C4
Wilson Mt. USGS Map
Coconino Forest Service Map

Driving Distance One Way: 7.7 miles *12.3 km* (Time 30 minutes)
Access Road: Most cars, Last 2.5 miles *4.0 km* medium dirt road
Hiking Distance One Way: 1.3 miles *2.1 km* (Time 45 minutes)
How Strenuous: Easy
Features: Scenic stroll through Arizona cypress forest

NUTSHELL: Located 7.7 miles *12.3 km* north of Sedona, this hike follows a closed road to a point near the southwest face of Wilson Mountain.

DIRECTIONS:
From the Sedona Y Go:
   Southwest on Highway 89A (toward Cottonwood) a distance of 3.2 miles *5.12 km* (MP 371) to the Dry Creek Road. Turn right on Dry Creek Road, and follow it to the 5.2 mile *8.4 km* point where FR 152 branches to the right. Take FR 152. Follow the road to the 7.7 miles *12.3 km* point where you will see a dirt road blocked with red boulders branching off to the right. The best parking is at the **Brins Mesa West** trailhead 0.1 mile *0.16 km* behind you.

TRAILHEAD: This trail is neither marked nor maintained. Walk the blocked road.

DESCRIPTION: FR 152 has been improved since the first edition of our book. It is still rough, but anything but a low rider can negotiate it. Another change is that the mouth of the road that you will hike has been blocked by boulders so that a car cannot enter it—a good thing for hikers.
   The road goes through a beautiful forest of Arizona cypress, juniper, manzanita, agave and cactus. The route ambles along, curving here and there to follow the terrain and you do not have a very good sense of its purpose. It primarily goes north, parallel to the base of Brins Mesa and then turns east toward Mt. Wilson. Just about the time you think that it is going to take you right to the mountain, it stops, where the road is deeply eroded at a steep bank. The stopping point does not make any sense. You will not feel that you have reached a destination. The road just ends. We explored all the likely routes from the end point but could find none.
   In spite of this strange end, the road provides a very easy pleasant walk,

far from the crowds. We have hiked it several times and found it a calming, easy stroll.

At the 0.90 mile *1.5 km* point, where the road makes a hairpin turn, there is a small clearing to the right. We walked over there and found a cairn that seemed to mark a trail down into a streambed. We tried to follow it but found no other cairns, and the streambed became choked with manzanita to the point that it was too difficult to hike through it.

How do you *lose* a mountain? Usually the term refers to a seldom seen aspect. In this case the name *Lost* Wilson refers to a nub projecting from the northwest face of the main mass of Wilson Mountain.

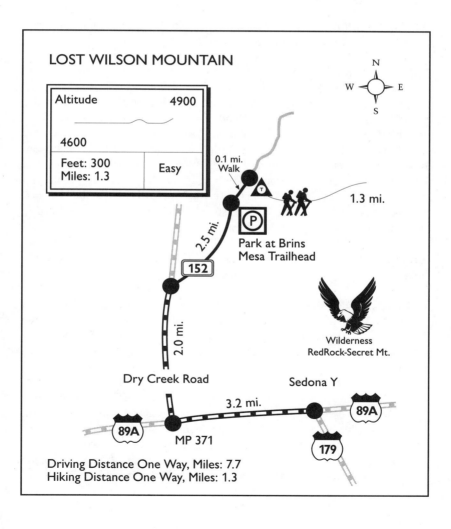

LOST WILSON MOUNTAIN

Altitude	4900
4600	
Feet: 300 Miles: 1.3	Easy

0.1 mi. Walk

1.3 mi.

2.5 mi.

152

Park at Brins Mesa Trailhead

Wilderness RedRock-Secret Mt.

2.0 mi.

Dry Creek Road

Sedona Y

3.2 mi.

89A

89A

MP 371

179

Driving Distance One Way, Miles: 7.7
Hiking Distance One Way, Miles: 1.3

LOY BUTTE (HONANKI RUINS)

General Information
Location Map C1
Loy Butte and Page Springs USGS Maps
Coconino Forest Service Map

Driving Distance One Way: 16.2 miles *25.92 km* (Time 45 minutes)
Access Road: All cars, Last 8.5 miles *13.6 km* good dirt road
Hiking Distance One Way: 0.25 miles *0.4 km* (Time 10 minutes)
How Strenuous: Easy
Features: Best Indian ruins in the Sedona area

NUTSHELL: Located 16.2 miles *25.92 km* northwest of Sedona, this is a short hike to excellent Indian ruins.

DIRECTIONS:
From The Y in Sedona Go:
    Southwest on Highway 89A (toward Cottonwood) a distance of 3.2 miles *5.12 km,* to the Dry Creek Road. Turn right on the Dry Creek Road and drive to the stop sign at 6.1 miles *9.76 km.* Turn left on the paved road and drive to the 7.7 mile *12.32 km* point, where the road to Enchantment Resort forks right. Go left here, on the unpaved road FR 152C, to Boynton Pass. You will come to a road junction at 11.7 miles *18.72 km,* where you turn right on FR 525. Near the end of this road you will come to the Hancock Ranch. The road goes through it and soon reaches the parking area for Loy Butte at the 16.2 mile point *25.92 km.*

TRAILHEAD: This trail is not marked with a sign but you will see a distinct path heading toward the nearby cliff.

DESCRIPTION: Don't be alarmed by the Hancock Ranch signs as you drive into the region of the ruins. An easement for the road runs through the ranch and you are welcome so long as you stay on the road and abide by the rules: no shooting, no hunting, no wandering around on the private property, etc.
    The ruins—the official name for which is the Honanki Ruins—are located in a large cave in the cliff face. There is no caretaker for them and over the years careless and malicious visitors have caused some damage. In recent years the Forest Service has done some work to stabilize the ruins, and they are well preserved and definitely worth a visit. You will see names carved and painted on the walls, some of them fairly old. The Smithsonian Institute did a survey of Indian ruins in northern Arizona in the 1920s, head-

ed by archaeologist Jesse Fewkes. He spent some time at this ruin and thought that it was a major find. In spite of his glowing reports, the government did little about the ruins except to preserve public access to them. They were little known and not very frequently visited until lately. Now they seem to be on the menus for all the jeep tours.

It is fun to explore the ruins and walk along the cliff face on both sides of the ruins. Try to imagine yourself as an occupant of the place centuries ago when the tribe of Indians lived there and picture the life you would have led. There is a small streambed running along the cliff bottom but it seldom carries water. Maybe in the days when these ruins were inhabited, water ran in the stream year around.

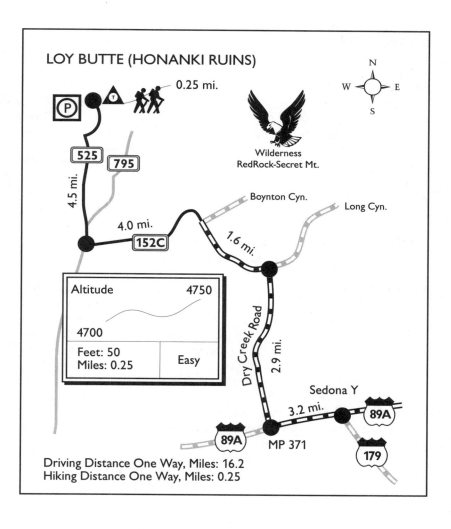

LOY BUTTE (HONANKI RUINS)

0.25 mi.

Wilderness
RedRock-Secret Mt.

525 795

4.5 mi.

4.0 mi.
152C

Boynton Cyn.

Long Cyn.

1.6 mi.

Altitude	4750
4700	
Feet: 50 Miles: 0.25	Easy

Dry Creek Road

2.9 mi.

Sedona Y

3.2 mi.

89A

89A MP 371

179

Driving Distance One Way, Miles: 16.2
Hiking Distance One Way, Miles: 0.25

LOY CANYON #5

General Information
Location Map C1
Loy Butte and Page Springs USGS Maps
Coconino Forest Service Map

Driving Distance One Way: 15.5 miles *24.8 km* (Time 40 minutes)
Access Road: All cars, Last 7.8 miles *12.48 km* good dirt road
Hiking Distance One Way: 4.0 miles *6.4 km* (Time 2.5 hours)
How Strenuous: Moderate
Features: Indian ruins, Scenic canyon, Views

NUTSHELL: Located 15.5 miles *24.8 km* northwest of Sedona, this trail takes you through a pleasant canyon to the base of the Mogollon Rim.

DIRECTIONS:
From The Y in Sedona Go:
Southwest on Highway 89A (toward Cottonwood) a distance of 3.2 miles *5.12 km,* to the Dry Creek Road. Turn right on the Dry Creek Road and drive this paved road to the stop sign at 6.1 miles *9.76 km.* Turn left on the paved road and drive to the 7.7 mile *12.32 km* point, where the road to Enchantment Resort forks right. Go left here, on the unpaved road FR 152C, to Boynton Pass. You will come to a road junction at 11.7 miles *18.72 km,* where you turn right on FR 525. Stay on FR 525 to the trailhead at the 15.5 mile point *24.8 km.*

TRAILHEAD: You will see a rusty sign marked, "Loy Canyon #5" on the right side of the road in front of a barbed wire fence.

DESCRIPTION: Since you are so close, drive on down the road another 0.7 miles *1.12 km* and visit the Honanki Indian ruins located at **Loy Butte** if you haven't seen them, as they are the Sedona area's finest Indian ruins.

The Loy Canyon trail was built as a cattle trail in the late 1890s. Like many other cattle trails now used for hiking, the purpose of this trail was to take cattle to the top of the Mogollon Rim. The cattle would be kept in the warm low country during the winter and then walked to the cool high country for the summer. The rim is over 1,000 feet high in most places, so it was hard to find spots where a trail could be built.

You start this hike by skirting the fence around a ranch for about half a mile, then begin to walk up the canyon bottom.

Look for a small Indian ruin set in a cave at 0.75 miles *1.2 km.* It is in a cliff face to your left.

The trail rises gradually through a forest for 4.0 miles *6.4 km*, and meanders across a creekbed a few times, so you don't want to make the hike when water is running high. Because the trail gains in altitude the vegetation along the trail also changes. It is very desert-like at the beginning, with cactus and low shrubs, then changing as you progress to a pine forest.

At the end of 4.0 miles *6.4 km* you are at the base of the cliffs forming the rim, where we stop for an easy day hike. To go to the top requires some serious work. The trail becomes much steeper and you climb about one thousand feet in a mile.

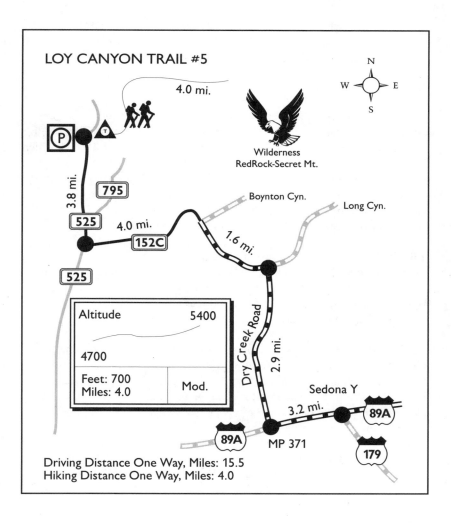

LOY CANYON TRAIL #5

4.0 mi.

N
W — E
S

Wilderness
RedRock-Secret Mt.

P   T   4.0 mi.

3.8 mi.

795

525   4.0 mi.

152C

Boynton Cyn.   Long Cyn.

1.6 mi.

525

Altitude	5400
4700	
Feet: 700 Miles: 4.0	Mod.

Dry Creek Road

2.9 mi.

Sedona Y

3.2 mi.   89A

89A   MP 371

179

Driving Distance One Way, Miles: 15.5
Hiking Distance One Way, Miles: 4.0

MARG'S DRAW

General Information
Location Map E5
Sedona USGS Map
Coconino Forest Service Map

Driving Distance One Way: 1.0 miles *1.6 km* (Time 5 minutes)
Access Road: All cars, 0.2 miles *0.32 km* unpaved bumpy road
Hiking Distance One Way: 1.6 miles *2.56 km* (Time 1 hour)
How Strenuous: Easy
Features: Views

NUTSHELL: Marg's Draw is a beautiful area in Sedona's backyard, a bowl surrounded by the Crimson Cliffs, Munds Mountain, Lee Mountain and Twin Buttes. This short hike takes you into the center of the area.

DIRECTIONS:
From the Sedona Y Go:
   (Note: the old trailhead at the end of Sombart Lane is no longer usable due to trespass problems.) Go South on Highway 179 (toward Phoenix) for a distance of 0.3 miles *0.48 km* (MP 313.1) to the Schnebly Hill Road, which is just across the bridge near Tlaquepaque. Turn left onto the Schnebly Hill Road, which is paved for the first half mile. There is a cattle guard at the end of the paving. Just beyond the cattle guard is a private driveway to the left. Go past it and look for the next road to the left, (0.2 miles *0.32 km* past the cattle guard) at 1.0 miles *1.6 km*. Turn left into the parking area.

TRAILHEAD: Directly across the Schnebly Hill Road from the parking place is the trailhead. It is unmarked, but look for a standbox for a telephone line. It is green and sticks up out of the ground about three feet. There is a sign on it reading, "Caution U. S. West Fiber Optic Cable...." At the side of this is the beginning of the trail.

DESCRIPTION: It helps to understand where you are going at the beginning of this hike. Directly in front of you are The Crimson Cliffs. You start by taking the **Snoopy Rock** trail for 0.75 miles *1.2 km*, to a point where there is a trail junction. The Snoopy Rock trail hugs the base of the cliffs and circles around them on their south face.
   The trail is easy to follow if you remember that it stays at the base of the cliffs. There are misleading cattle trails all over the place, but they go off onto the flat. After you have circled around the south face, look carefully for the trail junction at 0.75 miles *1.2 km*, because it is not easy to see, though

it is usually marked with a cairn. At the trail fork, the Snoopy Rock trail goes uphill. The fork you want to take goes downhill and moves south, away from the cliffs. Take it and you will come down onto a flat area, walking through junipers to get to a trail junction at 1.1 miles *1.76 km* from the point of beginning. Turn left on the broad well-defined path at the junction. If the place is not well-marked, you may want to put your personal marker here so you can find it on the way back.

From this point the trail is quite level and easy. It moves along east, then turns south to end on a redrock ledge, with strange quartz bubbles imbedded in its surface, where you can enjoy good views.

The Thompsons, earliest settlers in the area, had a mule named Marg. They used her to pull a wagon up the steep road to Flagstaff. Mules are pretty intelligent animals and Marg learned how to tell when the family was about to go somewhere. She would then gallop away into this draw to hide.

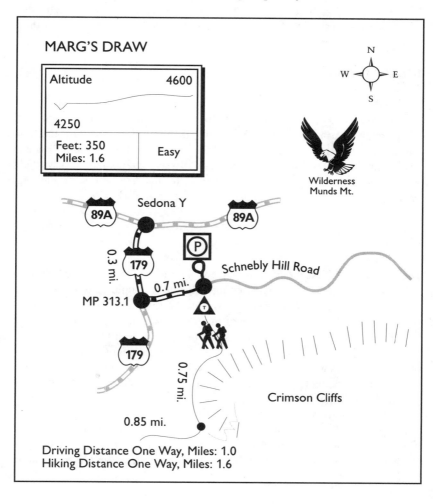

MERRY-GO-ROUND

General Information
Location Map E5
Munds Mt. and Munds Park USGS Maps
Coconino Forest Service Map

Driving Distance One Way: 5.0 miles *8.0 km* (Time 30 minutes)
Access Road: All cars, Last 4.2 miles *6.7 km* bumpy dirt road
Hiking Distance, Complete Loop: 1.0 miles *1.6 km* (Time 45 minutes)
How Strenuous: Moderate
Features: Historic road, Redrocks, Views

NUTSHELL: This hike takes you to a prominent landmark on the Schnebly Hill Road just east of Sedona, where you climb a rock formation and then hike part of an historic road.

DIRECTIONS:
From the Sedona Y Go:
    South on Highway 179 (toward Phoenix) for a distance of 0.3 miles *0.48 km* (MP 313.1) to the Schnebly Hill Road. It is just across the bridge past Tlaquepaque. Turn left onto the Schnebly Hill Road. It is paved for the first half mile and then turns into a dirt road that is all right for any car unless the road is muddy. At 5.0 miles *8.0 km* you will see a gate made of very thick steel pipes. This is used to close the road in winter. You will see a parking area on the left side of the road just before the gate. Park here.

TRAILHEAD: The trail starts at the parking place. It is unmarked and unsigned.

DESCRIPTION: At the parking place you will see a line of three boulders blocking what looks like a road going uphill to a couple of redrock spires just above your head. This hike has two levels. First take the uphill portion of the path, making a mental note of the fork downhill to the left (S).
    The uphill path takes you on a steep but short climb to the base of the two spires. It is fun to explore these. If you are adventuresome, you can climb them. This whole area on top is a good viewpoint from which to enjoy the eye-filling delights of the area. We sat here one memorable evening and watched a thrilling sunset.
    After you have finished enjoying the top, go back downhill and take the lower path. Although unmarked, it is well worn and you will have no trouble following it. In about 0.10 miles *0.16 km* you will intersect the old Schnebly Hill Road. Take the left fork first and follow the old road about

0.05 miles *0.08 km*, around the bend of a small arroyo that cuts it. When you look to your right here you will see the red butte whose top you just climbed. Circling the butte is a layer of rusty mauve stone about 12 feet thick. This is the Ft. Apache formation, a harder stone than the redrock above and below it. There are a couple of small windows in this layer. The old road ran along the top of this circular ledge around the butte and was referred to as the Merry-Go-Round.

Now go back to the trail fork and take the Merry-Go-Round. Step away from the road and go to the lip of the ledge anywhere along the way to enjoy many fine views into some of the most scenic areas around Sedona.

You will soon have girdled the butte. Keep following the old road uphill. You will see how the Merry-Go-Round was an ideal natural road, being flat and sandy, while the road above and below it was steep and rocky. You will intersect the present Schnebly Hill Road in about 0.25 miles *0.4 km* from the butte. From there walk back down the present road to your car.

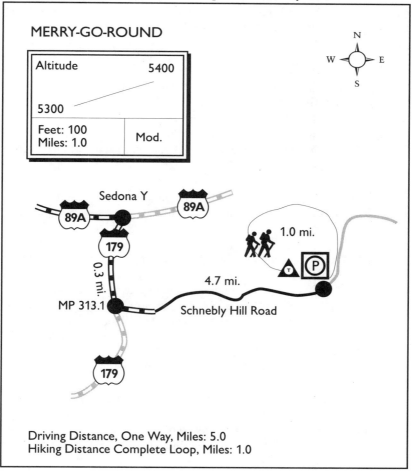

MERRY-GO-ROUND

Altitude 5400

5300

Feet: 100
Miles: 1.0

Mod.

Sedona Y

89A 89A

179

1.0 mi.

0.3 mi.

4.7 mi.

MP 313.1 Schnebly Hill Road

179

Driving Distance, One Way, Miles: 5.0
Hiking Distance Complete Loop, Miles: 1.0

MESCAL MOUNTAIN

General Information
Location Map C3
Wilson Mt. USGS Map
Coconino Forest Service Map

Driving Distance One Way: 6.7 miles *10.7 km* (Time 15 minutes)
Access Road: All cars, All paved
Hiking Distance One Way: 2.5 miles *4.0 km* (Time 90 minutes)
How Strenuous: Moderate
Features: Views, Indian ruins

NUTSHELL: Mescal Mountain is a small mesa at the mouth of Boynton Canyon 6.7 miles *10.7 km* northwest of Sedona. It takes a bit of scrambling to get to its top but the effort is worthwhile.

DIRECTIONS:
From the Sedona Y Go:
    Southwest on Highway 89A (toward Cottonwood) for a distance of 3.2 miles *5.12 km* (MP 371) to the Dry Creek Road. Turn right onto Dry Creek Road and follow it to the 6.1 mile *9.76 km* point, where there is a stop sign, where you turn right on the paved Long Canyon Road. Take it to the 6.7 miles *10.7 km* point, where you will see an unpaved road to your left, where you pull in and park.

TRAILHEAD: You will begin this hike on the marked and maintained trail Long Canyon Trail #122, for which you will see a rusty sign at the parking area.

DESCRIPTION: Start the hike by taking the **Long Canyon Trail**, which begins as a wide jeep road. In fact, the Forest Service has moved several boulders across the road at its entrance to keep vehicles from using it.
    At 0.30 miles *0.48 km* you will come to a 3-pronged fork. Take the left-most fork. At 0.60 miles *1.0 km* you will come to a big gate. This marks the entrance to the Redrock-Secret Mt. Wilderness Area. Instead of going through the gate, stay outside it and walk the old road that parallels the fence. At the 1.0 mile *1.6 km* point you will reach the foot of a butte, where the trail begins to climb sharply.
    On the way up, you will see a cave to your right that looks large enough to contain an Indian ruin. It is large enough but there is no ruin due to a large crack in the cave roof that allows water to pour into the cave when it rains. A side trail goes to this cave and it is worth taking for the fun of exploring.

The main trail zigzags to a saddle on Mescal Mountain. Just below the saddle, in a red ledge, you will see a shallow cave containing a rudimentary Indian ruin.

On top of the saddle, will see a distinct footpath marked with cairns going up to the left (S). A few yards along this trail there is the ruin of a pit house. Beyond it the trail winds right up to the face of the highest point on Mescal Mountain and then curves left, hugging the cliff at its base. It is fairly easy hiking, though steep, until you get to a point just below the top. There you will have to do some climbing if you want to go to the crest.

We don't do any rock climbing, as we are risk-averse and true rock climbing scares us. The small climb involved here is no worse than climbing a high ladder, though. Once you are on top, walk around the perimeter to enjoy the view. The distance to the top is 1.5 miles *2.4 km.* Fully exploring the top can add another mile to the hike.

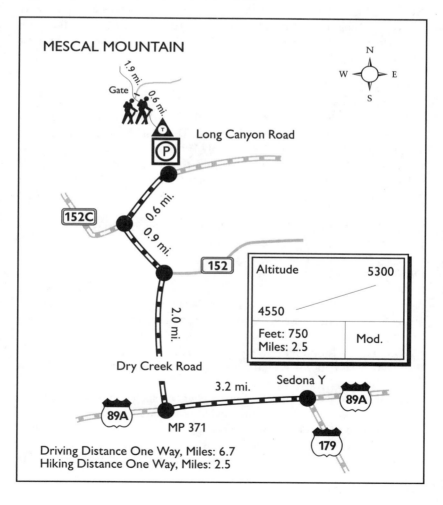

MITTEN RIDGE

VORTEX

General Information
Location Map E5
Munds Mt. and Munds Park USGS Maps
Coconino Forest Service Map

Driving Distance One Way: 3.8 miles *6.1 km* (Time 20 minutes)
Access Road: All cars, Last 3.0 miles *4.8 km* bumpy dirt road
Hiking Distance One Way: 2.5 miles *4.0 km* (Time 2 hours)
How Strenuous: Moderate
Features: Views, Fascinating rock formations and sculptures, Vortex

NUTSHELL: Just 0.3 miles *0.48 km* from the Y, the Schnebly Hill Road is enjoyed by thousands of people. The hike takes you part way up the road, then across Bear Wallow Canyon to explore the redrock buttes on the west side of the canyon.

DIRECTIONS:
From the Sedona Y Go:
    South on Highway 179 (toward Phoenix) for a distance of 0.3 miles *0.48 km* (MP 313.1) to the Schnebly Hill Road. It is just across the bridge past Tlaquepaque. Turn left onto the Schnebly Hill Road. It is paved for the first 0.5 miles *0.8 km* and then turns into a dirt road that is all right for any car unless the road is muddy. At the 3.8 mile *6.1 km* point, pull over and park. There is a bare redrock ledge off the road to your right.

TRAILHEAD: There are no signs. There is a trail going downhill off of the left side of the road (to the west). Follow it.

DESCRIPTION:
    As you drive up Schnebly Hill Road you will become conscious of a deep streambed to your left. This is Bear Wallow Canyon. You will also be aware of a big butte between the road and Sedona. This is Mitten Ridge, one of the major Sedona landmarks, and it is your goal on this hike.
    Parking is a little tricky. Try to find a place on the shoulder. Then take the hiker-made trail you see dropping down from the road. It heads toward Mitten Ridge.
    In about 200 yards you will come to a redrock shelf that was capped with a very thin layer of gray lava. This cap has broken up into small stones. This place is one of the Sedona Vortex spots and believers often arrange some of these gray stones into a huge medicine wheel.
    Thus far you are following the same trail that we have described for the

Cow Pies hike. At 0.50 miles *0.8 km*, the paths split. You will go straight instead of turning left as you would for the Cow Pies hike. You will walk toward ledges at the base of Mitten Ridge. Cairns usually mark the trail. It goes across several lower ledges to get up near the base of the cliffs. Once there you work your way west, at times ascending to a higher ledge. At first you will be walking through brush but at 1.5 miles *2.4 km* you will break out onto clear slickrock.

Here you will find an upper and lower trail. Try the lower one. You will soon see a saddle above you to the right. The saddle is a great viewpoint. You probably will not find a regular trail going to the saddle but it is easy and fun to walk up the sloping redrock face of the ridge to the saddle. The trail pinches out at the 2.5 miles *4.0 km* point.

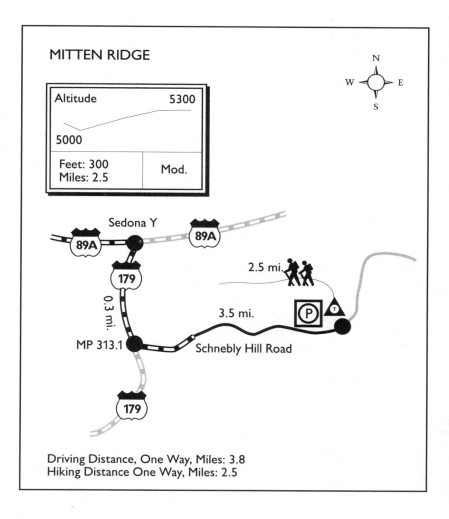

MITTEN RIDGE

Altitude   5300

5000

Feet: 300
Miles: 2.5

Mod.

N
W — E
S

Sedona Y

89A   89A

179

0.3 mi.

2.5 mi.

3.5 mi.

P T

MP 313.1   Schnebly Hill Road

179

Driving Distance, One Way, Miles: 3.8
Hiking Distance One Way, Miles: 2.5

MOONEY TRAIL #12

General Information
Location Map C1
Loy Butte USGS Map
Coconino Forest Service Map

Driving Distance One Way: 18.1 miles *29 km* (Time 30 minutes)
Access Road: All cars, Last 8.5 miles *13.6 km* good dirt road
Hiking Distance One Way: 3.75 miles *6.0 km* (Time 2.5 hours)
How Strenuous: Hard
Features: Views

NUTSHELL: This cattle trail starts at Black Tank 18.1 miles *29 km* southwest of Sedona and climbs to the base of the Mogollon Rim (or, alternatively, to the top)

DIRECTIONS:
From the Sedona Y Go:
Southwest on Highway 89A (toward Cottonwood) a distance of 9.6 miles *15.4 km* (MP 364.5) to the Red Canyon Road. Turn right on Red Canyon Road, also known as FR 525, and follow it to the 12.4 mile *19.8 km* point where FR 525C branches to the left. Sycamore Pass is your target. Turn left onto FR 525C. Follow it to the 18.1 mile *29 km* point, where FR 551 branches to the right. Pull in on FR 551 and park.

TRAILHEAD: This is a marked and maintained trail. You will see a rusty sign near the road reading, "Mooney Trail #12."

DESCRIPTION: You are near the trailhead when you see the red earth bank of a dam with fence posts on top on your right. This is Black Tank. Just as you curve around the tank there is a road to your right, FR 551. You will see the trail's rusty sign as you pull in.

Park near the tank. If you have a high clearance vehicle you can drive about 1.0 miles *1.6 km* on FR 551, parking just before the road crosses a gully. The gully is Spring Creek.

If you park at the tank, then walk through the fenced area toward the pumphouse, a small brick building. When you exit the gate at the other end of the tank area, turn right. You will see many trails because cattle are still run here and wherever they wander, they leave false trails. Follow the most heavily traveled jeep trail for 0.25 miles *0.4 km*, to a point where the road forks. Take the left fork marked FR 551A.

The trail goes along foothills, gradually climbing to a ridge top. Then you walk along the top of the ridge. The ridge is javelina country and you will see plenty of sign. It is hard to see these critters, as they are shy. Sometimes you may get a whiff of them. The javelina odor smells just like a cow barn. From the ridge top you get good distant views, particularly to the north, of the Mogollon Rim, but there isn't much to see close at hand. In fact, this is a rather drab trail.

You will reach another cattle tank called Sebra Tank. Beyond Sebra Tank you will come to the base of the Mogollon Rim, where the trail begins a steep ascent. There is an arch located in the cliff face here.

The trail to the top is hard. It is a severe climb and most of it is in the open, exposed to full sunlight. You wouldn't want to do this on a hot sunny day. At the top you will come out on a ridge at a place where the Mooney Trail, Taylor Cabin Trail and **Casner Mountain** trails all converge. If you turn left here, you will go to Casner Mountain; if you turn right, you will go to the top of the rim.

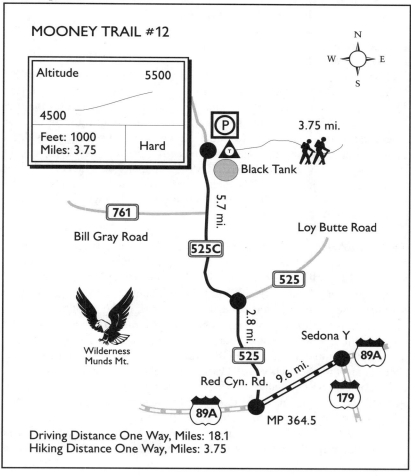

MOONEY TRAIL #12

Altitude	5500
4500	
Feet: 1000 Miles: 3.75	Hard

N
W—◇—E
S

3.75 mi.

Black Tank

5.7 mi.

761

Bill Gray Road

525C

Loy Butte Road

525

2.8 mi.

Wilderness Munds Mt.

Sedona Y

89A

525

Red Cyn. Rd. 9.6 mi.

179

89A MP 364.5

Driving Distance One Way, Miles: 18.1
Hiking Distance One Way, Miles: 3.75

MUNDS MOUNTAIN TRAIL #77

General Information
Location Map E5
Munds Mt. and Munds Park USGS Maps
Coconino Forest Service Map

Driving Distance One Way: 6.6 miles *10.6 km* (Time 30 minutes)
Access Road: All cars, Last 5.8 miles *9.3 km* bumpy dirt road
Hiking Distance One Way: 2.9 miles *4.64 km* (Time 2.5 hours)
How Strenuous: Hard
Features: Views

NUTSHELL: This hike takes you to the top of the north end of Munds Mountain, from where you have glorious views.

DIRECTIONS:
From the Sedona Y Go:
    South on Highway 179 (toward Phoenix) for a distance of 0.3 miles *0.5 km* (MP 313.1) to the Schnebly Hill Road. It is just across the bridge past Tlaquepaque. Turn left onto the Schnebly Hill Road. It is paved for the first 0.5 miles *0.8 km* and then turns into a dirt road that is all right for any car unless the road is muddy. At 5.0 miles *8.0 km* you will see a gate made of very thick steel pipes. This gate is locked across the road in winter, usually about mid-November to mid-April. (Call the Sedona Forest Service Ranger Station to find out whether it is open.) Drive to the top, 6.6 miles *10.6 km* from the Y, where you will find the Schnebly Hill Vista with a big parking area to your left. Park there.

TRAILHEAD: Your approach to the trailhead is over old jeep roads. From the parking area walk up the main road about 100 paces, where you will see a dirt road to your right (S). Take it. The route is the Old Schnebly Hill Road, following the alignment it had from 1902 until the 1930s. If you have a high clearance vehicle, you can drive a portion of it, though it has not been maintained for years and is very rough. At 0.88 miles *1.4 km* on this road you come to a fork. Go left (S) here. You will soon see a small microwave tower. At 1.2 miles *1.9 km* you will come to a fork. Here the old road goes right, to meet the **Schnebly Hill Trail.** Turn right and walk a short distance, to the point where the road makes a hairpin curve to your right. At this point you will see a footpath to the left (S) marked by a cairn. Take this path, which is the second leg of the Schnebly Hill Trail.
    From here the trail follows the edge of the rim, with many excellent viewpoints along the way. You will pass through two gates, the second

being located at Committee Tank. Soon after this the trail goes out on a thin ridge connected to Munds Mt. At 2.4 miles *3.9 km* you will find the trailhead sign, "Munds Mt. Trail 77," just beyond the point where the **Jacks Canyon Trail** meets the ridge.

DESCRIPTION: At the trailhead the trail splits. Take the right fork, a sandy groove. The footing on this trail is poor, as it is covered with small white slippery rocks. The cairns are hard to see. The trail goes to the top by switchbacks, improving about halfway up. Beyond the midpoint, you will get thrilling glimpses into the Mitten Ridge area. At the top you emerge onto a rather bare park. Move around its edge for unsurpassed views.

In winter, when the Schnebly Hill is closed above the 5.0 mile *8.0 km* point, you can use the Schnebly Hill Trail as your approach and still make this hike. The top is above 6,000 feet, meaning there may be snow or mud, so keep this in mind.

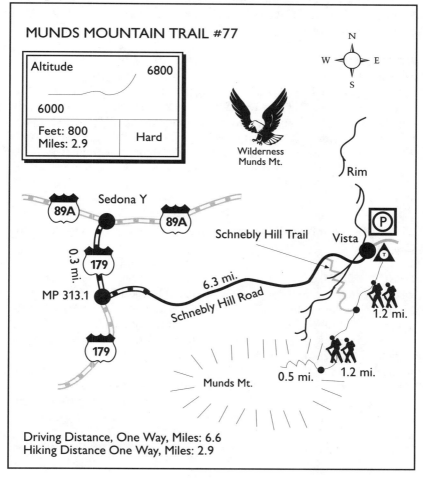

MUNDS MOUNTAIN TRAIL #77

Altitude

6800

6000

Feet: 800
Miles: 2.9

Hard

Wilderness
Munds Mt.

N
W — E
S

Rim

89A

Sedona Y

89A

Schnebly Hill Trail

Vista

P

T

0.3 mi.

179

MP 313.1

6.3 mi.

Schnebly Hill Road

1.2 mi.

179

0.5 mi.

1.2 mi.

Munds Mt.

Driving Distance, One Way, Miles: 6.6
Hiking Distance One Way, Miles: 2.9

MUSHROOM ROCK

General Information
Location Map C3
Wilson Mountain USGS Map
Coconino Forest Service Map

Driving Distance One Way: 8.0 miles *12.8 km* (Time 20 minutes)
Access Road: All cars, All paved
Hiking Distance One Way: 1.8 miles *2.9 km* (Time 90 minutes)
How Strenuous: Hard
Features: Gorgeous canyon, Indian Ruins, Vortex

NUTSHELL: A hike in **Boynton Canyon** 8.0 miles *12.8 km* northwest of Sedona. You branch off the main trail into a side canyon for a clifftop hike of eye-popping beauty.

DIRECTIONS:
From the Sedona Y Go:
Southwest on Highway 89A (toward Cottonwood) a distance of 3.2 miles *5.12 km* (MP 371), to Dry Creek Road, where you take a right turn onto Dry Creek Road. Follow it to the 6.1 mile *9.76 km* point, where it joins Long Canyon Road. Take a left here, staying on FR 152C. At the 7.7 mile *12.3 km* point, you reach another junction. Go right. At 8.0 miles *12.8 km*, just before the gatehouse to the Enchantment Resort, you will see a parking area to the right. Park there. There is also a small parking area on the left side of the road.

TRAILHEAD: It is marked at the parking area by a sign reading, "Boynton Canyon #47."

DESCRIPTION: Hike the Boynton Canyon Trail for 1.0 miles *1.6 km*, where the trail is a corridor through a thicket of head-high mazanitas. Take an unmarked narrow but distinct trail to the right (east) going downhill into a wash, on the other side of which is a canyon full of Arizona cypress trees.

On the far side of the wash the trail turns left (north), leaves the forest and climbs to a saddle on a ridge. At the saddle you will find that the ridge forms the south wall of yet another canyon. Go east, toward the head of the canyon, where you will find a walkable ledge under a ten foot high groove in the redrock. This groove is a magic place. Plants in natural "baskets" hang on its wall and we saw two pictographs there. Some hikers will want to stop at the groove's end.

For those unafraid of heights, who don't mind some redrock scrambling, deeper magic lies ahead. Follow cairns up a steep path. About half way up you will see a side path to your left. Take it to a pristine cliff dwelling in a large cave, then return to the main trail for a stiff climb to the next top.

You will emerge onto a terrace. Below you are ridges. Above you are ledges crowned with sheer cliffs. There are more ruins in a grooved ledge high above. You see into two canyons. Standing in this glorious place, we were transfixed with beauty. Following cairns, hike west along the north wall, climbing up and down to use walkable ledges. Some are wide as a street and some are narrow and scary. You round the corner of a giant reef at 1.8 miles *2.9 km* and, bang!, there is Mushroom Rock at the head of a steep V-shaped gorge, perfectly framed by giant rippling walls. You can bushwhack another 0.25 miles *0.4 km*.

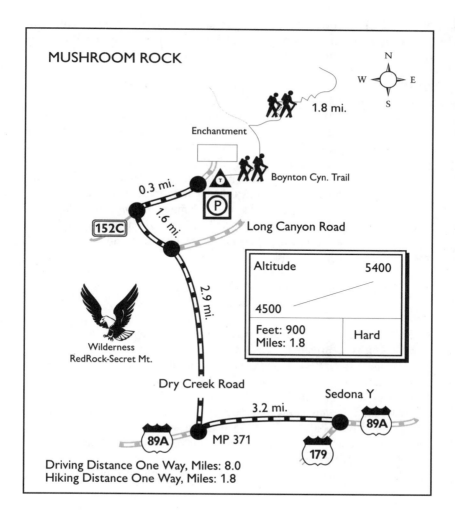

OAK CREEK & VERDE CONFLUENCE

General Information
Location Map G1
Cornville USGS Map
Coconino Forest Service Map

Driving Distance One Way: 22.2 miles *35.6 km* (Time 40 minutes)
Access Road: All cars, Last 4.0 miles *6.4 km* good dirt road
Hiking Distance One Way: 0.25 miles *0.4 km* (Time 15 minutes)
How Strenuous: Easy
Features: Indian ruins, River confluence

NUTSHELL: Located 22.2 miles *35.6 km* southwest of Sedona, this hike has no trail but offers interesting exploration along a stream bank to see a river confluence and an Indian ruin.

DIRECTIONS:
From The Y in Sedona Go:
Southwest on Highway 89A (toward Cottonwood) a distance of 17.0 miles *27.2 km* (MP 357), to a point where the Cornville Road intersects Highway 89A. Turn left on the Cornville Road (Yavapai County 30) and follow it one mile, to the 18.0 mile *28.8 km* point. Turn right there onto unpaved Tissaw Road. Follow this road to the 21.3 mile *34.08 km* point, where there is a three-pronged fork. Take the left fork onto Thede Lane, with a Dead End sign. Follow this road to the 22.0 mile *35.2 km* point, where two dirt roads fork to the right. Take FR 9813 to the ruin in another 0.2 miles *0.32 km*. The other fork, FR 9811, goes to the confluence in 0.4 miles *0.64 km*.

TRAILHEAD: No trail. You will see Indian ruins on a knob. View them and then hike or drive to the confluence.

DESCRIPTION: The Indian ruin is a two-story structure located near the riverbank. It is on private land and protected by a fence festooned with "No Trespassing" signs. You can get close enough for a good look without going onto the land. The ruin is the Atkeson Pueblo (formerly called Oak Creek Pueblo), containing 35 rooms, and was occupied 1300-1425.

From the ruin you can walk along the riverbank back to the confluence or you can drive there. To drive to the confluence just go back to the next fork in the road and turn left, from where it is 0.40 miles *0.64 km* to the spot where the rivers converge.

The two streams meet at a V-shaped point overlooked by a high white bluff. This bluff provides a natural perch, a place to sit and watch the meeting of the waters. As you sit on the point looking forward, Oak Creek is to your left and the Verde River is to your right. After a rain, Oak Creek runs red, while the Verde (true to its name, which means "green" in Spanish) runs green. It is fascinating to watch the waters mix.

This is not a wilderness experience. Right across the river is a big trailer and RV park and there are several ranches and homes in the area. You could actually make this trip with no hiking at all. It is an excellent hike, though, if you explore along the river bank for a couple of miles as we did.

Look sharp as you are walking and you may find pottery shards and arrowheads along the river rim, as this area was inhabited by Indians for hundreds of years. Leave artifacts in place. Never remove them.

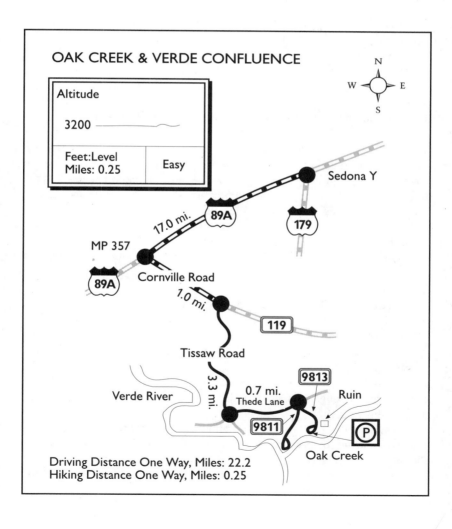

OLD JIM THOMPSON ROAD

General Information
Location Map D5
Munds Park, Wilson Mountain USGS Maps
Coconino Forest Service Map

Driving Distance One Way: 1.7 miles *2.72 km* (Time 10 minutes)
Access Road: All cars. Last 0.40 miles *0.64 km* rough dirt road
Hiking Distance One Way: 3.0 miles *4.8 km* (Time 1.5 hours)
How Strenuous: Moderate
Features: Historic road, Good views

NUTSHELL: This historic road is easy to reach and provides superb views while you hike around the base of Steamboat Rock.

DIRECTIONS:
From the Y in Sedona Go:
   North on Highway on 89A (toward Flagstaff) for 0.30 miles *0.48 km* to Jordan Road, in the middle of uptown Sedona. Turn left (N) and take Jordan Road to its end, at 1.1 miles *1.76 km*. Turn left at the stop sign, onto West Park Ridge, a paved road, which goes through a subdivision and ends at 1.3 miles *2.08 km*. Keep going on the rough but passable unpaved road. At the 1.6 mile *2.56 km* point, you will come to the old shooting range gate. At the time we checked this, it was unclear whether you can go inside and park. If you have any doubt, park outside the gate.

TRAILHEAD: Walk through the gate and up the road 0.1 miles *0.16 km*. You will see the trailhead in the bushes to your right. Large official cairns have been built here to mark the trail.

DESCRIPTION: The trail goes to your right, south, following the cairns. You will follow along this access, created in 1997, over mostly level terrain.
   At 0.14 miles *2.22 km*, you will intersect the Old Jim Thompson Road. Turn left here and go uphill. The downside leg of the road is blocked where it enters private property.
   You will come to a gate at 0.4 miles *0.64 km*, and at this point will have climbed high enough to begin to enjoy the wonderful views that are available on this hike.
   Soon after this, you will stop climbing at the 4,800 foot level and from this point the old road is wide and easy to walk. You will move right over to the base of Steamboat Rock and curve around it.
   At the 1.0 mile *1.6 km* point, you will walk under a power line. Here the

only private hiking trail in Sedona takes off to the right, going down to the Red Rock Lodge in 1.0 miles *1.6 km.*

At 2.0 miles *3.2 km* you will be just below Steamboat Tank, which you can identify by the deciduous trees sticking up from it. A short detour to it is worthwhile. The road ends where it comes down to **Wilson Canyon**.

Jim Thompson was the first settler in Oak Creek, arriving at Indian Gardens in 1876. He built a road to Sedona along the creek banks, but saw it washed away by floods, causing him to build this road, far from the creek, in 1887.

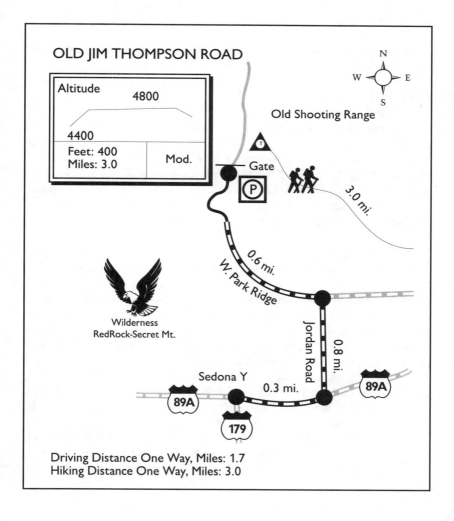

OLD JIM THOMPSON ROAD

Altitude
4800
4400
Feet: 400
Miles: 3.0
Mod.

Old Shooting Range

Gate

3.0 mi.

0.6 mi.

W. Park Ridge

Wilderness
RedRock-Secret Mt.

Jordan Road

0.8 mi.

Sedona Y

0.3 mi.

89A

89A

179

Driving Distance One Way, Miles: 1.7
Hiking Distance One Way, Miles: 3.0

PACKARD MESA TRAIL #66

General Information
Location Map F1
Clarkdale and Sycamore Basin USGS Maps
Coconino Forest Service Map

Driving Distance One Way: 34.3 miles *54.9 km* (Time 1 hour)
Access Road: All cars, Last 10.5 miles *16.8 km* good dirt road
Hiking Distance One Way: 5.6 miles *8.96 km* (Time 4 hours)
How Strenuous: Hard
Features: This livestock trail dips into Sycamore Canyon, then climbs the opposite bank and goes over the top of the canyon rim, coming down into Sycamore Basin.

NUTSHELL: Sycamore Canyon is one of the great scenic features of the area. This trail gives seldom seen views of the canyon's majesty.

DIRECTIONS:
From The Y in Sedona Go:
   Southwest on Highway 89A a distance of 19.4 miles *31 km*, which will take you into the town of Cottonwood. Go straight through Cottonwood on Main Street and then on Broadway, headed toward Tuzigoot National Monument. At 23.4 miles *37.5 km* you will reach the road to Tuzigoot. Turn right onto it and follow it to the 23.8 mile *38.1 km* point, just over the bridge. Turn left on the first dirt road, FR 131. Stay on FR 131 to the 34.3 mile *54.9 km* point, a parking area at the top of Sycamore Canyon.

TRAILHEAD: The trail is well marked at the parking area, where there is a common trailhead for the **Parsons Trail** and the Packard Trail.

DESCRIPTION: At the trailhead, look across the canyon at the top of a small mesa, and you will see the Packard Mesa Trail coming out of the canyon bottom and working its way across. It is a shadeless trail (too hot for comfort in summer). The water in the canyon bottom forms a pool. The best place to cross the creek is where the water runs out of the pool.
   You will first hike down to the stream level, where you will find a trail junction. The Packard Trail #66 goes to the left here down a flight of steps made out of logs, while the Parsons Trail #65 goes to the right, parallel to the stream. Go left.
   At the bottom of the stairs, you will find that the trail heads across a boulder field, where you cannot see the path. Turn right and work your way toward the muddy bank of the pool, crossing along its southern margin to get

to the running water. You must wade across the creek to get onto the Packard Trail, and no bridges or stepping stones have been provided; so come prepared with a towel and a walking stick. Once across, you will see a barbed wire fence with a squeeze-through opening.

From the gate turn right and walk along the fence for a short distance. The trail then turns left and begins climbing out of the canyon. From this point it is well marked and maintained and you will have no difficulty following it.

The trail winds back and forth as it climbs up the rim. The higher you climb, the better views you have. The crest is reached at the 2.5 mile *4.0 km* point. From here the trail continues north along the top of Packard Mesa on fairly level ground to reach the Sycamore Basin trailhead, another 3.1 miles *4.96 km* from the top (see Sycamore Basin in *Flagstaff Hikes*).

We think that the full trail is too long and hard for a day hike and recommend stopping at the crest, at 2.5 miles *4.0 km.*

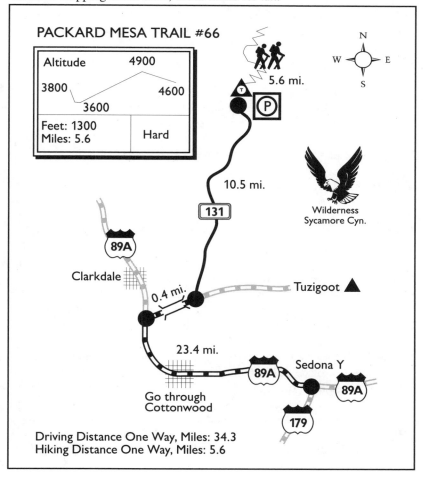

PACKARD MESA TRAIL #66

Altitude 4900
3800   4600
    3600
Feet: 1300
Miles: 5.6   Hard

5.6 mi.

N
W   E
S

10.5 mi.

131

89A

Clarkdale

Wilderness
Sycamore Cyn.

0.4 mi.

Tuzigoot ▲

23.4 mi.

89A   Sedona Y

89A

Go through
Cottonwood

179

Driving Distance One Way, Miles: 34.3
Hiking Distance One Way, Miles: 5.6

PAGE SPRINGS CREEKSIDE TRAIL

General Information
Location Map F2
Page Springs USGS Map
Coconino Forest Service Map

Driving Distance One Way: 14.0 miles *22.4 km* (Time 30 minutes)
Access Road: All vehicles, All paved
Hiking Distance One Way: 0.75 miles *1.2 km* (Time 30 minutes)
How Strenuous: Easy
Features: Oak Creek, Beautiful old cottonwoods, Birding area

NUTSHELL: One of the few walks in the area that goes along the banks of Oak Creek. After an easy drive, you hike past the Fish Hatchery, ending at a place where an unusual rock outcrop furnishes a welcome touch of color.

DIRECTIONS:
From the Sedona Y Go:
    Southwest on Highway 89A (toward Cottonwood) for a distance of 11.25 miles *18 km* to the Page Springs Road (Yavapai Country Road 50). Turn left and follow the Page Springs Road to the 14.0 mile *22.4 km* point, the beginning of a bridge across Oak Creek. There are parking places along the right shoulder before you go over the bridge.

TRAILHEAD: There are no signs. You will see a trail going downhill to the creek on the south side, in the shadow of the bridge.

DESCRIPTION: This is a hiker-made trail, so there are no signs. When you get to creekside, move south, away from the trailer park. The trail is distinct here and easy to follow. In many places it runs along quite close to the water, always a refreshing treat in the Arizona desert.
    Just past the bridge you will notice a cable strung across the creek, with a cage fastened to a tree. This is a gaging station. At times, a person will get into the cage and travel out over the middle of the creek to get a reading on the water depth and flow.
    The banks of Oak Creek are lined with immense old cottonwood trees, giving abundant shade and making a habitat for many birds. It is a good birding area. We enjoyed the sight of half a dozen blue herons as we made our walk, plus many lesser birds.
    You will soon see the Arizona Game and Fish facility across the creek. (The entrance to the Hatchery is only 0.5 miles *0.8 km* from the bridge. It is open to the public and visitors are welcome. Call 634-4805 for visiting

hours. Recommended.)

As you move past the Hatchery, the hike feels more "woodsy," away from homes and road noises. The path is less distinct, but it can be followed for the full distance unless high waters cut off part of it. At one point it moves toward the creek and cuts across an irrigation ditch. A log across the ditch makes an effective bridge.

After moving south, the creek and path make a bend to the east. You will see some interesting rock formations at water level on the other side of the creek. Not long after that, a hillside rises along the right edge of the trail. The shelf of land you are walking on eventually tapers to a point against this hillside, cutting off further travel. You will see a rocked-up irrigation ditch in this area. It is in this vicinity that the trail ends. You walk out onto strange rock outcrops here. The rock seems volcanic, but is an unusual burnt mauve laced with seams of a white quartz-like material. It is unusual and fascinating. This is a good place to sit, watch the birds, and listen to the stream.

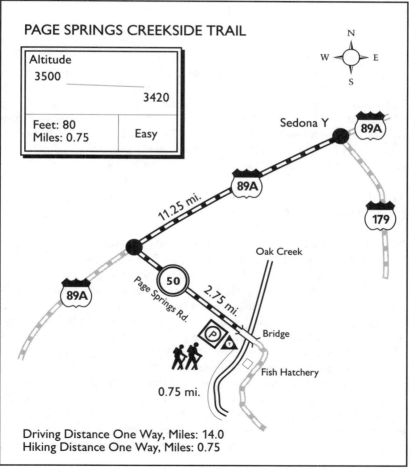

PAGE SPRINGS CREEKSIDE TRAIL

Altitude	
3500	
	3420
Feet: 80 Miles: 0.75	Easy

N
W E
S

Sedona Y 89A

89A

11.25 mi.

179

Oak Creek

89A

50

Page Springs Rd.

2.75 mi.

Bridge

Fish Hatchery

0.75 mi.

Driving Distance One Way, Miles: 14.0
Hiking Distance One Way, Miles: 0.75

PARSONS TRAIL #65

General Information
Location Map F1
Clarkdale and Sycamore Basin USGS Maps
Coconino Forest Service Map

Driving Distance One Way: 34.3 miles *54.9 km* (Time 1 hour)
Access Road: All cars, Last 10.5 miles *16.8 km* good dirt road
Hiking Distance One Way: 4.0 miles *6.4 km* (Time 2 hours)
How Strenuous: Moderate
Features: Tremendous colorful canyon, Year around stream

NUTSHELL: This trail enters the south end of Sycamore Canyon, 34.3 miles *54.9 km* SW of Sedona. It is the easiest trail into the canyon.

DIRECTIONS:
From The Y in Sedona Go:
   Southwest on Highway 89A a distance of 19.4 miles *31 km*, which will take you into the town of Cottonwood. Go straight through Cottonwood on Main Street and then on Broadway, headed toward Tuzigoot National Monument. At 23.4 miles *37.5 km* you will reach the road to Tuzigoot. Turn right onto it and follow it to the 23.8 mile *38.1 km* point, just over the bridge. Turn left on the first dirt road, FR 131. Stay on FR 131 to the 34.3 mile *54.9 km* point, a parking area at the top of Sycamore Canyon.

TRAILHEAD: The trail is well marked at the parking area. A rusty sign reads, "Parsons Trail #65."

DESCRIPTION: You hike into the south end of Sycamore Canyon, where the walls are not as tall as they are upstream. The walls display fascinating rock formations. The hue of the red stone is rosier than the rock in Sedona and is mixed with white rock and is very rough, grainy and chunky. Basalt is blended in, rather than being a cap as it is in Sedona.
   The trail follows along Sycamore Creek, usually on the right bank, though it does cross the creek twice and it is fairly level. In all but extremely dry years, water runs year around up to Parsons Spring at 4.0 miles *6.4 km*, so you have the pleasant experience of walking beside running water. The vegetation is lush and cows often graze through the area.
   The canyon for the first two miles seems wide and spacious. At 1.3 miles *2.1 km* you will reach Summers Spring which usually seeps water across the trail. Although the water looks clear and pure, the Forest Service advises not to drink it unless you treat it. Also be careful about eating the watercress

growing there: wherever there are cows, giardia is a threat.

Upstream from Summers Spring the trail gets rough. A heavy flood in 1980 tore out a lot of the trail and it has not been completely rebuilt. In spots you must scramble over boulders. Stay near the streambed and you will pick up the surviving parts of the trail every time you pass one of the washouts. There are large pools that hold fish.

Sycamore Canyon is in a mineralized zone and before it became a Wilderness Area some mining occurred there. You will pass the entrance to an agate mine at 2.7 miles *4.3 km*. It has been plugged but bits of hardware are still around.

The canyon narrows and the walls get steeper as you work your way upstream. You will reach Parsons Spring at 4.0 miles *6.4 km*. Above this point the stream is only intermittent. The spring is the place to stop for a day hike. The trail continues but becomes very difficult.

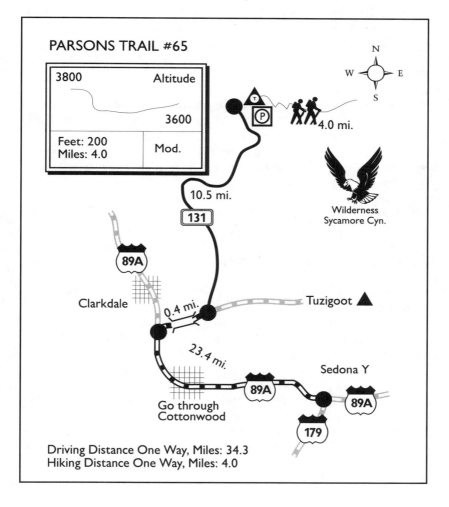

PARSONS TRAIL #65

3800 — Altitude — 3600
Feet: 200 Miles: 4.0 — Mod.

N W E S

4.0 mi.

10.5 mi.
131

Wilderness Sycamore Cyn.

89A

Clarkdale

Tuzigoot

0.4 mi.

23.4 mi.

Sedona Y

89A

89A

Go through Cottonwood

179

Driving Distance One Way, Miles: 34.3
Hiking Distance One Way, Miles: 4.0

PINK SAND CANYON

General Information
Location Map B5
Mountainaire USGS Map
Coconino Forest Service Map

Driving Distance One Way: 12.7 miles *20.3 km* (Time 20 minutes)
Access Road: All cars, All paved
Hiking Distance One Way: 0.25 miles *0.4 km* (Time 30 minutes)
How Strenuous: Easy
Features: Scenic canyon

NUTSHELL: Starting at the Pine Flat Campground in upper Oak Creek Canyon, this hike takes you across the creek and up an unusual narrow canyon, the floor of which is covered with pink sand.

DIRECTIONS:
From the Sedona Y Go:
    North on Highway 89A (toward Flagstaff) for a distance of 12.7 miles *20.3 km* (MP 386.9) to the Pine Flat Campground. On your left at the upper end of the campground on the shoulder of the highway, you will see a stand-pipe, a structure about 5 feet high and 4 feet square made of round stones that houses a spring. Park anywhere near here. There are wide aprons on both shoulders in this area.

TRAILHEAD: Go into the campground at the north entrance just below the standpipe. A paved driveway branches to the right as you enter. Take it. It becomes unpaved and goes down to Oak Creek, where you will find the remains of a concrete driveway going across the creek. This is the unmarked trailhead.

DESCRIPTION: The water in the spring at the Pine Flat campground is pure. Caution: with any spring water, even though it tests pure, there are nat-ural microbes in the water. Local residents are used to these microbes and their immune systems can handle them. This may not be true of visitors; so be careful. Just because you see someone drinking from a spring doesn't mean that the water is good for *you*.
    The center of the concrete driveway was ripped out by heavy floods in 1993, but you can walk across on rocks. Follow the old sunken road you will find on the other side. After walking it a short distance you will come to a three-way fork. Take the center road here, which is a sunken lane, which curves to the north, running parallel to the creek. In about 0.1 mile *0.16 km*

this road will wind around to a point under a power line, where it turns into a footpath heading west into a canyon.

Follow this trail into the canyon. Although the trail is not posted, it is distinct at the entrance to the canyon. It goes up on the top of the bank until it is about half way up the canyon. There it reaches a place where it is better to hike down into the canyon bottom and follow it the rest of the way.

You will find the bottom of this attractive canyon covered with an unusual pink sand, almost a coral color. The canyon is narrow, getting narrower as it goes. A thousand feet above your head are soaring white cliffs, though you will be walking in redrock.

At a point 0.25 miles *0.4 km* from the beginning, the canyon becomes a narrow slot choked with boulders. It would take a lot of effort to scramble over these boulders, so most hikers will want to quit in this spot, where you can see the canyon end a few hundred yards ahead of you in a beautiful box.

This hike is shaded all the way and would be cool even in summer.

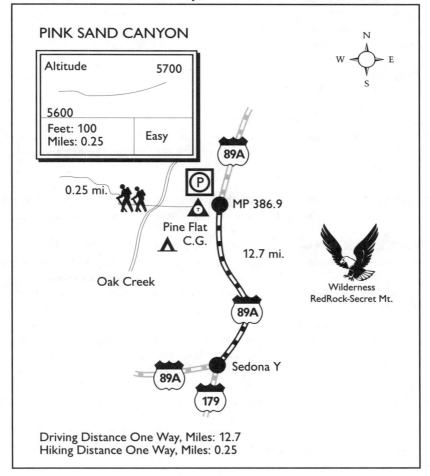

PUMPHOUSE WASH

General Information
Location Map B5
Mountainaire USGS Map
Coconino Forest Service Map

Driving Distance One Way: 13.5 miles *21.6 km* (Time 20 minutes)
Access Road: All cars, All paved
Hiking Distance One Way: 1.5 miles *2.4 km* (Time 1.5 hours)
How Strenuous: Moderate
Features: Scenic canyon

NUTSHELL: Pumphouse Wash is a tributary canyon meeting Oak Creek at the bottom of the Highway 89A switchbacks. There is no trail. You rock hop along the canyon bottom, enjoying the sight of immense towering cliffs, redrock sculptures and a get-away-from-it-all feeling.

DIRECTIONS:
From the Sedona Y Go:
    North on Highway 89A (toward Flagstaff) for a distance of 13.5 miles *21.6 km* (MP 387.7) to the bridge that spans Pumphouse Wash. It is posted. Below (S) of the bridge there is a wide apron that will hold a couple of cars on the right hand side of the road (E), or you can cross the bridge and park on a wide apron on the left side of the road (S).

TRAILHEAD: There is no marking or official trail. Look for a way down into the bottom of the wash. There are paths from both parking areas.

DESCRIPTION: Once you are in the canyon bottom, you walk along the streambed in an upstream direction, east, away from Oak Creek. The bottom is strewn with large boulders and you have to hop from rock to rock. As a result of this, the hike is harder than the mileage and altitude would seem to indicate.
    Pumphouse Wash does not carry water year around. During the spring snowmelt it can run high, but after the first of June it is usually dry except for a few pools. The trick is to make the hike when there is enough water in the wash to add to the enjoyment of the hike but not so much as to make it impassable. Try mid-May. If you see water running under the bridge, there is too much water to make the hike.
    Soon after you enter the canyon, your attention will turn from the boulders under your feet to the heights overhead. The walls of the canyon are extremely high and sheer, giving the hiker a real awestruck feeling of just

how small humans are in the scale of things.

At about 0.3 miles *0.48 km* you will reach the first of a chain of half a dozen pools. These are situated so that you cannot bypass them, but must go through them. Depending on how much water is present, this can mean walking, wading or swimming. When the water is low, an old pair of tennies is good gear. You just wade through and keep on going, walking in wet shoes. If the water is deep enough, there are some good swimming holes.

You will be out of the pool zone in about 0.6 miles *1.0 km* and soon after will see a transition. The rock you hike on changes from white to red. We love this middle part of Pumphouse Wash. It seems virgin and primitive. Oak Creek Canyon itself must have looked like this before it was commercialized. The cutting action of the water has carved chutes and swirls and all kinds of fascinating sculptures in this red stone. You may see evidence of beaver activity.

We think that the 1.5 mile *2.4 km* point is a good place to stop.

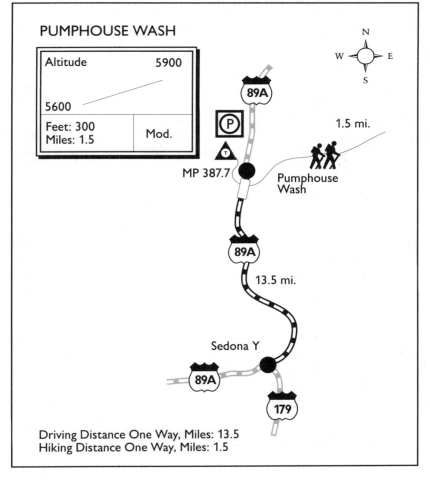

PUMPHOUSE WASH

Altitude	5900
5600	
Feet: 300 Miles: 1.5	Mod.

89A

P

MP 387.7

Pumphouse Wash

1.5 mi.

89A

13.5 mi.

Sedona Y

89A

179

Driving Distance One Way, Miles: 13.5
Hiking Distance One Way, Miles: 1.5

PURTYMUN TRAIL

General Information
Location Map B5
Munds Park and Wilson Mt. USGS Maps
Coconino Forest Service Map

Driving Distance One Way: 8.4 miles *13.5 km* (Time 20 minutes)
Access Road: All cars, All paved
Hiking Distance One Way: 1.0 miles *1.6 km* (Time 1 hour)
How Strenuous: Hard
Features: Views

NUTSHELL: This hard hike climbs the east wall of Oak Creek Canyon from a point directly across Highway 89A from the Junipine Resort in the upper canyon, 8.4 miles *13.5 km* north of Sedona. The trail is in poor condition.

DIRECTIONS:
From the Sedona Y Go:
   North on Highway 89A (toward Flagstaff) for a distance of 8.4 miles *13.5 km* (MP 382.6) to the entrance to the Junipine Resort, which is on your left (W). Parking is very limited. There is a place for one car to nose in just across from the entrance. A bit south of the entrance there is a wide spot on the shoulder on the west side.

TRAILHEAD: There are no markings for this trail. Go across the highway to the Fire Station. The trail starts there.

DESCRIPTION: The trailhead is not conspicuous. You will see a Fire Station across the highway from the resort. The trail starts at the south side of the Fire Station between the building and a yellow fire plug.
   This trail was built by the Purtymun family, which homesteaded the Junipine property in 1896. Like other families in the canyon they needed a way to get to the rim in order go to Flagstaff, so they built this trail. They did not have sophisticated equipment, just picks, shovels, crowbars and maybe a little dynamite, so the trail was crude. Their practice was to leave a wagon at the top. When they wanted to go to town they would walk a horse to the top, hitch it to the wagon and then drive to Flagstaff. In town they would load the wagon with goods, perhaps bartering some of the vegetables and fruits they had grown for flour and coffee. They would then drive the wagon back to Oak Creek Canyon and chain it to a tree at the top of the trail. After that they would carry the goods down in saddlebags. Such a trip could

take three or four days.

In spite of the hardships of using the trail, the alternative was worse. There was no convenient wagon road from Sedona to Flagstaff until the Schnebly Hill Road was built in 1902. Before that the only wagon road was the old **Beaverhead** route several miles farther south. Highway 89A did not come onto the scene until much later. It was built in phases starting in the early 1920s, and took a decade to complete.

This trail is so steep and so rough that we don't see how the Purtymuns could ever have gotten a horse up and down it. It is hard climbing for humans, who can grab onto trees for support. We rate this the worst kept and most difficult trail in the book. We do not recommend this hike but we include it as an historic trail.

If you want a good hike up the east rim of upper Oak Creek Canyon try **Cookstove**, **Harding Spring** or **Thomas Point**.

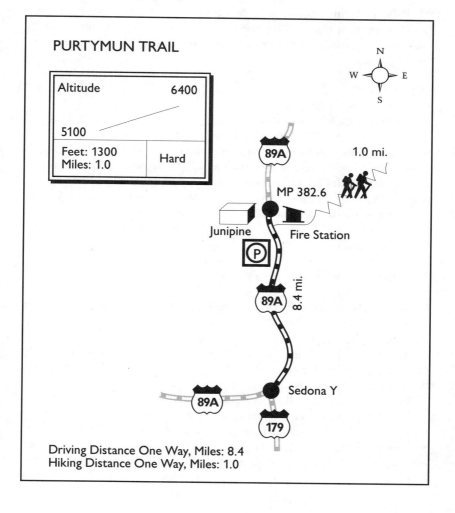

PURTYMUN TRAIL

Altitude 6400

5100

Feet: 1300
Miles: 1.0

Hard

89A   1.0 mi.

MP 382.6

Junipine   Fire Station

89A   8.4 mi.

89A   Sedona Y

179

Driving Distance One Way, Miles: 8.4
Hiking Distance One Way, Miles: 1.0

RACHEL'S KNOLL

General Information
Location Map C3
Wilson Mt. USGS Map
Coconino Forest Service Map

Driving Distance One Way: 7.7 miles *12.32 km* (Time 20 minutes)
Access Road: All cars, Last 0.1 miles *0.16 km* good dirt road
Hiking Distance One Way: 0.5 miles *0.8 km* (Time 20 minutes)
How Strenuous: Easy
Features: Very simple, Very Sedona

NUTSHELL: This is an unusual trail, privately owned but open to the public. Its creator intends it as a monument to peace and has posted signs requesting that it be a quiet area for meditation. It is easy to reach, beautiful, and inspiring.

DIRECTIONS:
From the Sedona Y Go:
Southwest on Highway 89A (toward Cottonwood) for a distance of 3.2 miles *5.12 km* (MP 371) to the Dry Creek Road. Turn right onto Dry Creek Road and follow it to the 6.1 mile *9.76 km* point, where there is a stop sign. Turn right on the paved Long Canyon Road and follow it to the end of the paving at 7.6 miles *12.16 km,* and keep going on the dirt road beyond the paving. There is a fork just beyond the end of the paving, where you go left. Soon afterwards you will come to the parking area at the entrance to the Canon del Oro subdivision, at 7.7 miles *12.32 km* where you see a sign "Park Here and Walk."

TRAILHEAD: Walk up the main road.

DESCRIPTION: About halfway up the hill, you will pass from private land to Forest Service land. At 0.2 miles *0.32 km* you will be at the top of the knoll, and re-enter private land, where you will find a sign giving the rules of the area, the "Hill Etiquette:" (1) Dedicated to Meditation & Prayer, (2) Honor the Silence, (3) Stay on the Trail, (4) Groups over 7 Require Permit. Go to the right here, still walking the road.

In a few yards you will reach a place where you may see some vehicles. Some of the jeep tours are permitted to come up here, but they can drive no farther. At 0.37 miles *0.59 km,* you will see a footpath veer off to the right. Stay on the road here and continue heading west. You are now entering the zone where beautiful views unfold. At 0.5 miles *0.8 km* you will be at the end of the road, where you have a choice of footpaths going down a few feet to bare redrock ledges which are absolutely perfect for sitting, enjoying the unspoiled beauty of the cliffs to the north, and meditating.

The paths below the road are marked, and you can enjoy meandering around. You will probably find medicine wheels and other artifacts. As you curve back toward the way you came in, you will find a Peace Pillar. When we passed by, a group of six women were holding hands in a circle around it, and wished us well. You will also find a donation box at the top. Drop in a dollar or two and help support this inspired project.

People come to Sedona for many reasons. A substantial number of them visit because of their belief that Sedona is a special place, endowed with cosmic powers. See the discussion on vortexes on page 255. We have been told that Rachel's Knoll is regarded as a vortex site, but we have not had this confirmed by any of the experts, so we do not include it on our list. However, there is no doubt that it is a place of sublime beauty and spiritual power.

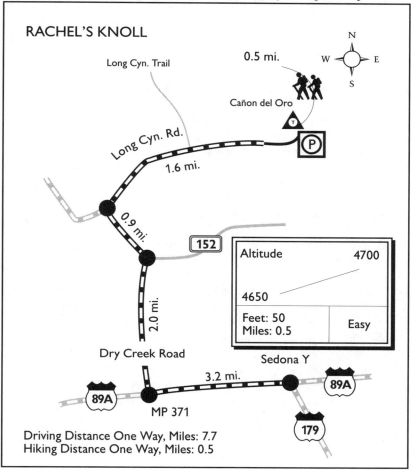

RATTLESNAKE CANYON

General Information
Location Map G5
Munds Mt. USGS Map
Coconino Forest Service Map

Driving Distance One Way*: 23.0 miles *36.8 km* (Time 45 minutes)
Access Road*:* All cars, Last 1.0 miles *1.6 km* medium gravel
Hiking Distance One Way*:* 0.75 miles *1.2 km* (Time 30 minutes)
How Strenuous*:* Moderate
Features*:* Remote scenic canyon

NUTSHELL: This trail takes you to the bottom of Rattlesnake Canyon, a little known beautiful spot.

DIRECTIONS:
From the Sedona Y Go:
    South on Highway 179 (toward Phoenix) for 14.7 miles *23.5 km*, to the I-17 Interchange. Turn north and head toward Flagstaff on I-17. At the 22.0 mile *35.2 km* spot you will see Exit 306 "Stoneman Lake" (MP 306.1). Make this exit. Go under I-17 into the lane marked south, to Phoenix, but look for a dirt road to your right (west), FR 647, just beyond the underpass. Turn off onto FR 647. For the first 0.75 miles *1.2 km* it is in good condition except for one gully. At the 22.75 mile *36.4 km* point you reach a T. Turn right here. The road becomes much worse, bare dirt with lots of ruts and rocks. Most cars should be able to make it to the 23.0 mile *36.8 km* point, beyond which the road is too rough. Pull off the road and park.

TRAILHEAD: There are no signs. You walk the road to the canyon rim and then hike down to the bottom.

DESCRIPTION: If you park at the 23.0 mile *36.8 km* point as we recommend, then you must walk about 0.25 miles *0.4 km* to the canyon.
    You won't have to ask *what* canyon. As you near the rim you can see it plainly. This is one of those hidden canyons that you don't see from anywhere unless you fly over it. But it is a deep and interesting canyon. The walls are quite sheer and are made of successive layers of columnar-jointed basalt. There are many such canyons in northern Arizona, but this one has more color and character than most.
    At the canyon rim you will see that the road goes down into the canyon but that no one drives it. Walk down the road. The road will disappear in about 0.10 miles *0.16 km*.

Beyond this point you will find a footpath in good condition. It is a real walking path, with erosion control and other improvements and you can see that a lot of work has been done on it. It is not a recreational trail, but is used to provide access to the gaging station that you will find at the bottom.

We think the rock walls you pass by are interesting and have some beautiful markings, including accents made by lichens and mosses.

At the bottom is a cable strung across the canyon and the gaging station, which is a sort of tall corrugated tube with a box on top. There is a depth gauge on the front of the tube showing depths as high as ten feet.

Beyond this there is a waterfall with a thirty foot drop. Water was running over it while we were there and it seemed dangerous to climb. Other sources indicate that one can climb down it, but we do not recommend dangerous climbing. From this point, Rattlesnake Canyon joins **Woods Canyon** in about 2.25 miles *3.6 km*. It is a satisfying hike if you just sit at the waterfall. If you want to explore the canyon, go upstream.

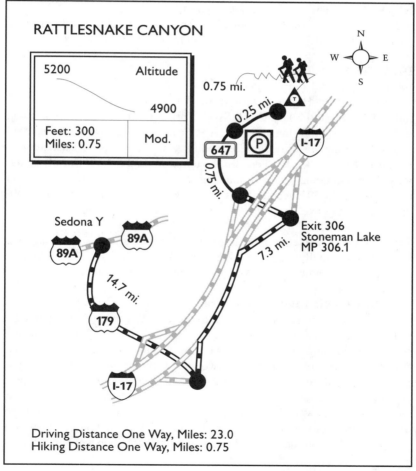

RATTLESNAKE CANYON

5200	Altitude
	4900
Feet: 300 Miles: 0.75	Mod.

0.75 mi.

0.25 mi.

647 · P · I-17

0.75 mi.

Sedona Y

89A · 89A

Exit 306
Stoneman Lake
MP 306.1

7.3 mi.

14.7 mi.

179

I-17

Driving Distance One Way, Miles: 23.0
Hiking Distance One Way, Miles: 0.75

RED CANYON (PALATKI) RUINS

General Information
Location Map C2
Loy Butte and Page Springs USGS Maps
Coconino Forest Service Map

Driving Distance One Way: 13.5 miles *21.6 km* (Time 25 minutes)
Access Road: All cars, Last 5.8 miles *9.28 km* good dirt road
Hiking Distance: Trail #1 is a 0.6 mile *1.0 km* loop; **Trail #2** is 0.3 miles *0.48 km* one way
How Strenuous: Both hikes are Easy
Features: Indian ruins, Pictographs, Caves

NUTSHELL: This adventure takes you to the Palatki Indian Ruins 13.5 miles *21.6 km* northwest of Sedona for a short jaunt to cliff dwellings and a meander along the base of Bear Mountain to see caves full of rock art.

DIRECTIONS:
From the Sedona Y Go:
Southwest on Highway 89A (toward Cottonwood) a distance of 3.2 miles *5.12 km,* to the Dry Creek Road. Turn right on the Dry Creek Road and drive to the stop sign at 6.1 miles *9.76 km.* Turn left on the paved road and drive to the 7.7 mile *12.32 km* point, where the road to Enchantment Resort forks right. Go left here, on the unpaved road FR 152C, to Boynton Pass. You will come to a road junction at 11.7 miles *18.72 km,* where you turn right on FR 525. About 0.1 mile *0.16 km* from this junction, turn right on FR 795 and travel to the parking lot at 13.5 miles *21.6 km.*

TRAILHEAD: There are three trails signed at the parking area, though we think there are really only two hikes here. The Palatki Vista Trail is a connecting loop, at either end of which are the real hiking trails.

DESCRIPTION: Palatki Ruins Trail, 0.6 miles *1.0 km*, complete loop. This trail takes you to the Palatki ruins, and is the harder trail. After 0.20 miles *0.32 km* of level walking you will make a short steep climb, requiring some rock-hopping, to the ruins. The ruins are in two shallow caves. The first ruin is the larger one, with a two story structure that contained eight rooms. The walls are well preserved—even to the juniper poles that support doors and windows. The second ruin is smaller and also contained eight chambers, but its walls have collapsed and you cannot enter the area. Date of construction of both ruins is about 1200 A.D. The site housed about 100 people. Retrace your path to the bottom and finish the loop back to the parking lot.

Rock Art Trail, 0.3 miles *0.48 km*, one way. This trail zigzags up to the base of tall red cliffs to the left of and above the ranch house, taking you to a series of caves at the base of a butte. Behind (north of) the first cave you will find what appears to be a high-walled ancient ruin but is really a 1920s dwelling which was a temporary residence before the ranch house was built. The string of caves continues to the west. These caves contain the largest collection of rock art in the Verde Valley, ranging from art of the ancient Sinagua to the more modern Apaches. They also contain inscriptions by Anglo pioneers—and modern vandals.

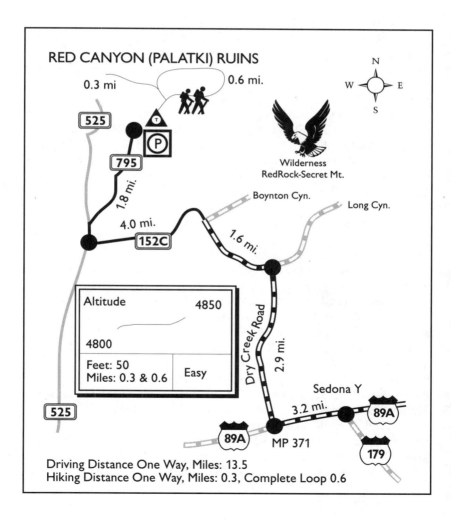

RED CANYON (PALATKI) RUINS

0.3 mi   0.6 mi.

525

795

Wilderness
RedRock-Secret Mt.

Boynton Cyn.

Long Cyn.

1.8 mi.

4.0 mi.   152C

1.6 mi.

Altitude   4850

4800

Feet: 50
Miles: 0.3 & 0.6   Easy

Dry Creek Road

2.9 mi.

Sedona Y

525

3.2 mi.   89A

89A   MP 371

179

Driving Distance One Way, Miles: 13.5
Hiking Distance One Way, Miles: 0.3, Complete Loop 0.6

RED ROCK STATE PARK

General Information
Location Map F3
Sedona USGS Map
Coconino Forest Service Map

Drive Distance One Way: 8.8 miles *14.1 km* (Time 15 minutes)
Access Road: All vehicles, All paved
Hiking Distance, Complete Loop: Six hikes of various distances, see map
How Strenuous: Easy-Moderate, except Eagles' Nest, which is Hard
Features: Oak Creek, Red Rock State Park, Views

NUTSHELL: These six trails are located in Red Rock State Park 8.8 miles *14.1 km* southwest of Sedona. They range from easy to hard and offer a variety of features. A good family destination.

DIRECTIONS:
From the Sedona Y Go:
    Southwest on Highway 89A (toward Cottonwood) for a distance of 5.5 miles *8.8 km* (MP 368.6) to the Lower Red Rock Loop Road. Turn left on the Lower Red Rock Loop Road and follow it to the 8.5 miles *13.6 km* point, where you will see the entry to Red Rock State Park. Turn right into the park. You will come to a toll booth where an admission is charged. From that point, drive to the Visitor Center and park there, at 8.8 miles *14.1 km.*

TRAILHEAD: All hikes start at the Visitor Center.

DESCRIPTION: Go through the Visitor Center and turn right on the paved trail. At 0.08 miles *0.13 km* you will come to the first junction. (Note: our mileage includes connections to the trails.)
    (1) **Smoke Trail** forks to the right. It is 0.4 miles *0.64 km* long, and easy. You walk down to the creek and then turn right for a pleasant creekside stroll. Sometimes trail guides are dispensed from a box.
    (2) **Kisva Trail.** This trail is 1.0 miles *1.6 km* long and easy. From the Visitor Center walk the main path to Kingfisher Crossing bridge. Go across the creek on the bridge to the trail junction for the Apache Fire Trail and the Eagles' Nest Trail. Turn right here. You will see a sign identifying the Kisva Trail, which follows an old ranch road parallel to the creek.
    (3) **Eagles' Nest Trail.** The hardest trail in the park, 3.23 miles *5.2 km* for a complete loop, requiring a 200 ft. climb. Take the Kisva Trail to its end. You will see the Eagles' Nest Trail going uphill there. You must make a steep climb to the top, where you will enjoy the views. You then loop around

to join the Kisva Trail at its midsection, though you could take Coyote Ridge over to Apache Fire.

(4) **Apache Fire.** From the Visitor Center, go across Kingfisher bridge. Once across you will come to the trail junction where Kisva and Eagles' Nest go to the right. Go left there to the base of the knoll on which the house is located. A short flight of redrock steps and a sign lead you to the Apache Fire trail. It is 1.7 miles *2.7 km* for a complete loop, and is moderate because of the 100 ft. climb required.

(5) **Javelina.** 2.0 mile *3.2 km* loop, Moderate. Just before the Apache Fire trail begins climbing out of the creek bed, the **Javelina Trail** takes off to your left, making a loop.

(6) **Yavapai.** 1.58 miles *2.5 km,* Moderate. Walk across Kingfisher bridge to the point where the Apache Fire Trail starts. Here you take the left fork, on the unpaved East Gate Road. In a short distance you will reach the Yavapai Trail, going to the left (N). The Javelina Trail joins the road here.

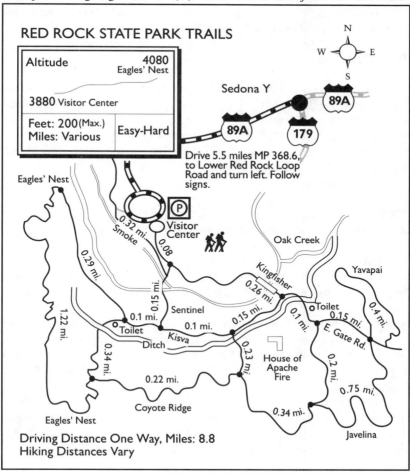

RED TANK DRAW

General Information
Location Map G6
Casner Butte USGS Map
Coconino Forest Service Map

Driving Distance One Way: 16.1 miles *25.8 km* (Time 30 minutes)
Access Road: All cars, All paved
Hiking Distance One Way: 0.9 miles *1.5 km* (Time 1 hour)
How Strenuous: Moderate
Features: Intermittent stream, Picturesque cliffs

NUTSHELL: This hike follows the course of Red Tank Draw, 16.1 miles *25.8 km* southeast of Sedona, in the Wet Beaver Creek country. You walk along the streambed enjoying a beautiful little canyon.

DIRECTIONS:
From the Sedona Y Go:
South on Highway 179 (toward Phoenix) for 14.7 miles *23.52 km*, to the I-17 Interchange. Instead of going onto I-17, go underneath it onto the paved road. At 15.2 miles *24.3 km*, you will come to a junction. The right fork goes to Montezuma Castle. Take the left fork (FR 618), staying on the paved road. At 16.1 miles *25.8 km*, you will see a sign reading, "Red Tank Draw" located just in front of a small bridge. There is a dirt road to the left here. Pull in on it and park.

TRAILHEAD: There is no designated or marked trail. You go down into the streambed and walk the canyon upstream (north).

DESCRIPTION: From the parking place, you simply walk down to the streambed at any place you choose. It is easy to enter it anywhere in this area because the canyon walls are low. Farther upstream the walls become higher.

The best time we found for this hike was in late April, when the stream was carrying just enough water to be interesting. We tried it in early April and the runoff waters were too high for hiking. You can hike it when it is dry also, which is most of the year, but we think a little running water adds interest.

At the place where you go into the canyon there are two forks. It doesn't much matter which fork you choose to hike, as they will merge upstream. This is a rock hopping hike, as the bottom of the draw is boulder strewn. Such hikes can be fun but they are hard on the feet.

As you move upstream, the canyon will deepen. At about 0.6 miles *1.0 km* you come to a narrow spot with sheer red walls, not tremendously high as Northern Arizona canyons go, about thirty feet, but very pleasing to the eye. The area is one of geologic uplifts, the result of which has been to twist the rock into some very interesting angles. Look for swallows' nests throughout this area. The birds make their nests by cementing countless beakfuls of mud into globular nests that hang from the underside of rock shelves. They are about the size of a baseball.

You will move out of the most scenic part of Red Tank Draw soon afterwards. At 0.9 miles *1.5 km* you will come to an old barbed wire fence with a gate. We think this is a good stopping place for the hike, though we have gone much farther.

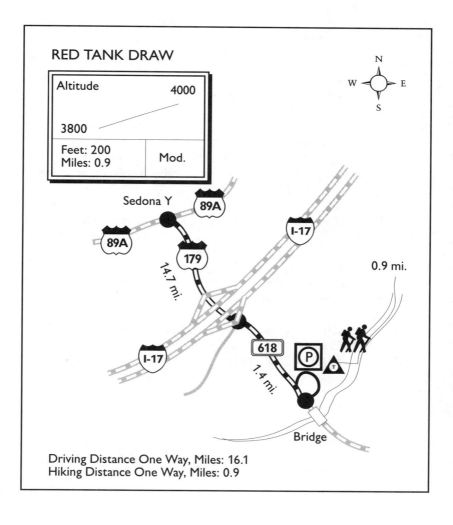

RED TANK DRAW

Altitude

4000

3800

Feet: 200
Miles: 0.9

Mod.

Sedona Y

89A

89A

I-17

179

14.7 mi.

I-17

618

1.4 mi.

0.9 mi.

P

T

Bridge

Driving Distance One Way, Miles: 16.1
Hiking Distance One Way, Miles: 0.9

ROBBERS ROOST

General Information
Location Map C1
Loy Butte and Page Springs USGS Maps
Coconino Forest Service Map

Driving Distance One Way: 19.2 miles *30.7 km* (Time 30 minutes)
Access Road: All cars, Last 9.6 miles *15.4 km* good dirt road
Hiking Distance One Way: 1.5 miles *2.4 km* (Time 45 minutes)
How Strenuous: Easy
Features: Fascinating cave with unique window

NUTSHELL: This is a short hike to an interesting cave in a red butte located 19.2 miles *30.7 km* northwest of Sedona.

DIRECTIONS:
From the Sedona Y Go:
   Southwest on Highway 89A (toward Cottonwood) a distance of 9.6 miles *15.4 km* (MP 364.5) to the Red Canyon Road. Turn right on Red Canyon Road, also known as FR 525, and follow it to the 12.4 mile *19.8 km* point where FR 525C branches to the left. Turn left on FR 525C and follow it to the 19.2 miles *30.7 km* point. There you will see a rough road branching to the right marked FR 9530. Take this but drive it only a short distance to the top of the hill, where you will park.

TRAILHEAD: You walk up the road, FR 9530, for 1.1 miles *1.8 km*. There you will see the trail going down into a ravine to your right. It is not signed.

DESCRIPTION: If you have a high clearance vehicle and tough tires you can drive right up to the trailhead and save a mile of walking, but don't try to make it in an ordinary passenger car.
   As you walk up the road you approach Casner Mountain. Your target is the muffin shaped red butte just in front of and on the right hand side of the mountain. Robbers Roost is located on the far side of that butte.
   At the trailhead you will see an area to your left where the vegetation is matted down because of cars parking there. Look for the trail to your right. Usually there are cairns marking the beginning of the trail. The trail goes straight downhill into the bottom of a ravine, then goes up the other side.
   The trail, after rising from the bottom of the ravine, curls around to the north side of the butte and climbs about two-thirds of the way to the top of it. At 0.35 miles *0.56 km* from the beginning of the trail, the trail forks. The right fork goes to the top. Ignore it for now and take the left fork. This will

require that you walk out on the face of the butte on the slickrock (a misnomer, as the rock actually gives very good traction, like sandpaper). The two metal rods that used to stick vertically out of the rock face and acted as handholds were gone the last time we hiked here, but we had no trouble because of it.

After that you will see the cave. Rock walls have been built at the mouth of the cave to support dirt fill that was placed there to make the floor of the cave level. There are even steps to the "door" of the cave.

The cave looks out to the northeast, toward Bear Mountain and Maroon Mountain. Down below it there is a cattle tank.

There is a circular window in the cave that looks more to the south. This window is unique. There is nothing else like it in the Sedona area. The cave gets its name, Robbers Roost, from the fanciful notion that this would be a good hideout for robbers, who could use the window as a lookout. It was used by a moonshiner during Prohibition.

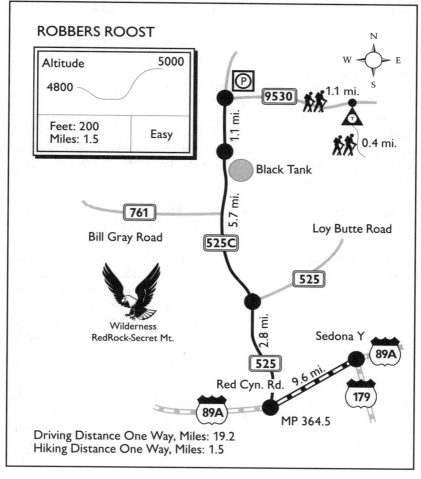

SACRED MOUNTAIN

General Information
Location Map G6
Casner Butte USGS Map
Coconino Forest Service Map

Driving Distance One Way: 18.0 miles *28.8 km* (Time 30 minutes)
Access Road: All cars, Last 0.8 miles *1.3 km* good dirt road
Hiking Distance One Way: 0.35 miles *0.56 km* (Time 30 minutes)
How Strenuous: Moderate
Features: Indian ruins, Views

NUTSHELL: Located 18.0 miles *28.8 km* southeast of Sedona, this special mountain takes moderate effort to climb. At the top are pueblo ruins and fine views.

DIRECTIONS:
From the Sedona Y Go:
    South on Highway 179 (toward Phoenix) for 14.7 miles *23.5 km*, to the I-17 Interchange. Instead of going onto I-17, go underneath it onto a paved road, FR 618. Stay on FR 618. The paving ends at the bridges at the Beaver Creek Campground. Half a mile beyond, at 17.9 miles *28.6 km*, as the road is curving right, you will see a dirt road, FR 9201A, to your left. Pull off on 9201A. You will see that it leads to a fence. Try to get as close to the fence as you can (it's about 0.2 miles *0.32 km*) and park.

TRAILHEAD: You will not see a trail sign. Go through the gate and turn right and walk parallel to the fence. The path is obvious.

DESCRIPTION: The mountains that fill the northern horizon as you drive through the Beaver Creek area are all part of the Mogollon Rim, a giant uplift that runs from Silver City, New Mexico to Ashfork, Arizona. As you come around a curve in the road, Sacred Mountain appears. It is really more of a butte than a mountain in this country full of mountains, and it stands alone in front of the rim. It is set apart by its color—white—against the darker colors of the rim, which are gray, black and red.
    At times, when the low evening sun hits Sacred Mountain, the mountain seems to glow. We saw a beautiful example of this one March evening when we were at the nearby Montezuma's Well (worth a visit). From the top of the well we looked northwest and saw Sacred Mountain shining as if it were lit by a spotlight—magic. One can well understand why the ancient Indians thought that the mountain was sacred.

At the fence surrounding Sacred Mountain there is a small sign indicating that the ruins are protected by Federal law. Go through the gate and immediately turn right, walking along parallel to the fence. You will pick up the trail there and will see it going up the toe of the mountain that faces the road. The trail will take you to a sign with a visitors' register to which you may add your name. At the top of the mountain you will find extensive ruins that have been partially excavated. They have also been thoroughly pot hunted, more's the pity. Please do not disturb them.

The site has not been restored, just investigated. The remains of many walls have been uncovered so that you can see the outline of the pueblo. It was a fairly large site, perhaps as large as Tuzigoot.

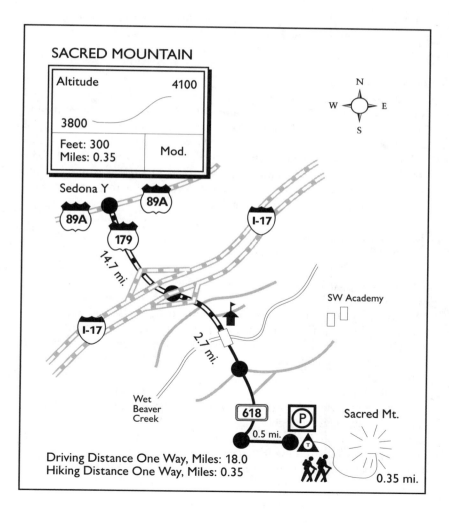

SCHEURMAN MOUNTAIN #56

General Information
Location Map E3
Sedona USGS Map
Coconino Forest Service Map

Driving Distance One Way: 4.5 miles *7.2 km* (Time 10 minutes)
Access Road: All vehicles, All paved
Hiking Distance One Way: 1.1 miles *1.76 km* (Time 1 hour)
How Strenuous: Moderate
Features: Views

NUTSHELL: This sprawling mountain southwest of Sedona is rather drab but is a platform for great views.

DIRECTIONS:
From the Sedona Y Go:
Southwest on Highway 89 (toward Cottonwood) for a distance of 4.2 miles *6.72 km* (MP 368.9) to the Upper Red Rock Loop Road, the road to the high school. Turn left on the Upper Red Rock Loop Road and follow it to the 4.45 miles *7.12 km* point, where you turn right on Scorpion Way. (You will pass Scorpion Drive first, then come to Scorpion Way.) You will see a sign for the trailhead at the turn. In another 0.05 miles *0.08 km*, turn left into the parking area, also signed. The parking place is just across from the high school's Building B, Administration Center.

TRAILHEAD: You will see a rusty trailhead sign on the south side of the parking lot, and the trail leading toward the mountain.

DESCRIPTION: In order to guide hikers onto the trail, the Forest Service has erected official cairns in wire cages. Look for them and you won't be misled. At 0.15 miles *0.24 km*, you will come to a gate. Beyond the gate the trail climbs up to a saddle. It is a good trail, winding its way uphill so that the climb is gradual. Almost immediately you are rewarded with good views. After a steep but short climb of 0.5 miles *0.8 km*, you will reach the top.

At the top you will see that the trail has two branches. Each is worth exploring and is about 0.3 miles *0.48 km* long. The one we enjoy the most is the trail to the left. This goes out onto an overlook from where you will enjoy good views of Cathedral Rock and Oak Creek. The viewpoint is about 0.3 miles *0.48 km* from the fork. (About 30 paces from the beginning you will intersect a trail going to the right. It goes about 2.0 miles *3.2 km* SW to join the Lower Red Rock Loop Road near the place where you park for the **Goosenecks** hike. We find it colorless and not very interesting. Not recommended.)

After enjoying the views, return to the main trail junction and take the trail that goes westerly out into another lookout point. You have to pick your way out to the edge, but navigating is easy.

The mountain is named after Sedona pioneer Henry Schuerman, a German who spelled his name Schürman. The standard way to Americanize that spelling is to place an e after the u, making the correct spelling Schuerman, and this was the way Henry spelled his name. Map makers goofed and spelled it Scheurman. We regret this error, but go with the flow, using the incorrect but now-established spelling. Scheurman Mountain is an old shield volcano. Instead of exploding violently and forming a tall cone, shield volcanoes ooze up, making a low tapering shape.

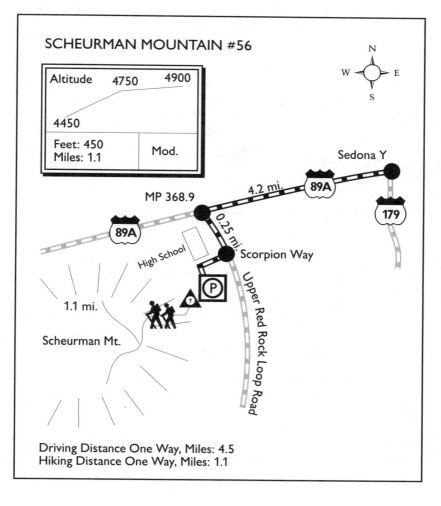

SCHEURMAN MOUNTAIN #56

Altitude   4750   4900
4450
Feet: 450
Miles: 1.1   Mod.

Sedona Y

MP 368.9   4.2 mi.   89A

89A   179

0.25 mi.

High School   Scorpion Way

P   T

1.1 mi.   Upper Red Rock Loop Road

Scheurman Mt.

Driving Distance One Way, Miles: 4.5
Hiking Distance One Way, Miles: 1.1

SCHNEBLY HILL BUTTES

General Information
Location Map E5
Munds Mt. and Munds Park USGS Maps
Coconino Forest Service Map

Driving Distance One Way: 5.5 miles *8.8 km* (Time 30 minutes)
Access Road: All cars, Last 4.7 miles *7.5 km* bumpy dirt road
Hiking Distance One Way: 0.60 miles *1.0 km* (Time 45 minutes)
How Strenuous: Moderate
Features: Views, Fascinating rock formations and sculptures

NUTSHELL: This is a scrambling, bushwhacking experience just off the Schnebly Hill Road, only a mile east of Sedona as the crow flies.

DIRECTIONS:
From the Sedona Y Go:
    South on Highway 179 (toward Phoenix) for a distance of 0.3 miles *0.48 km* (MP 313.1) to the Schnebly Hill Road. It is just across the bridge past Tlaquepaque. Turn left onto the Schnebly Hill Road. It is paved for the first half mile and then turns into a gravel road that is all right for any car unless the road is muddy. At the 5.0 mile *8.0 km* point, you will see a gate. At 5.5 miles *8.8 km* is a knoll to your left fronted by an apron big enough to hold three or four cars. Park on this apron.

TRAILHEAD: At the parking place.

DESCRIPTION: You park at the foot of a knoll. There you will see a foot-path going straight up to the top of the knoll. Climb up it. On top you will see some fine views and you will find several paths heading toward the cliffs to the west.
    Look straight ahead to the west and you will see a tall butte nearby. Pick out the main trail going toward the butte. You will hike across a narrow ridge to the base of a thick red ledge. Move to your right along the base until you come to a climbable fault-crack. It is a steep but short haul up this crevice.
    You will top out on a saddle. To your left (S) you can go to a point jutting out into Bear Wallow Canyon. The right hand trail goes up to a taller butte.
    Try the trail to the south butte first. The ledges are narrow and have several stages or landings. You can walk around a pinnacle for magnificent views. This is a real "Ah!" experience.

If you are afraid of heights, adjust your comfort level as to how far out on the point you want to go. Daredevils can walk right out to the can-tilevered tip of a "diving board" where it is 1200 feet straight down to join Elvis. Sissies can stay well back on solid footing and still get great views.

It's fun to watch cars coming up the Schnebly Hill Road from this point. If they see you they will wonder how you got there and why you're foolish-ly risking your neck.

From the diving board it's back to the saddle, then up to the higher butte. It is an easier climb than you would expect from its appearance. The main path is quite distinct and gentle. The views are not as good as you would hope because another butte to the west partially blocks southward sights. You do have good views to the north.

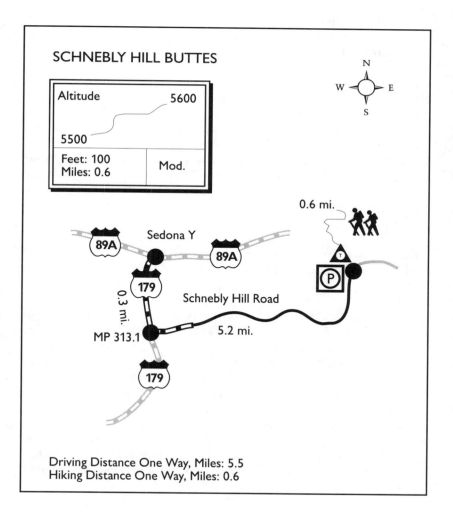

SCHNEBLY HILL BUTTES

Altitude 5600

5500

Feet: 100
Miles: 0.6   Mod.

0.6 mi.

89A   Sedona Y   89A

179

0.3 mi.

Schnebly Hill Road

MP 313.1   5.2 mi.

179

Driving Distance One Way, Miles: 5.5
Hiking Distance One Way, Miles: 0.6

SCHNEBLY HILL TRAIL #158

General Information
Location Map E5
Munds Mt. and Munds Park USGS Maps
Coconino Forest Service Map

Driving Distance One Way: 5.5 miles *8.8 km* (Time 30 minutes)
Access Road: All cars, Last 4.7 miles *7.5 km* bumpy dirt road
Hiking Distance One Way: 2.4 miles *3.9 km* (Time 1.5 hours)
How Strenuous: Moderate
Features: Historic road, Views

NUTSHELL: This trail climbs to the top of Schnebly Hill, on an old road, then swings south and follows the edge of the rim to join the **Munds Mountain Trail**.

DIRECTIONS:
From the Sedona Y Go:
    South on Highway 179 (toward Phoenix) for a distance of 0.3 miles *0.48 km* (MP 313.1) to the Schnebly Hill Road. It is just across the bridge past Tlaquepaque. Turn left onto the Schnebly Hill Road. It is paved for the first half mile and then turns into a dirt road that is all right for any car unless the road is muddy. At 5.0 miles *8.0 km* you will see a gate made of very thick steel pipes used to close the road in winter. At 5.5 miles *8.8 km*, you will see a low redrock butte to your left with a parking area big enough for four cars. Park there.

TRAILHEAD: Walk down the road about twenty yards from where you have parked. You will see the trailhead marker to your left, on the uphill side.

DESCRIPTION: The first half of the trail is the original 1902 alignment of the Schnebly Hill Road, and as you walk along it, you will have fascinating and ever changing views. First you will look down into the Bear Wallow-Mitten Ridge area. As you move farther south (uphill) you will begin to see around the south end of the ridge into Sedona. At the top you can see right through a natural corridor into the Verde Valley. There are many superb vista points.
    At the 1.2 miles *1.92 km* point look to your right just as you come to the top of the grade, at a hairpin curve. Here you will see a footpath going to your right (S), into the trees. Follow it. This is the new leg of the trail. It is marked by cairns and takes you south along the rim. In some places you are

right on the rim and have choice views into colorful country. At others you go inland a bit. You will pass through two gates. The second gate is at Committee Tank, located to your left (E), a favorite spot for wildlife.

Soon after, the trail reaches a thin ridge connecting to Munds Mountain. This ridge is a wonderful and unusual land feature. From the ridge you can see to the north into the Schnebly Hill area and south into Jacks Canyon, a great double-header. You are high enough to have sweeping views out over the landscape on top of the Mogollon Rim. The San Francisco Peaks stand out and are very attractive from here. The ridge then dips down to join the **Munds Mountain Trail** at the 2.4 miles *3.9 km* point, a place marked by a super cairn. The **Jacks Canyon Trail** terminates here, coming up from the bottom of Jacks Canyon.

The Munds Mountain Trail is steep, climbing 500 feet in half a mile to the top.

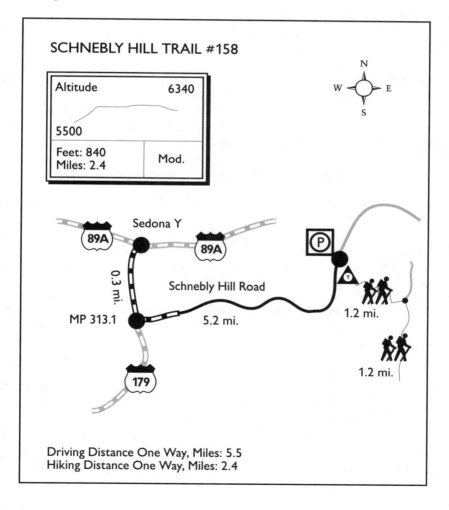

SCHNEBLY HILL TRAIL #158

Altitude	6340
5500	

| Feet: 840
Miles: 2.4 | Mod. |

N
W — E
S

89A Sedona Y 89A

P

0.3 mi.

Schnebly Hill Road

MP 313.1 5.2 mi. 1.2 mi.

T

179 1.2 mi.

Driving Distance One Way, Miles: 5.5
Hiking Distance One Way, Miles: 2.4

SECRET CANYON #121

General Information
Location Map C4
Loy Butte and Wilson Mt. USGS Maps
Coconino Forest Service Map

Driving Distance One Way: 8.6 miles *13.8 km* (Time 30 minutes)
Access Road: Most cars, Last 3.4 miles *5.5 km* bumpy dirt road
Hiking Distance One Way: 2.5 miles *4.0 km* (Time 90 minutes)
How Strenuous: Moderate
Features: Views, Remote canyon

NUTSHELL: This beautiful canyon, 8.6 miles *13.8 km* northwest of uptown Sedona, provides a delightful hike along a streambed through the redrocks. **A Personal Favorite.**

DIRECTIONS:
From the Sedona Y Go:
　　Southwest on Highway 89A (toward Cottonwood) for 3.2 miles *5.12 km* (MP 371) to Dry Creek Road. Turn right on Dry Creek Road and proceed to the 5.2 mile *8.4 km* point. Turn right on FR 152, the Vultee Arch Road, and follow it to the 8.6 mile *13.8 km* point. You will see a road sign pointing to the trail turnoff. Make a sharp turn to your left into the parking area.

TRAILHEAD: There is a rusty sign at the roadside where you turn in reading, "Secret Canyon #121."

DESCRIPTION: The access road to this hike, FR 152, is rough but has been improved since the first edition of this book. We frequently see people in ordinary passenger cars driving this road, but be on the lookout for ruts and rocks.
　　Watch carefully for the turnoff to the Secret Canyon trailhead. The road in this area is lined with a screen of brush and trees and the entry is a brief opening in this screen. A large sign has been installed, making this trailhead easier to find.
　　The parking space is limited. It can hold only about five cars.
　　From the parking area the trail goes immediately to Dry Creek and then turns right (E) and runs along the bottom of Dry Creek, going up (NE) toward its headwater. If water is running in Dry Creek you may not be able to make this hike, as the trail winds back and forth across the creek several times.
　　The trail takes you through some beautiful back country, passing through

impressive redrocks. At 0.60 miles *1.0 km* you will see the **H S Canyon** trail taking off to the left.

We like the first part of the Secret Canyon hike the best, where you are going through the redrocks. There are several side canyons that are fun to explore, and are recommended.

At about 2.25 miles *3.6 km* you come up out of the canyon bottom and walk along the side of the canyon. At 2.5 miles *4.0 km* you will enter a pine forest. Up to this forest, the hike has been unshaded, but from this point the pines provide ample shade.

For the purposes of this book, which features day hikes, we have you stop in the cool pines at 2.5 miles *4.0 km*, although the trail goes farther.

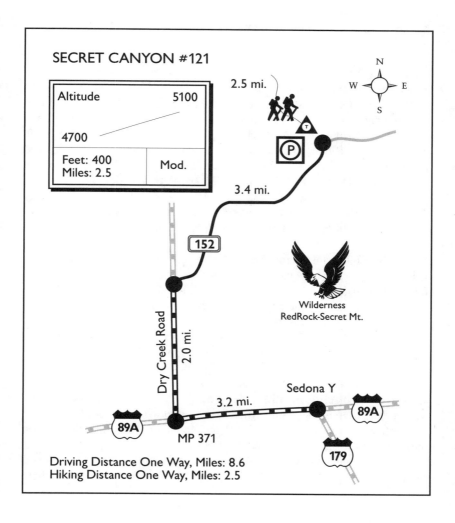

SECRET CANYON #121

Altitude 5100

4700

Feet: 400
Miles: 2.5

Mod.

2.5 mi.

N
W E
S

3.4 mi.

152

Dry Creek Road

2.0 mi.

Wilderness
RedRock-Secret Mt.

Sedona Y

89A

89A

3.2 mi.

MP 371

179

Driving Distance One Way, Miles: 8.6
Hiking Distance One Way, Miles: 2.5

SHOOTING RANGE RIDGE EAST

General Information
Location Map D4
Wilson Mountain USGS Map
Coconino Forest Service Map

Driving Distance One Way: 1.6 miles *2.56 km* (Time 10 minutes)
Access Road: All cars. Last 0.30 miles *0.48 km* medium gravel
Hiking Distance One Way: 0.7 miles *1.12 km* (Time 40 minutes)
How Strenuous: Moderate
Features: Easy to reach, Good views

NUTSHELL: You climb to the top of a 300 foot high ridge for excellent views.

DIRECTIONS:
From the Y in Sedona Go:
   North on Highway on 89A (toward Flagstaff) for 0.30 miles *0.48 km* to Jordan Road, which is in the middle of uptown Sedona. Turn left (N) and take Jordan Road to its end, at 1.1 miles *1.76 km*. Turn left at the stop sign, onto West Park Ridge, a paved road, which ends at 1.3 miles *2.08 km*. Keep going on the unpaved road, which is rough but passable. You will reach the old Shooting Range gate at 1.6 miles *2.56 km*. Park outside.

TRAILHEAD: This is not a signed trail. The trail starts on a side road located just in front of the gate to the old shooting range.

DESCRIPTION: Just before you reach the gate to the old shooting range you will see a road to your left (W). Park and walk back to this road, then follow it. You will find that it is a jeep trail. Keep following it uphill as far as it goes. It soon ends and a foot path starts. This path was marked by cairns when we hiked it and was easy to follow.
   On the way up you will begin to enjoy views that are even better at the top. You will reach a well-defined trail on the top of the ridge at 0.46 miles *0.74 km*. From here turn to the left and follow the trail out to its end, which is on the toe of the ridge. Along the way you will enter an area where there are steep redrock cliffs to either side. We enjoy looking down on these. The trail ends at a great viewpoint where you look down on upper Sedona. To your left you have fine views of Wilson Mountain. To your right you see into the Capitol Butte and Coffee Pot Rock areas.
   After you have had your fill of the views you can go back the way you came or you can check out the balance of the ridge. From the point where

you came up to the ridgetop trail, you walk along the top for a short distance. Then the trail dips down to a saddle, and rises again, taking you to a fence at 0.1 miles *0.16 km*. From there the trail generally follows the fence line. You will come to a gate at 0.23 miles *0.37 km*, where the **Shooting Range Ridge West Trail** takes off downhill to your left.

Go beyond this point about five paces, where you will see a trail in a deep groove going downhill to your right. This is the trail to take on the way back. It intersects the Brins Mesa Trail at 0.4 miles *0.64 km*, at a point that is only 0.05 miles *0.08 km* from the gate.

If you want to go on out to the far end of the ridge, you will get to it at 0.5 miles *0.8 km*. From there you will have exceptionally fine views of Brins Mesa and Wilson Mountain.

This is a nice little hike, a good choice when the backroads are too muddy or you don't have time to drive far out into the country.

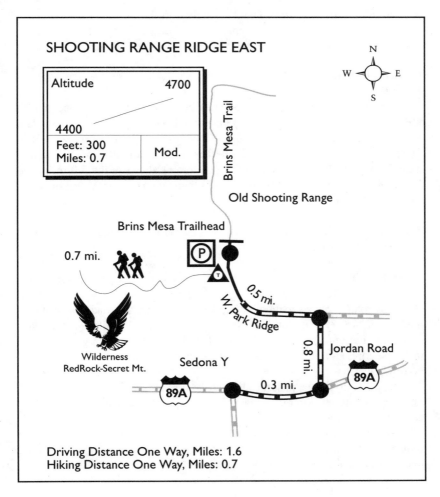

SHOOTING RANGE RIDGE EAST

Altitude	4700
4400	
Feet: 300 Miles: 0.7	Mod.

Brins Mesa Trail

Old Shooting Range

Brins Mesa Trailhead

0.7 mi.

W. Park Ridge

0.5 mi.

0.8 mi.

Jordan Road

Wilderness RedRock-Secret Mt.

Sedona Y

0.3 mi.

89A

89A

Driving Distance One Way, Miles: 1.6
Hiking Distance One Way, Miles: 0.7

SHOOTING RANGE RIDGE WEST

General Information
Location Map D4
Sedona and Wilson Mt. USGS Maps
Coconino Forest Service Map

Driving Distance One Way: 3.0 miles *4.8 km* (Time 10 minutes)
Access Road: All cars, All paved
Hiking Distance One Way: 1.5 miles *2.4 km* (Time 1 hour)
How Strenuous: Moderate
Features: Views

NUTSHELL: Starting from Devil's Kitchen in the Soldier Pass area, this moderate hike takes you to a scenic ridge dividing Soldier Pass from the upper Jordan Road area of Sedona.

DIRECTIONS:
From the Sedona Y Go:
Southwest on Highway 89A (toward Cottonwood) for a distance of 1.25 miles *2.0 km* (MP 372.8) to Soldier Pass Road. Turn right onto Soldier Pass Road and follow it to the 2.75 mile *4.4 km* point, where it intersects Rim Shadows Drive, where you turn right. The roads and road signs turn funky here. Disregard the street names and go straight ahead to the 3.0 miles *4.8 km* point. Take the paved road to your left there and park in the parking area. This is well defined and spacious.

TRAILHEAD: You will see a rusty sign at the parking area reading, "Soldier Pass Trail #66."

DESCRIPTION: The first leg of this trail has been changed, as the Forest Service has created a new route for the Solder Pass Trail, which used to run along the road. Now a separate hiking trail away from the road has been created, a much nicer experience for the hiker. In only 0.15 miles *0.24 km* you will come out onto bare redrock at the Devil's Kitchen the largest sinkhole in the Sedona area. Look to the east here and you can see the ridge that is your destination.

The jeeps drive east past the sinkhole to turn around. Follow their blackened path along the top of the redrock to the point where the tracks end, in about two hundred yards.

Keep walking on the redrocks at roughly the same level, and you will see foot and bike tire tracks marking your way. Continue along the redrock ledges until the ledges pinch out, at a point where you will see distinctly ahead of you the trail you are to take. Usage has made the trail easy to see and follow. After winding through the trees, you will end up in a streambed. From there you will turn left and walk up the floor of the streambed.

As you near the ridge, do not take the first trail going to your right. Stay in the bed for a distance, where you will see the path start to go up the ridge. Take it. You will reach an intermediate top at 0.90 miles *1.5 km,* where there is a fence. Uphill a few feet from this place there is a gate in the fence. Go through the gate, then turn right and follow the fence to the true top of the ridge.

From the top, you will come out onto red slickrock, where you get great views.

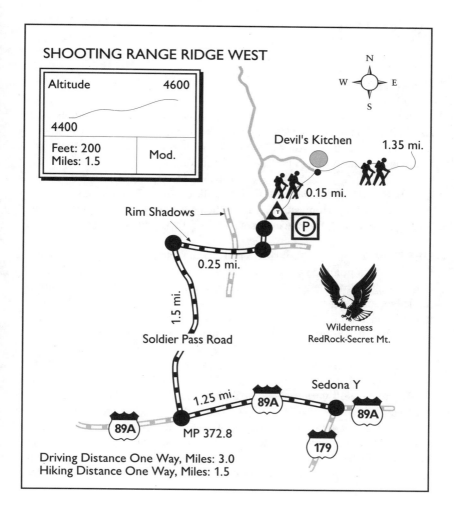

SHOOTING RANGE RIDGE WEST

Altitude	4600
4400	
Feet: 200 Miles: 1.5	Mod.

Devil's Kitchen 1.35 mi.

0.15 mi.

Rim Shadows

0.25 mi.

1.5 mi.

Soldier Pass Road

Wilderness
RedRock-Secret Mt.

Sedona Y

1.25 mi. 89A

89A

89A
MP 372.8

179

Driving Distance One Way, Miles: 3.0
Hiking Distance One Way, Miles: 1.5

SLIDE ROCK

General Information
Location Map C5
Wilson Mt. USGS Map
Coconino Forest Service Map

Driving Distance One Way: 6.9 miles *11.1 km* (Time 15 minutes)
Access Road: All cars, All paved
Hiking Distance One Way: 0.5 miles *0.8 km* (Time 30 minutes)
How Strenuous: Moderate
Features: Slide Rock State Park

NUTSHELL: You enjoy two hiking trails in Slide Rock State Park 6.9 miles *11.1 km* north of Sedona, one at water's edge and the other on the cliffs above Oak Creek.

DIRECTIONS:
From The Y in Sedona Go:
    North on Highway 89A (toward Flagstaff) a distance of 6.9 miles *11.1 km* (MP 381.1) to the entrance to Slide Rock State Park. The park is well marked and signed and you will have no trouble finding it. Pull in to the park (there is an entry fee) and park on the large lot.

TRAILHEAD: From the parking lot, walk upstream along a paved walk-way, the Pendley Homestead Trail. When you get to the Apple Packing Shed, you will be at the place where the Cliff Top and Creekside trails start.

DESCRIPTION: (1) **Creekside Trail**: At the Packing Shed you will see a flight of steps going down to Oak Creek. Take the steps. You will emerge onto a long redrock ledge going upstream. It is easy and fun to walk along the ledge, enjoying the water and the redrock cliffs on either side. This is a favorite place for visitors and is likely to be crowded. You will see a place in the creek where the water has cut a channel into the bedrock. This is the *slide* of Slide Rock and you will probably see people using it, as they sit in the water at the beginning of the channel and let the current sweep them down to its end in a deep pool.
    There are well-worn trails at the base of the cliffs and also at the edge of the water. When the water is low, you can walk across the creek on a duck-board bridge, but we think the best sights are on the west bank, the side you start on. The trails end at an interesting old shed built of rock in front of an irrigation flume at about 0.5 miles *0.8 km*. From there you can rock hop upstream for a considerable distance depending on the depth of the water

and your desire to explore.

(2) **Clifftop Trail**: Now go back to the top of the stairs. There you will see a sign for the Cliff Top Trail. The trail runs along the top of the cliffs parallel to the creek, providing several places where you can step off the trail and go over to the cliff tops to look down on Slide Rock. The Cliff Top Trail ends at about 0.10 mile *0.16 km* at the ruins of a concrete gatehouse that controlled the flow of water in the irrigation ditch. You can go a few paces beyond this for a view of the irrigation flume winding its way around the face of cliffs, but can go no farther due to a *No Trespassing* sign.

Slide Rock has been a popular spot for years, but its use soared when the state bought it and improved the access and parking. In the height of the tourist season, it can be so crowded as to be annoying. We like to visit it in the off season in order to avoid the throngs.

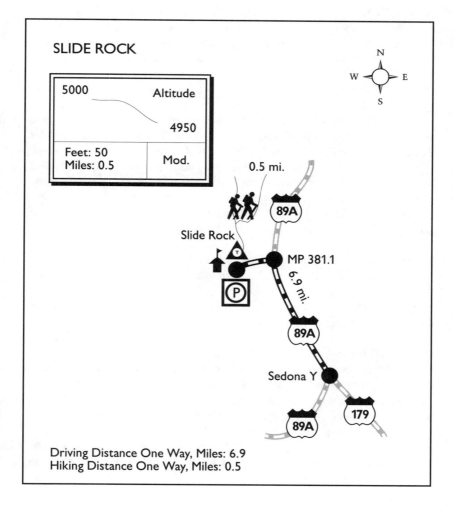

SNOOPY ROCK

General Information
Location Map E5
Sedona and Munds Mt. USGS Maps
Coconino Forest Service Map

Driving Distance One Way: 1.0 miles *1.6 km* (Time 5 minutes)
Access Road: All cars, 0.2 miles *0.32 km* unpaved bumpy road
Hiking Distance One Way: 1.1 miles *1.8 km* (Time 60 minutes)
How Strenuous: Moderate
Features: Views, Red cliffs, Favorite rock formation

NUTSHELL: This very nice, very accessible hike takes you to Snoopy Rock, which is located on the Crimson Cliffs at the north end of Marg's Draw, a short distance from downtown Sedona. This hike is fun, a good one when you don't have much time or the roads are muddy.

DIRECTIONS:
From the Sedona Y Go:
   (Note: the old trailhead at the end of Sombart Lane is no longer usable due to trespass problems.) Go South on Highway 179 (toward Phoenix) for a distance of 0.3 miles *0.48 km* (MP 313.1) to the Schnebly Hill Road, which is just across the bridge near Tlaquepaque. Turn left onto the Schnebly Hill Road, which is paved for the first half mile. There is a cattle guard at the end of the paving. Just beyond the cattle guard is a private driveway to the left. Go past it and look for the next road to the left, (0.2 miles *0.32 km* past the cattle guard) at 1.0 miles *1.6 km*. Turn left into the parking area.

TRAILHEAD: Directly across the Schnebly Hill Road from the parking place is the trailhead. It is unmarked, but look for a standbox for a telephone line. It is green and sticks up out of the ground about three feet. There is a sign on it reading, "Caution U. S. West Fiber Optic Cable...." At the side of this is the beginning of the trail.

DESCRIPTION: As you begin the hike, you will note that you are headed toward tall red buttes, a formation known as The Crimson Cliffs. The trail winds around the south face of these cliffs.
   You start by going downhill into a dry wash. The trail goes up out of the wash and begins circling the cliffs. The Crimson Cliffs are beautiful and the trail hugs their base closely, giving you some wonderful views. You know you are not very far out into the country, however, for to your right is the town of Sedona, nearby. There are a lot of meandering cattle paths in

through here, so pay attention. Your trail never veers away from the cliffs, but stays right at their base.

As you begin turning around the south tip of the cliffs, at about 0.5 miles *0.8 km*, you come to a very agreeable place where the trail follows along the top of a redrock ledge. From here you begin to get views to the south, to Twin Buttes and the big bowl that is Marg's Draw.

The trail is easy to follow up to the 0.75 mile *1.2 km* point, where you have to look closely for a trail junction. The junction is located in a place where the path is littered with small rocks, and is not easy to see. It usually is marked with cairns and lines of rock. Take the left-hand fork, which goes uphill. The right fork goes south onto the flat, joining the **Marg's Draw** trail.

The path has been mild up to here, but now it begins to climb about 200 feet, winding its way up to Snoopy Rock. At the end of the trail you are standing just below Snoopy's foot— a fine viewpoint.

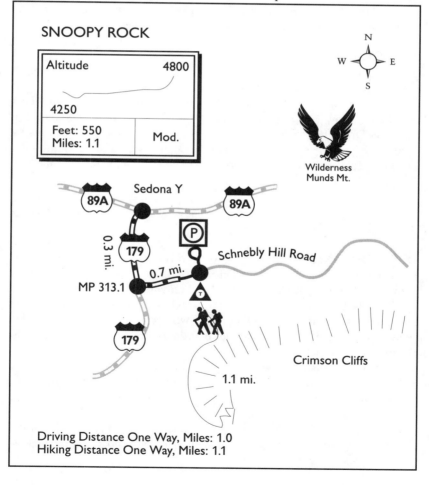

Driving Distance One Way, Miles: 1.0
Hiking Distance One Way, Miles: 1.1

SOLDIER PASS ARCHES

General Information
Location Map D4
Sedona and Wilson Mt. USGS Maps
Coconino Forest Service Map

Driving Distance One Way: 3.0 miles *4.8 km* (Time 10 minutes)
Access Road: All cars, All paved
Hiking Distance One Way: 1.5 miles *2.4 km* (Time 60 minutes)
How Strenuous: Moderate
Features: Views, Arches

NUTSHELL: Located off of Soldier Pass Road, the trailhead for this hike is only 3.0 miles *4.8 km* from the Y. The hike follows an old jeep road most of its way, then climbs up to a trio of interesting arches.

DIRECTIONS:
From the Sedona Y Go:
   Southwest on Highway 89A (toward Cottonwood) for a distance of 1.25 miles *2.0 km* (MP 372.8) to Soldier Pass Road. Turn right onto Soldier Pass Road and follow it to the 2.75 mile *4.4 km* point, where it intersects Rim Shadows Drive, where you turn right. The roads and road signs turn funky here. Disregard the street names and go straight ahead to the 3.0 miles *4.8 km* point. Take the paved road to your left there and park in the parking area. This is well defined and spacious.

TRAILHEAD: You will see a rusty sign at the parking area reading "Soldier Pass Trail #66."

DESCRIPTION: Since the last edition of this book, the Forest Service has created a new trail here, so that hikers no longer have to share the road with jeeps. The trail is higher than the road and provides much better views.
   The first leg of the trail takes you to Devil's Kitchen, the area's biggest sinkhole, in 0.15 miles *0.24 km*. Look for white diamond markers from this point onward. They will lead you around the rim of the sinkhole and onto the main part of the trail.
   At the 0. 55 mile *0.88 km* point you will come out onto a bare redrock where the Seven Sacred Pools are located in a little canyon to your left. These natural scoops, though small, hold water even in dry periods and are important to birds and animals.
   From here, you will hike to the 1.25 mile *2.0 km* point, the end of the marked trail, at the Wilderness Boundary. The path forks at this point. A

broad trail goes straight ahead, uphill, and is the path to the Soldier Pass Arches. A minor path to the left, is the continuation of the Soldier Pass Trail.

You will climb out of the wash onto a large red slickrock ledge, which provides good views in all directions. You are in a box canyon at this point, with interesting and colorful cliffs on all sides except east (toward Sedona). Walk up to the left edge of the ledge. If you look up at the cliffs to your left from this spot you will see one arch.

From there the trail is narrow and steep (180 feet) up to the arch, but it is a short climb (0.2 miles *0.32 km*). When you arrive you will see two arches. You can walk under the first one. It is fun to explore, as it forms a sort of cave. There is a third arch that you can't see. You can reach it by walking along the cliff face on a faint trail. The third arch is the smallest and least interesting. Just above you on top of the rim is the **Brins Mesa Trail**.

This is a good hike to take when the roads are muddy because the access road is all paved and it is near town.

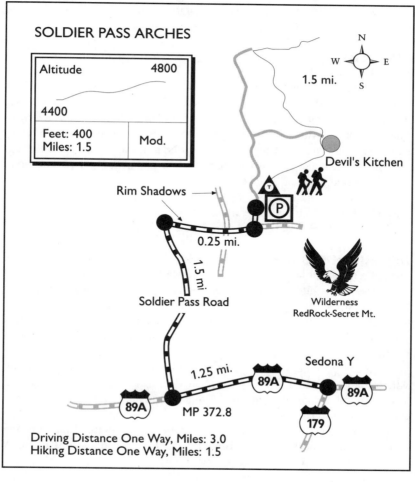

SOLDIER PASS TRAIL #66

General Information
Location Map D4
Sedona and Wilson Mt. USGS Maps
Coconino Forest Service Map

Driving Distance One Way: 3.0 miles *4.8 km* (Time 10 minutes)
Access Road: All cars, All paved
Hiking Distance One Way: 1.9 miles *3.04 km* (Time 1 hour)
How Strenuous: Moderate
Features: Views

NUTSHELL: Located off Soldier Pass Road, the trailhead for this hike is easily reached. The trail takes you through colorful redrock country, and climbs to the top of Brins Mesa, a Sedona landmark.

DIRECTIONS:
From the Sedona Y Go:
Southwest on Highway 89A (toward Cottonwood) for a distance of 1.25 miles *2.0 km* (MP 372.8) to Soldier Pass Road. Turn right onto Soldier Pass Road and follow it to the 2.75 mile *4.4 km* point, where it intersects Rim Shadows Drive, where you turn right. The roads and road signs turn funky here. Disregard the street names and go straight ahead to the 3.0 miles *4.8 km* point. Take the paved road to your left there and park in the parking area. This is well defined and spacious.

TRAILHEAD: You will see a rusty sign at the parking area reading, "Soldier Pass Trail #66."

DESCRIPTION: Since the last edition of this book, the Forest Service has created a new trail here, so that hikers needn't hike along the jeep-infested road. The trail is higher than the road and provides much better views.

The first leg of the trail takes you to Devil's Kitchen, the area's biggest sinkhole, in 0.15 miles *0.24 km*. Look for white diamond markers from this point onward. They will lead you around the rim of the sinkhole and onto the main part of the trail.

At the 0. 55 mile *0.88 km* point you will come out onto a bare redrock where the Seven Sacred Pools are located in a little canyon to your left. These natural scoops, though small, hold water even in dry periods and are important to birds and animals.

From here, you will hike to the 1.25 mile *2.0 km* point, the end of the marked trail, at the Wilderness Boundary. The path forks at this point. A broad trail goes straight ahead, uphill, and is the path to the **Soldier Pass Arches**.

Take the smaller trail, which goes to your left, along the canyon bottom. (You will now climb 370 feet in 0.4 miles *0.64 km*). At about 1.3 miles *2.08 km*, look to your right and you will see the three Soldier Pass Arches clearly. The trail from here follows along the crest of a ridge that rises gently to the top of Brins Mesa. As you climb, you lift out of the bottom and get some great views.

At 1.5 miles *2.4 km* you will reach a gate in a barbed wire fence. You top out on a redrock shelf at 1.6 miles *2.56 km*. From this point you can follow the trail to link up with the **Brins Mesa Trail** at 1.9 miles *3.04 km*.

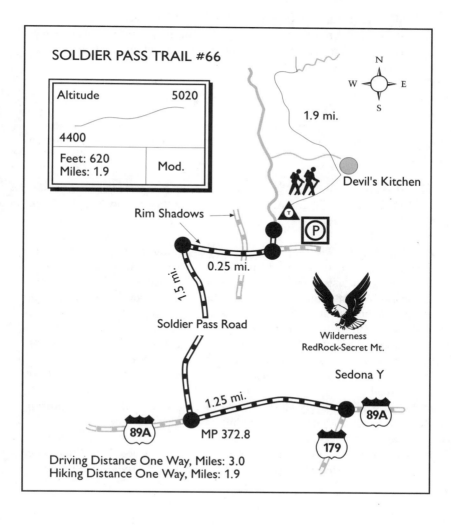

STEAMBOAT ROCK

General Information
Location Map D5
Munds Park USGS Map
Coconino Forest Service Map

Driving Distance One Way: 1.1 miles *1.8 km* (Time 5 minutes)
Access Road: All cars, All paved
Hiking Distance One Way: 1.5 miles *2.4 km* (Time 1.5 hours)
How Strenuous: Hard
Features: Views

NUTSHELL: Located 1.1 miles *1.8 km* north of Sedona, Steamboat Rock is one of the area's most famous landmarks. This hike takes you near the top, just below the "funnel" for breathtaking views and an unforgettable adventure. *For experienced hikers only.*

DIRECTIONS:
From the Sedona Y Go:
    North on Highway 89A (toward Flagstaff) for a distance of 1.1 miles *1.8 km* (MP 375.9). Go just across Midgley Bridge and turn left into the parking area.

TRAILHEAD: You will see a rusty sign at the parking lot. It reads, "Wilson Canyon #49." Start this hike by taking the **Wilson Canyon Trail** for 0.5 miles *0.8 km* .

DESCRIPTION: The trailhead is as easy as pie to locate. Just walk toward the picnic tables at the end of the parking lot. There you will find the Wilson Monument, a bronze plaque set in stone, and two rusty signs. The sign to the left marks **Wilson Canyon #49** and is the one you want for this hike. The other sign marks an uphill trail, Wilson Mountain #10, which is called **Wilson Mountain South** in this book.
    Take note of how far it is to the first point where the trail crosses the streambed (0.25 mi. *0.4 km*), which is just beyond the old bridge abutment. Walk another 0.25 miles *0.4 km* along the trail to a point where you will see an old road coming down from your left. This road is badly eroded, with rocks sticking out everywhere. It is a piece of the **Old Jim Thompson Road.** Turn left (W) here and go uphill on the old road.
    You will top out at 0.75 miles *1.2 km*. Go left on the road you find here. In about 20 yards you will reach another intersection. Avoid both of the wide trails here and instead take the narrow footpath going right, uphill, toward

the nearest red butte. Look carefully for the trail, as it is rather faint and you must follow it to take advantage of the only two approaches on the face of the butte that allow you to go to the top.

As you come onto the slickrock, look for cairns. They lead you up the east face of Steamboat Rock. After a short stretch of scrambling, you'll be on top of the butte, where walking is easy and the trail is wide. Ahead is the towering "funnel" of the "steamboat." Near it you will find a talus slope going up to a band of mauve Ft. Apache sandstone forming a ledge (the "deck") at the funnel's base. If you are afraid of heights, stop here. You can scramble up the talus, but the ladder that used to be there was removed, which makes climbing up to the top of the Ft. Apache difficult and risky.

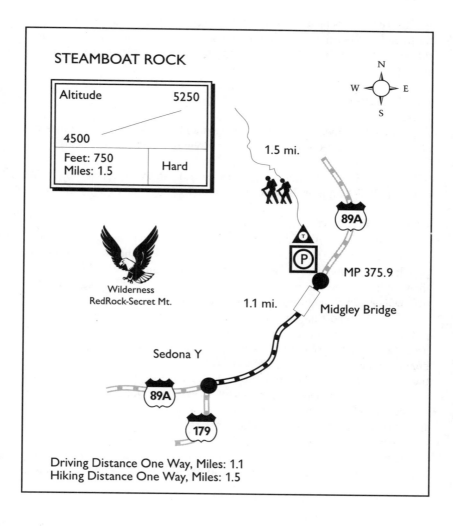

STERLING PASS #46

General Information
Location Map C5
Munds Park and Wilson Mt. USGS Maps
Coconino Forest Service Map

Driving Distance One Way: 6.2 miles *9.9 km* (Time 10 minutes)
Access Road: All cars, All paved
Hiking Distance One Way: 1.65 miles *2.7 km* (Time 60 minutes)
How Strenuous: Hard
Features: Views, Great rock formations

NUTSHELL: Located 6.2 miles *9.9 km* north of Sedona, just above the north end of Manzanita Campground, and just below Canyon Wren Lodge, this steep but beautiful hike climbs through a heavy forest to a mountain pass.

DIRECTIONS:
From the Sedona Y Go:
    North on Highway 89A (toward Flagstaff) for a distance of 6.2 miles *9.9 km* (MP 380.4). Park anywhere you can along the roadside in this area.

TRAILHEAD: There is a rusty sign in a little alcove marking this maintained trail. The sign reads, "Sterling Pass #46."

DESCRIPTION: There is very little parking at the roadside near the trailhead. You have to pick out a wide spot on the shoulder and do your best.
    This trail rises steeply, climbing all the way. For the first portion you parallel a little side canyon, which may contain running water during spring thaw. When it does, it creates a charming waterfall near the highway. The trail wanders back and forth over the streambed four times.
    For those who think of the Oak Creek area as sun swept expanses of redrock dotted with cactus, this trail will be an eye-opener. It goes through a cool pine forest. While you will cross over a bit of red slickrock at the beginning and will see some gorgeous red cliffs and buttes as you progress, the soil underfoot will be a rich brown loam. The forest is heavy. In addition to the familiar ponderosa pine you will see some Douglas fir and a few spruces. After about the first 0.25 miles *0.4 km* you are far enough away from the road so that you can no longer hear its sounds and can see no signs of human activity. The area feels primeval and is truly delightful.
    Because the forest is so heavy, you can't see much until you have gone about 1.25 miles *2.0 km*. Until then you get glimpses of giant white cliffs

ahead of you (W) and red cliffs on your right and left. Then you rise above the trees for great views across Oak Creek Canyon and nearby. The cliffs here are a treat to the eye, highly sculptured, with many interesting lines and angles. You will find a viewpoint at a bend of the trail where you can look over into an adjacent canyon to your left for views of soaring white cliffs.

The crest is at about 1.65 miles *2.7 km*, where you come onto a saddle. There is a heavy stand of trees here with oaks on the east side and oaks and maples on the west wide. Because of these trees the views are not as good at the top as they are just below the top. This is a true mountain pass, there being a decided gap in the cliffs here.

The trail continues down the other side, another 0.75 miles *1.2 km*, to intersect the **Vultee Arch Trail.** If you do go down the west side you might as well go on to Vultee Arch, which is only 0.20 miles *0.32 km* from the trail junction. Many hikers will stop at the saddle.

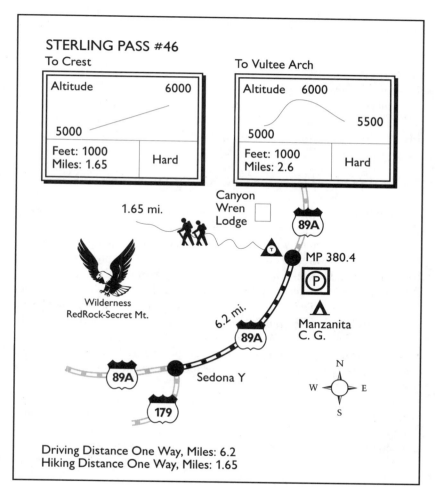

STERLING PASS #46

To Crest

Altitude	6000
5000	
Feet: 1000 Miles: 1.65	Hard

To Vultee Arch

Altitude 6000	5500
5000	
Feet: 1000 Miles: 2.6	Hard

1.65 mi.

Canyon Wren Lodge

89A

MP 380.4

P

Manzanita C. G.

Wilderness RedRock-Secret Mt.

6.2 mi.

89A

89A

Sedona Y

179

N
W — E
S

Driving Distance One Way, Miles: 6.2
Hiking Distance One Way, Miles: 1.65

SUBMARINE ROCK

General Information
Location Map E5
Sedona USGS Map
Coconino Forest Service Map

Driving Distance One Way: 2.1 miles *3.36 km* (Time 10 minutes)
Access Road: All cars, Last 0.1 mile *0.16 km* good dirt road
Hiking Distance One Way: 1.0 miles *1.6 km* (Time 30 minutes)
How Strenuous: Easy
Features: Interesting rock formation, Views

NUTSHELL: Located only a couple of miles southeast of uptown Sedona, this interesting rock formation is fun to climb and pretend that you are Captain Nemo.

DIRECTIONS:
From the Sedona Y Go:
    South on Highway 179 (toward Phoenix) for 1.4 miles *2.3 km* (MP 312.1) to Morgan Road in the Broken Arrow Subdivision. Turn left (east) on Morgan Road and follow it to its end, at 2.0 miles *3.2 km*, then proceed another 0.1 mile *0.16 km* to the parking lot.

TRAILHEAD: The trailhead for the **Broken Arrow Trail.**

DESCRIPTION: Since the previous editions of this book the Forest Service has changed the entrance for this hike. There is now a nice big parking lot, although you may find it full on weekends. The main purpose in creating the Broken Arrow Trail, it seems, was to avoid the problem that used to exist here and was becoming steadily worse: jeep tours use the road and it was harder and harder for hikers and bikers to have a quality experience. The Broken Arrow Trail provides a footpath so you can now avoid the jeeps.
    The Broken Arrow Trail is well marked and you will have no trouble finding and following it. At first it takes you close to Battlement Mesa, where you will enjoy looking at the red cliffs. The trail climbs so that you will also have enjoyable views out over the area to your left, including the town of Sedona.
    At 0.5 miles *0.8 km* you will come downhill to a hole enclosed by a barbed wire fence. This is the Devil's Dining Room, a natural sinkhole that is considered a local landmark. We used to include the hike to this point as a separate excursion but now it is just a waypoint on the Broken Arrow Trail.
    At 0.75 miles *1.2 km* you will come to a trail junction. The trail to the

right goes to Chicken Point. You want to take the left fork, going downhill to Submarine Rock. The trail crosses the road and then works its way to the north end of the rock. We found no distinct trail going up to the top of the rock, but that is not a problem because it is easy to pick a way up. Once you are on top of it you can have great fun walking around it, getting the views from the top of the "conning tower." The jeep tours come in on the other (lower) end of the rock.

Submarine Rock is located at the south end of **Marg's Draw**, a scenic bowl. This is a beautiful natural area and the home of several good hikes. Marg's Draw is remarkable, being unspoiled and yet close to developed parts of Sedona. Land barons would love to get their hands on it and subdivide it but—fortunately for outdoor lovers—part of it is protected by being included in the Munds Mt. Wilderness Area.

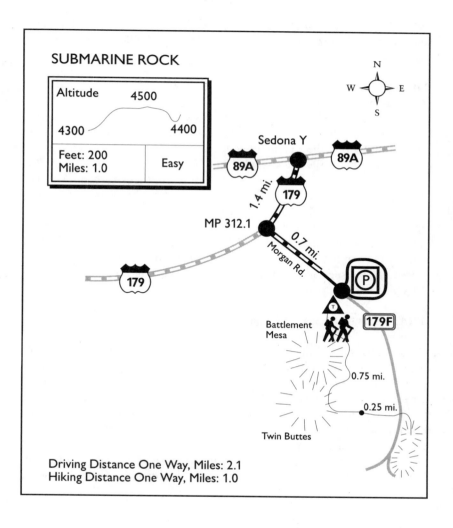

SUBMARINE ROCK

Altitude 4500
4300 4400
Feet: 200
Miles: 1.0 Easy

Sedona Y

89A 89A
1.4 mi. 179
MP 312.1 0.7 mi.
Morgan Rd.
179
P
179F
Battlement Mesa T
0.75 mi.
0.25 mi.
Twin Buttes

Driving Distance One Way, Miles: 2.1
Hiking Distance One Way, Miles: 1.0

SUGARLOAF AT BLACK MT.

General Information
Location Map C1
Loy Butte and Sycamore Basin USGS Maps
Coconino Forest Service Map

Driving Distance One Way: 29.8 miles *47.7 km* (Time 60 minutes)
Access Road: High clearance vehicles, Very rough roads
Hiking Distance One Way: 0.33 miles *0.5 km* (Time 30 minutes)
How Strenuous: Moderate
Features: Ruins, Views

NUTSHELL: Located 29.8 miles *47.7 km* southwest of Sedona, this small mountain is moderately easy to climb. There are Indian ruins at the top. Great views.

DIRECTIONS:
From the Sedona Y Go:
Southwest on Highway 89A (toward Cottonwood) a distance of 16.0 miles *25.6 km* (MP 358) to FR 761, the unpaved Bill Gray Road. Turn right and take FR 761 to the 25.5 miles *40.8 km* point, which is the junction of FR 761 and FR 258A, the Buckboard Road. Go right here, staying on FR 761. At 26.2 miles *41.9 km*, you will see a road to your left marked FR 761A. Turn left onto this road. Up to this point, the road has been good, but now it gets quite rough. A high clearance vehicle with sturdy tires is recommended, and you should drive it only when the road is dry. Go under the power line and turn right. At 27.6 miles *44.2 km*, you reach a Y fork, with FR 761A going right and FR 761C going left. Drive FR 761A, to the right. This is a very rough but spectacular road. You will see a good turnoff to the left at the 29.8 mile *47.7 km* point, where you park.

TRAILHEAD: No trail. You bushwhack up the mountain.

DESCRIPTION: Although this Sugarloaf (there are two other buttes named "Sugarloaf" near Sedona) is a small mountain, the south face is not easy to climb because of some thick eroded ledges there. On the east face, where we have had you park, the access to the top is much easier.

You will have to contend with two ledges here, one of redrock and the other of buff colored stone, but they both narrow down on this face and it is easy to get around them.

At the top you will find a small ruin, just a short wall about three feet high filled with sand. Hikers have also built a cairn at the top. Add a stone to the cairn to show you've been here. There is another ruin on the west side of the crest, downhill a bit.

The area at the top is small, so you can easily walk around it and get good views in all directions. The views to the north, east and south are terrific.

Since you are so close to it, you should also visit the **Black Mountain Mystery House** while you are here.

The early settlers in Sedona were hard pressed to come up with names for the multitude of hills, mountains, rock formations and other land features they found and they used the name Sugarloaf three times. See **Sugarloaf in Sedona** for an explanation of what a sugarloaf is.

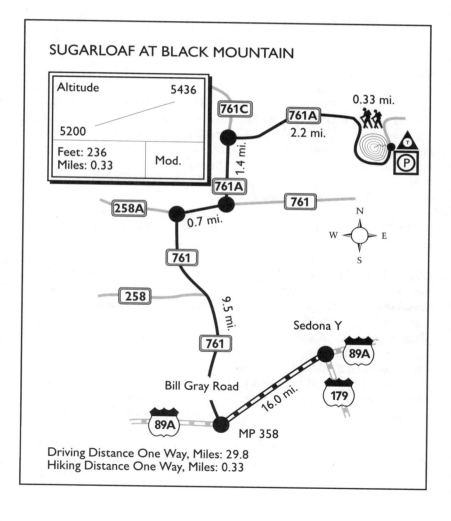

SUGARLOAF AT BLACK MOUNTAIN

Altitude	5436
5200	
Feet: 236 Miles: 0.33	Mod.

761C   761A   0.33 mi.

2.2 mi.

1.4 mi.

761A   761

258A   0.7 mi.

N
W ← → E
S

761

258

9.5 mi.

Sedona Y

761

89A

179

Bill Gray Road

16.0 mi.

89A   MP 358

Driving Distance One Way, Miles: 29.8
Hiking Distance One Way, Miles: 0.33

SUGARLOAF IN SEDONA

General Information
Location Map D4
Sedona and Wilson Mt. USGS Maps
Coconino Forest Service Map

Driving Distance One Way: 2.6 miles *4.2 km* (Time 10 minutes)
Access Road: All cars, All paved
Hiking Distance One Way: 0.70 miles *1.12 km* (Time 30 minutes)
How Strenuous: Moderate
Features: Rock formation, Views

NUTSHELL: This ramp-shaped landmark located a couple of miles west of uptown Sedona can be climbed with moderate effort for great views.

DIRECTIONS:
From the Sedona Y Go:
   Southwest on Highway 89A (toward Cottonwood) for a distance of 1.7 miles *2.72 km* (MP 372.5), to Mt. Shadows Street. Turn right onto Mt. Shadows Street. Follow it to the 2.6 mile *4.2 km* point where you will find a large water storage tank and a transmitter inside a chain link fence. The road intersects Fabulous Texan Way here (the streets in this area were named after movies filmed in Sedona). Drive across the street onto the dirt apron around the fenced area and park there.

TRAILHEAD: At the parking area. There are no signs, but you will see a crawl-through in the fence; it looks like a picture frame.

DESCRIPTION: Squeeze through the crawl-through and walk uphill along the fence. The path forks just past the fence. Take the left fork (W), which goes uphill. It circles the base of Sugarloaf and takes you around to the north side, where you will find the low point of the "ramp," which is the obvious place to begin the ascent to the top. You will find this in a clearing where the old road ended. There is a line of flat red rocks blocking the entrance to a road going up Sugarloaf. You want to walk this "ramp."
   It is as if Sugarloaf was created to be a viewpoint, because you have the ramp to allow easy hiking to the top, and natural forces have sheared off the east face of the butte to give you unobstructed views once you reach the crest.
   There is another Sugarloaf in the Sedona area, which we call **Sugarloaf at Black Mountain** in this book to distinguish the two. It is also a good hike.
   The early settlers in Sedona were hard pressed to come up with names

for the multitude of hills, mountains, rock formations and other land features they found and they can be forgiven for using the name Sugarloaf more than once. There is yet a third Sugarloaf adjacent to the **Airport Saddle Loop Trails** hike.

One hundred years ago, when these pioneers came, people didn't buy granulated sugar as we know it today. In those days molasses was boiled down until it began to crystallize and was poured into cone-shaped molds, where it hardened. These "loaves" of sugar, about the size of a golf ball, were their sugar. The loaves became very hard as they aged and it was usually the job of the children in a family to break up the loaves with a hammer so that the sugar could be measured and used in cooking. Eating a bit of the sugar was their reward. A sugarloaf was a blunt-tipped cone, a shape that aptly describes these buttes.

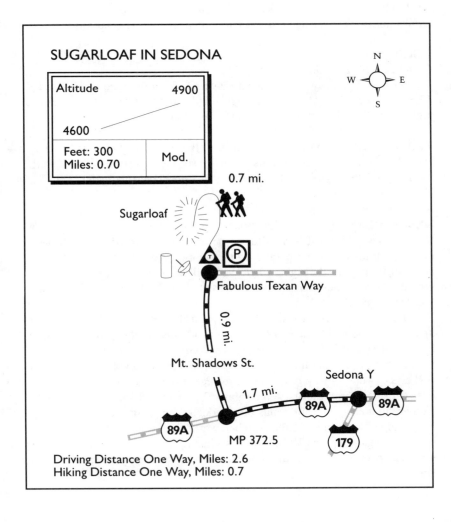

TELEPHONE TRAIL #72

General Information
Location Map B5
Munds Park USGS Map
Coconino Forest Service Map

Driving Distance One Way: 10.9 miles *17.5 km* (Time 20 minutes)
Access Road: All cars, All paved
Hiking Distance One Way: 1.25 miles *2.0 km* (Time 2.0 Hours)
How Strenuous: Hard (Very steep)
Features: Interesting rock formations, Views

NUTSHELL: This is a marked and posted trail in upper Oak Creek. It climbs northerly to a ridge top and then turns east to reach the rim.

DIRECTIONS:
From the Sedona Y Go:
    North on Highway 89A (toward Flagstaff) for a distance of 10.9 miles *17.5 km* (MP 385.1). Here you will see a wide apron on the right side of the highway under a twenty foot high cliff. Park here.

TRAILHEAD: From the parking place, walk up Highway 89A on the right shoulder about one hundred yards. You will see the typical rusty metal trailhead sign off the highway a few feet to your right. The sign reads, "Trail 72, Telephone."

DESCRIPTION: From the sign look sharp and you will see cairns marking the trail. The trail itself is hard to see because it is covered with pine needles. The trail runs along parallel to the highway for about 0.05 mile *0.08 km*, then swings to the right, where you will walk along an old road bed, probably a construction road that was created while the old telephone line was being installed.
    At 0.1 miles *0.16 km* you will walk under the new phone line. The trail up to here is obvious and easy to follow. From this point on, the trail is difficult to find, and is *for experienced hikers only.*
    The next leg of the hike takes you sharply uphill, to your left (N). You will zigzag your way up to the top of a finger ridge that runs west from the East Rim, reaching the first top at about 0.5 miles *0.8 km*. Turn right (E). You are in a zone of white sandstone studded with fossils. You stay on top of the ridge for a while and then dip below it. At 0.6 miles *0.96 km*, you will be on top again, and will come to a fascinating little reef about thirty feet long and twelve feet high that contains several windows, called the Peep Holes.

There is a rough spot beyond this, where the trail dips again and gets difficult. There are several confusing game trails. Be sure to follow the flags and cairns. You will find one of the old phone pole stubs, with guy wire and support sleeve where the trail turns back to the top. Hard scrambling in here.

When you get back to the ridge top, the trail becomes more obvious. At about 0.75 miles *1.2 km*, you move along another intermediate top. Soon after that, you begin the very steep climb to the top of the rim. This is in a beautiful fir forest, which lasts all the way to the tip top. Along the way here you will see the remains of several old phone poles.

The trail ends at the top at 1.25 miles *2.0 km*, at a large cairn. You can walk out to the rim in several places here for wonderful views out toward the cliffs of West Fork.

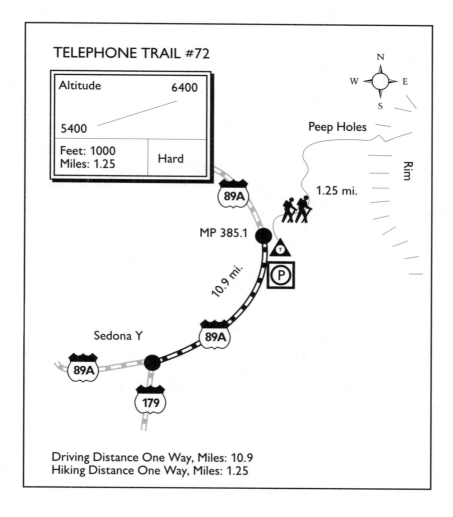

TELEPHONE TRAIL #72

Altitude 6400

5400

Feet: 1000
Miles: 1.25   Hard

Peep Holes

Rim

N
W — E
S

89A

MP 385.1

1.25 mi.

10.9 mi.

Sedona Y

89A

89A

179

Driving Distance One Way, Miles: 10.9
Hiking Distance One Way, Miles: 1.25

THOMAS POINT #142

General Information
Location Map B5
Munds Park USGS Map
Coconino Forest Service Map

Driving Distance One Way: 10.5 miles *16.8 km* (Time 20 minutes)
Access Road: All cars, All paved
Hiking Distance One Way: 1.0 miles *1.6 km* (Time 60 minutes)
How Strenuous: Hard
Features: Views

NUTSHELL: This is a marked and posted trail that climbs the east wall of upper Oak Creek Canyon 10.5 miles *16.8 km* north of Sedona.

DIRECTIONS:
From the Sedona Y Go:
    North on Highway 89A (toward Flagstaff) for a distance of 10.5 miles *16.8 km* (MP 384.7) You will see a road sign for the West Fork parking area, which requires a sharp turn to your left (W).

TRAILHEAD: There is a fee for parking in the lot. The driveway forms a loop, and you want to park at the farthest point, the south end of the loop. Walk the trail you will see heading south, parallel to the highway and not very far from it. The trail will fork soon. Take the left (SE) fork and walk to Highway 89A. Cross over the paving, turn right (S) and walk along the east shoulder of Highway 89A about 100 yards. You will find the trailhead to your left, uphill a bit from the road.

DESCRIPTION: The start of the trail looks like a groove worn into the soil bank with the trailhead sign at the beginning of the groove. Look sharp, for the sign is hard to see.
    Like the other trails that climb the east wall of the canyon, this trail goes nearly straight up, with little artfulness. You start the hike in a pine and spruce forest. The trail zigzags in such a way that it isn't a killer trail like the **Purtymun Trail** or Thompson's Ladder.
    After hiking a short distance you will climb high enough to get good views of the sheer white cliffs of the West Fork and East Pocket areas across the canyon to the west, and can see the path of Oak Creek and glimpse bits of the highway.
    At about the half mile point the trail winds around onto an unshaded south face of the canyon wall. Here the pines disappear and you enter the

chaparral and juniper life zone. These plants are small compared to the pines so you have better views along this part of the trail. Near the top you come back into the pine and spruce forest.

At the top, pine needles may cover the trail and make it indistinct, so look for cairns. They mark an extension of the trail to a viewpoint to the left (N), where Thomas Point is located. Thomas Point is well named, for it is a peninsula or tongue pointing west. Standing at the tip of the point you will have good views north, west and south. Particularly good are the views of the San Francisco Peaks and the head of Oak Creek Canyon. Since you are on top of the rim, you might enjoy walking along it in both directions to find different viewpoints and places of interest.

The point was named after J. L. V. "Dad" Thomas, who bought the West Fork Ranch in 1888 and built this trail in 1890.

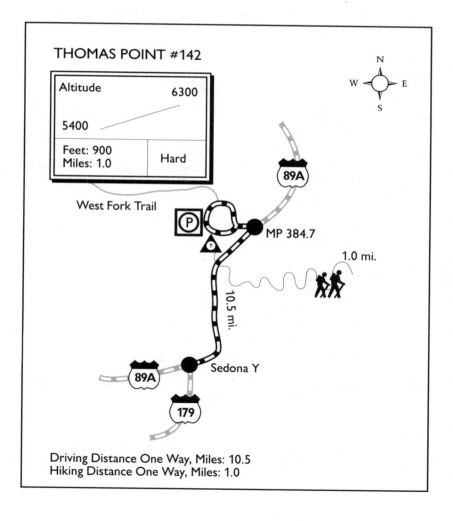

TOWEL CREEK TRAIL #67

General Information
Location Map G6
Hackberry Mt. and Horner Mt. USGS Map
Coconino Forest Service Map

Driving Distance One Way: 44.2 miles *70.72 km* (Time 1.0 hours)
Access Road: All cars, Last 8.8 miles *14.08 km* good dirt road
Hiking Distance One Way: 7.0 miles *11.2 km* (Time 7 Hours)
How Strenuous: Strenuous due to grades and distance
Features: Scenic rugged back country trail to the Verde River

NUTSHELL: This long trail winds around through broken hills and canyons to the Verde River.

DIRECTIONS:
From the Sedona Y Go:
    South on Highway 179 (toward Phoenix) for 14.7 miles *23.5 km*, to the I-17 Interchange. Turn south on I-17 and go to the 23.6 miles *37.8 km* point, where you take Exit 289 for Camp Verde. Go into Camp Verde, where you will come to a stop light at 27.3 miles *43.7 km*. Turn left here and go east on Highway 260 to the 35.4 mile *56.6 km* point (MP 228.5), where you turn right (south) on unpaved FR 708. It is signed. Follow this narrow winding mountain road to the 44.0 mile *70.4 km* point, where you come onto a little flat just beyond Needle Rock. There is a barbed wire fence to your right and a road going into a ranch. Turn right on this road, then turn left at the first junction and left again almost immediately afterward. You will be in sight of the ranch house but will turn away from it. The last little leg to the parking area is rougher than the rest but not too bad. You will see a trail sign [giving incorrect distances] and beyond it a loop, where you park.

TRAILHEAD: At the parking loop. (There is a secondary trailhead at the 44.2 mile 70.72 km point on FR 780. No parking area here, but you can park on a wide shoulder nearby. Go through the fence at a gate made of tall steel poles and go straight up the hill to intersect the jeep road,)

DESCRIPTION: From the place where you parked, just hike up the continuation of the road. The first part of this trail uses an old jeep road, which is very rugged, but it is nice to have an open trail in this area because walking through the brush is very difficult without a trail.
    You will climb a couple of hundred feet and then the trail becomes more level, turning away from the main road. At about a mile you will reach a

point above Pambo Tank, which usually contains water. From here the trail winds around Hackberry Mountain, reaching Towel Tank at 2.0 miles *3.2 km* in a flat meadow bounded by a fence. This is the high point on the trail.

From Towel Tank you begin a long downhill descent to the Verde River following the drainage of Towel Creek. The scenery becomes much more interesting on this leg of the hike, as you enter some really rugged wilderness and feel that you are miles away from civilization. There is a tricky patch where the trail becomes indistinct, crossing to the north side of the creek, but keep following the drainage and you will pick it up where it crosses to the other side.

If you do the entire hike, you will walk 14.0 miles *22.4 km* over rugged undulating country, with a 1,000 foot descent and climb; this is a substantial hike and will take all day. A way to make this shorter yet still enjoyable is to turn back at the Towel Creek boulder fields, which is at the 6.0 miles *9.6 km* point.

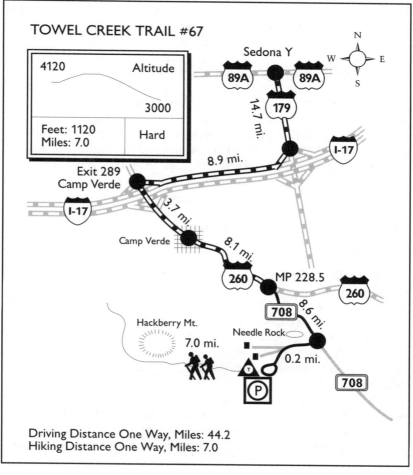

TOWEL CREEK TRAIL #67

4120	Altitude
	3000
Feet: 1120 Miles: 7.0	Hard

Sedona Y

89A 179 89A

I-17

14.7 mi.

8.9 mi.

Exit 289 Camp Verde

I-17

3.7 mi.

Camp Verde

8.1 mi.

260 MP 228.5 260

708

8.6 mi.

Hackberry Mt.

Needle Rock

7.0 mi.

0.2 mi.

P

708

Driving Distance One Way, Miles: 44.2
Hiking Distance One Way, Miles: 7.0

TURKEY CREEK TRAIL #92

General Information
Location Map F3
Sedona USGS Map
Coconino Forest Service Map

Driving Distance One Way: 11.9 miles *19.0 km* (Time 30 minutes)
Access Road: All cars, Last 1.7 miles *2.72 km* good dirt roads
Hiking Distance One Way: 3.5 miles *5.6 km* (Time 2.0 hours)
How Strenuous: Hard
Features: Rock formations, Views

NUTSHELL: Located 11.9 miles *19.0 km* southwest of Sedona, behind the Verde Valley School, this moderate hike has you climb 1,000 feet in about a mile through interesting redrocks to the top of House Mountain.

DIRECTIONS:
From the Sedona Y Go:
　　South on Highway 179 (toward Phoenix) for 7.2 miles *11.5 km* (MP 306.1), to the Verde Valley School Road, where there is a stoplight. Turn right (W) onto Verde Valley School Road. The first 3.0 miles *4.8 km* of this road are paved. Follow it to the 11.3 mile *18.08 km* point where you will see a sign marking the **Turkey Creek Trail**. Just beyond the sign you will see FR 9216B, a dirt road to your left. Turn onto FR 9216B. Any vehicle with medium clearance can handle the road. At 11.9 miles *19.0 km* you will reach a V fork. Turn left here and park on the shoulder of the little loop.

TRAILHEAD: The trailhead is at Turkey Creek Tank and is marked with a rusty sign, but you have to walk 1.5 miles *2.4 km* to get there.

DESCRIPTION: At the parking place, you will see an old road to the south that is closed by a barrier of stones. Walk down this road for 0.25 miles *0.4 km*, where you will find a V junction. The fork to your right (SW) is the trail to Turkey Creek. The fork to the left (SE) goes to **Twin Pillars**.
　　You will soon see a faint unmarked trail coming on to the road from your right, which is the alternate trail that goes to the gate at the rear entrance of Redrock State Park and then skirts around it. Continue walking the main road south.
　　When you get near Turkey Creek Tank you will recognize its presence because it is encircled by cottonwood trees. It is a pleasant oasis, though it goes dry in summer. The hiking trail starts at its farthest edge and goes along a former jeep road, winding through some fine redrocks. It changes to a foot-

path in about half a mile (*0.8 km*).

Soon after this you begin to climb House Mountain. The path is fairly steep but the footing is good. The path is an old stock trail. It zigzags to a saddle on the top, where you crest out on the rim of an extinct volcanic crater, a rather flat and shallow one. From that point you can take the trail down into the bowl of the crater, though there isn't much to see there. We prefer to bushwhack along the rim to the north for the fine views of Sedona, which are magnificent from there. The mountain's high point is to the north, a basalt tower worth scaling.

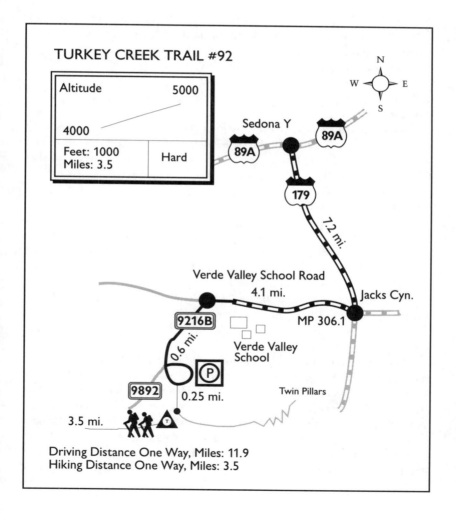

TWIN BUTTES

General Information
Location Map E5
Sedona USGS Map
Coconino Forest Service Map

Driving Distance One Way: 2.1 miles *3.36 km* (Time 10 minutes)
Access Road: All cars, All paved
Hiking Distance One Way: 1.5 miles *2.4 km* (Time 1.25 hours)
How Strenuous: Hard
Features: Views

NUTSHELL: The Twin Buttes formation is located a couple of miles south of the Sedona Y. The famous Chapel of the Holy Cross was built near its south face. It is a hard haul to the top of the north face over an unmaintained trail but once there you will enjoy superb views.

DIRECTIONS:
From the Sedona Y Go:
   South on Highway 179 (toward Phoenix) for 1.4 miles *2.3 km* (MP 312.1) to Morgan Road in the Broken Arrow Subdivision. Turn left (E) on Morgan Road and follow it to its end, at 2.0 miles *3.2 km*, then go another 0.1 miles *0.16 km* to the parking area.

TRAILHEAD: Use the **Broken Arrow Trail**, at the parking lot.

DESCRIPTION: The Forest Service has changed this area since the previous editions of our book, by creating a nice large parking lot and the **Broken Arrow Trail**. You no longer approach this hike by walking down the road; instead, you begin it by hiking the Broken Arrow Trail.
   From the parking lot, walk southwest across the road and follow the markers and cairns for the Broken Arrow Trail, to the west and south. The trail soon moves over near the redrock cliffs of Battlement Mesa, and the trail then curves around its base.
   At 0.5 miles *0.8 km* you will come down a steep hill to a sinkhole surrounded by a barbed wire fence. The sinkhole is called the Devil's Dining Room and is a local landmark. From this point you continue on the Broken Arrow Trail for another 0.13 miles *0.2 km*. Look carefully, because the trail you are seeking is sometimes camouflaged. You need to leave the Broken Arrow Trail and take a distinct well-worn trail to the right, going uphill, the first such trail you will encounter after leaving Devil's Dining Room. Once you locate the trail you will have no trouble following it because it is dis-

tinct. The trail will take you up a canyon toward a saddle between Battlement Mesa and Twin Buttes, winding its way through a pleasant forest. On the route you will enjoy looking from numerous viewpoints.

Climb the trail to the saddle, where you will have great views to the north toward Sedona and to the south toward Poco Diablo. The Twin Buttes Trail takes off to the left from the saddle. It is easy to see because it is located on a bare spot and is usually marked with a cairn. You can see it clearly as it goes sharply uphill, while the Battlement Mesa Trail goes off to your right on the level.

Take this left-hand trail and begin climbing. Moderately steep up to now, the trail gets much steeper. Your target is the big saddle in the Twin Buttes to your left, and you have 0.5 miles *0.8 km* of hard hiking to get there.

Once you top out and see the views, we think you will be happy you made the effort.

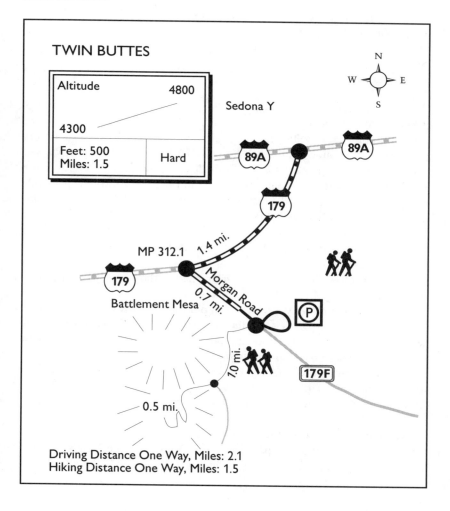

TWIN PILLARS

General Information
Location Map F4
Sedona USGS Map
Coconino Forest Service Map

Driving Distance One Way: 11.9 miles *19.0 km* (Time 30 minutes)
Access Road: All cars, Last 1.7 miles *2.72 km* good dirt roads
Hiking Distance One Way: 1.0 miles *1.6 km* (Time 45 minutes)
How Strenuous: Moderate
Features: Rock formations, Views

NUTSHELL: Located 11.9 miles *19.0 km* southwest of Sedona, behind the Verde Valley School, this moderate hike has you climb through interesting redrocks to the top of a ridge overlooking the school.

DIRECTIONS:
From the Sedona Y Go:
South on Highway 179 (toward Phoenix) for 7.2 miles *11.5 km* (MP 306.1), to the Verde Valley School Road, where there is a stoplight. Turn right (W) onto Verde Valley School Road. The first 3.0 miles *4.8 km* of this road are paved. Follow it to the 11.3 mile *18.08 km* point where you will see a sign marking the **Turkey Creek Trail**. Just beyond the sign you will see FR 9216B, a dirt road to your left. Turn onto FR 9216B. Any vehicle with medium clearance can handle the road. At 11.9 miles *19.0 km* you will reach a V fork. Turn left here and park on the shoulder of the little loop.

TRAILHEAD: Not marked. The trail begins where you park.

DESCRIPTION: The access road for this hike is the same up to a point as that for the **Turkey Creek Trail**, which is a recommended hike.
At the parking place, you will see an old road to the south that is closed by a barrier of stones. Walk down this road for 0.25 miles *0.4 km*, where you will find a V junction. The fork to your right (SW) is the trail to Turkey Creek. You want to take the fork to the left (SE).
You will continue to walk down a closed road that takes you ever closer to a redrock butte. The road ends at the foot of the butte, 0.5 miles *0.8 km* from the parking place, against a red wall, where you will see a foot trail going uphill.
There are always hoof prints on this trail and we would guess that the trail was created as a horse path for the students at Verde Valley School, which is on the other (E) side of the butte. It makes a good hiking trail.

Though the trail was not marked, we had no trouble following it. The path winds around in such a fashion that it makes good use of the terrain to climb the butte gradually. It is not very steep, rising 200 feet in 0.35 miles *0.6 km.* As you climb you rise high enough to get good views of some pretty country.

At the top you come onto the saddle. The Twin Pillars for which we named the hike are to your right (S). We could find no name for this place on any map, so we christened it after these prominent redrock pillars. From the saddle you look down onto the school, white buildings with red roofs in a beautiful setting.

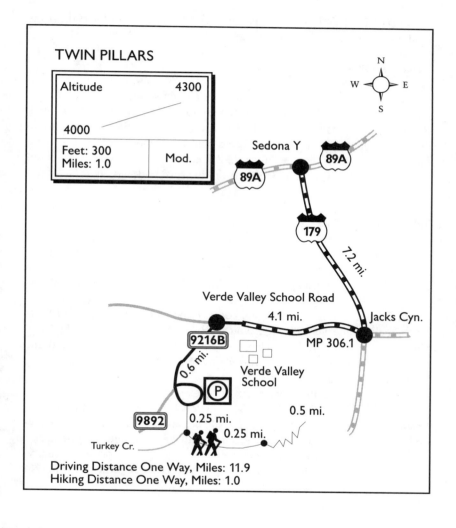

VAN DEREN CABIN

General Information
Location Map C4
Wilson Mt. USGS Map
Coconino Forest Service Map

Driving Distance One Way: 7.6 miles *12.2 km* (Time 30 minutes)
Access Road: Most cars, Last 2.4 miles *3.9 km* medium dirt road
Hiking Distance One Way: 0.30 miles *0.5 km* (Time 15 minutes)
How Strenuous: Easy
Features: Historic cabin, Views

NUTSHELL: This is a short easy hike to a historic cabin located off the road to Vultee Arch, 7.6 miles *12.2 km* northwest of Sedona.

DIRECTIONS:
From the Sedona Y Go:
    Southwest on Highway 89A (toward Cottonwood) a distance of 3.2 miles *5.12 km* (MP 371) to the Dry Creek Road. Turn right on Dry Creek Road, and follow it to the 5.2 mile *8.32 km* point where FR 152 branches to the right. Take FR 152. You will see a sign for Vultee Arch on this road. Follow the road to the 7.6 miles *12.2 km* point, where you will see an unmarked road to your left. Turn left on this road and park as soon as you can.

TRAILHEAD: There are no trail signs. Walk the road, which is FR 9917.

DESCRIPTION: Jeep tours regularly come here and drive FR 9917 all the way to the cabin. However, we recommend that you park just off the main road and walk to the cabin because the road is uneven and rough and this is a book of hikes.
    At 0.16 miles *0.26 km* you will come to the place where the road fords Dry Creek. If the water is high you might want to wait for another day. Upstream to your right there is a broad redrock ledge cut by the action of the creek into charming sculptures. It is well worth a short detour to walk along it and enjoy the shapes.
    When you cross the creek the road goes to the top of the bank on the other side. The road forks there. Take the left fork and follow it to its end. From there you will see the cabin. The old homestead was composed of several acres, but the Forest Service purchased the cabin site only, and has devoted it to public use. The remainder of the old ranch is private property. This private land has been enclosed by a fence that is garlanded with No

Trespassing signs. Don't worry about these, because access to the cabin site is open to the public.

The cabin was built by pioneer Earl Van Deren in the 1890s. The oldest part is nearest to the new fence. After he built the cabin, Earl fell in love but his fiancee refused to marry him until he expanded the place. He added a second unit and connected the two units with a roof, forming a breezeway. This expansion satisfied his fiancee, and they married.

Earl ranched and made some money as a movie extra. In the 1940s he bought acreage in what turned out later to be uptown Sedona, where there is a Van Deren Road honoring him. At the back of the cabin site, you can see the remains of Earl's root cellar. Legend says that the cellar was used by a bootlegger after Earl moved to town and that the bootlegger was murdered there.

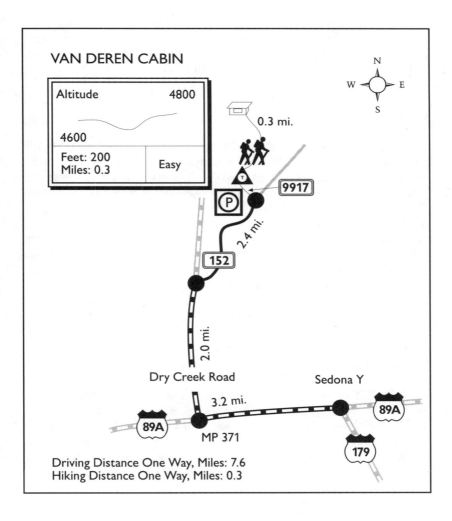

VERDE HOT SPRINGS

General Information
Location Map G6
Verde Hot Springs USGS Map
Coconino Forest Service Map

Driving Distance One Way: 55.8 miles *89.3 km* (Time 1.5 hours)
Access Road: All cars, Last 20.4 miles *32.7 km* good dirt road
Hiking Distance One Way: 1.25 miles *2.0 km* (Time 40 minutes)
How Strenuous: Easy, but you have to wade across the Verde River
Features: Historic site, Permanent river, Wide easy trail, Views, Hot springs

NUTSHELL: This adventure is worth making for the sake of the drive alone, but is spiced by the addition of wild country, an historic electrical power plant and flume, a hot spring, a river and the ruins of a former resort. NOTE: You must be equipped with wading shoes and shorts to go to the springs.

DIRECTIONS:
From the Sedona Y Go:
   South on Highway 179 (toward Phoenix) for 14.7 miles *23.5 km*, to the I-17 Interchange. Turn south on I-17 and go to the 23.6 miles *37.8 km* point, where you take Exit 289 for Camp Verde. Go into Camp Verde, where you will come to a stop light at 27.3 miles *43.7 km*. Turn left here and go east on Highway 260 to the 35.4 mile *56.6 km* point (MP 228.5), where you turn right (south) on unpaved FR 708. It is signed. Follow this narrow winding mountain road to the 49.5 mile *79.2 km* point, where it meets FR 502. Turn right (SW), toward Childs. You will drive a very winding road down to the 55.8 mile *89.3 km* point, where the road splits, with the right hand road going into the power plant. You want to go left down to the campground here, but washouts have made the last 0.15 mile *0.24 km* stretch very rough. High clearance is necessary. You may want to park here and walk down.

   TRAILHEAD: At the campground by the Verde River bank, you will see a trail sign.

   DESCRIPTION: The trail moves up to the historic power plant, built in 1916 to serve Jerome, Prescott and Phoenix. You pass over a catwalk in front of the power house, where the waters of Fossil Creek (channeled into the seven mile flume you saw while driving in) come surging through hydro-electric turbines and discharge into the Verde. Then the trail goes down to the river bank. Soon after, it climbs away from the river and goes up on a ridge to meet a road. You turn left and follow this road down to its end, where it joins the river. There is a campground here.

You will see a ranch house to your right on the opposite bank. The rancher drives across the river here, so it is usually the best place to wade across, but be careful. At normal levels, the river will be from knee to waist deep, but when it is high, it may be dangerous to cross. Once over, you climb up onto a trail and turn left, going back downstream. You will soon come onto a bench that was created as the site for a resort that flourished here decades ago, before burning down in 1962. Keep following the trail. You will see a number of white pillars marking the trail as it dips down to the river. At the end of the trail is the main spring.

The spring water is contained in a green pool sitting atop a rock bath house. It is open to public use and is an interesting place. Be aware that many people who use the spring like nudity. That explains the anti-nudity signs you saw on the trail earlier.

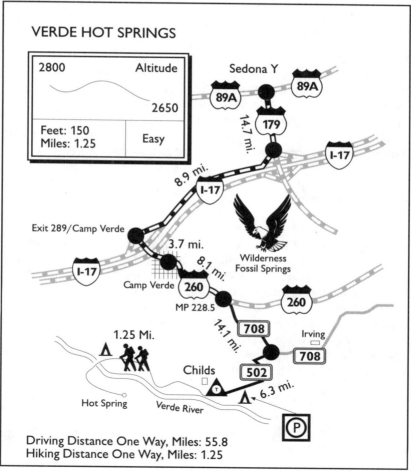

VERDE HOT SPRINGS

2800	Altitude
	2650
Feet: 150 Miles: 1.25	Easy

Sedona Y

89A · 89A

14.7 mi. · 179

8.9 mi. · I-17 · I-17

Exit 289/Camp Verde

I-17

3.7 mi.

Camp Verde 260 · 8.1 mi.

MP 228.5 · 260

Wilderness Fossil Springs

1.25 Mi.

14.1 mi. · 708

Childs · 502 · Irving · 708

Hot Spring · Verde River · 6.3 mi. · ℗

Driving Distance One Way, Miles: 55.8
Hiking Distance One Way, Miles: 1.25

VULTEE ARCH #22

General Information
Location Map C4
Loy Butte and Wilson Mt. USGS Maps
Coconino Forest Service Map

Driving Distance One Way: 9.6 miles *15.4 km* (Time 45 minutes)
Access Road: Last 4.4 miles *7.0 km* rocky, bumpy, but OK for most cars
Hiking Distance One Way: 1.6 miles *2.6 km* (Time 1 hour)
How Strenuous: Moderate
Features: Arch, Historic marker, Scenic canyon

NUTSHELL: Located 9.6 miles *15.4 km* north of Sedona, this hike takes you to a natural arch and a commemorative plaque in a beautiful box canyon. **A personal favorite**.

DIRECTIONS:
From the Sedona Y Go:
    Southwest on Highway 89A (toward Cottonwood) for 3.2 miles *5.12 km* (MP 371) to Dry Creek Road. Turn right on Dry Creek Road and proceed to the 5.2 mile *8.3 km* point. Turn right on FR 152, the Vultee Arch Road, and follow it to the 9.6 mile *15.4 km* point. Here there is a parking loop, with the **Vultee Arch** Trailhead at the tip. Parking is provided at the trailhead.

TRAILHEAD: This is a marked and maintained trail. You will see a rusty sign at the parking place reading, "Vultee Arch #22."

DESCRIPTION: FR 152 has been improved since the first edition of this book was issued. We feel that almost any passenger car, except one that is very low slung, can make this trip now. Even so, go slowly and keep your eyes open for ruts and rocks, as this situation changes with every storm.
    The hiking trail is sandy and gives nice soft footing. The trail climbs as it progresses, passing through several life zones, which causes interesting changes in the vegetation surrounding the trail. When you begin the trail you are in a forest of Arizona cypress. After that you will go through oak and pine and finally you will find Douglas fir. The route is shaded the entire way, which makes it a good trail in hot weather.
    The trail crosses a creekbed several times, so don't try to hike it when a lot of water is running in the creek. The creek is dry except for a few weeks in the spring, generally in March and April or after a hard summer rain.
    At 1.4 miles *2.3 km* you will reach the junction of this trail and the **Sterling Pass Trail**, which forks to the right.

At the end of the trail you will break out into a clearing in a box canyon and the trail will climb onto redrock ledges. You will see Vultee Arch against a far wall (N) of the box canyon. There is a trail leading to it that you can easily pick up. It is possible to walk right up to the arch and even to climb on top of it.

The historical plaque is cast in bronze and fastened to the face of a redrock ledge, the second ledge above you as you enter the box canyon. The plaque commemorates the airplane crash that killed Gerald Vultee, an aviation pioneer, and his wife in 1938. They did not crash here, but on nearby East Pocket, when they were caught in a storm at night. Had Vultee been flying one of today's planes with modern instruments, he probably would have brought it in safely.

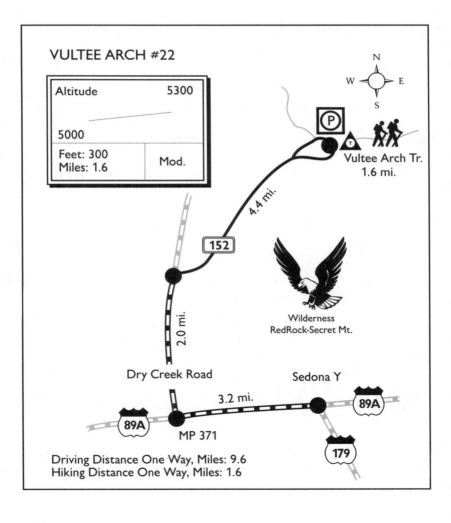

VULTEE ARCH #22

Altitude	5300	
5000		
Feet: 300 Miles: 1.6	Mod.	

Vultee Arch Tr. 1.6 mi.

4.4 mi.

152

2.0 mi.

Wilderness RedRock-Secret Mt.

Dry Creek Road

Sedona Y

89A

3.2 mi.

89A

MP 371

179

Driving Distance One Way, Miles: 9.6
Hiking Distance One Way, Miles: 1.6

WALKER BASIN TRAIL

General Information
Location Map G6
Walker Mtn. USGS Map
Coconino Forest Service Map

Driving Distance One Way: 31.8 miles *50.9 km* (Time 1.25 hours)
Access Road: All cars, Last 14.6 miles *23.4 km* good dirt road
Hiking Distance One Way: 8.0 miles *12.8 km* (Time 4.5 hours)
How Strenuous: Hard
Features: Views

NUTSHELL: This trail runs from a point 5,960 feet high on the Mogollon Rim to the bottom, a 2,000 foot drop in 8.0 miles *12.8 km.*

DIRECTIONS:
From the Sedona Y Go:
   South on Highway 179 (toward Phoenix) for 14.7 miles *23.5 km*, to the I-17 Interchange. Go underneath onto FR 618 (paved for 2.5 miles *4.0 km*) and follow it. At the 19.7 mile *31.5 km* point you will see a sign for the Walker Basin Trail and a road going left. Pass by. At the 24.5 mile *39.2 km* point, take a road left, FR 214, "Cedar Flat." FR 214 takes you to the top of the Mogollon Rim, a 2,000 foot climb. You will come to the high point at about 30.0 miles *48 km*, then go downhill. Just past a cattle guard, at the 31.8 mile *50.9 km* point, you will see a dirt road to your left (W) marked 214B. Pull in and park. Do not try to drive 214B.

TRAILHEAD: There is a sign where you park.

DESCRIPTION: This is a hard hike. We recommend doing this hike with two cars, in which case it is still pretty strenuous, but is an enjoyable experience instead of an ordeal. The way to do this is to take two cars in to the lower trailhead, at the 19.7 mile *31.5 km* point on FR 618, mentioned above. You can drive in about 0.9 miles *1.5 km*, to the parking place. Leave one car there and take the other to the top.
   There is one trick at the top, and an important one. After you have hiked about 0.1 miles *0.16 km*, you will come to a gate. Go *inside* the gate. There is a path outside as well, but it is not your trail. The gate is not signed, so be sure to follow these instructions.
   The first leg of the hike is on a mesa top. The area has been cleared, giving fine views in all directions. At 1.75 miles *2.8 km* you come to a drop-off where you descend to a lower bench. As you drop, you will see a pond down

to your right. This is Walker Basin.

You reach the pond at 2.5 miles *4.0 km*, where the trail gets a little tricky, not well marked. Up to now it has been a jeep road, but here it becomes a footpath. Walk around the right shoulder of the pond, and take the trail to the right, at the end of the fence. You will see cairns and limbs cut from trees. The path goes north from the pond.

From here you climb to the 3.3 mile *5.3 km* point, then walk across a fairly level stretch. At 4.2 miles *6.7 km* you come upon a mysterious trailless sign, "Jacobs Tank 1/4 mi." At 4.75 miles *7.6 km* you come to another drop-off, where you have great views west. As you wind down from here, the views to the south open, to the Verde Valley.

At 5.4 miles *8.7 km* you reach the final drop-off where you enter an area of beautiful sandstone ledges with impressive sights both near at hand and far away. You reach the bottom at 7.25 miles *11.6 km* and walk across level country to get back to your waiting car at 8.0 miles *12.8 km*.

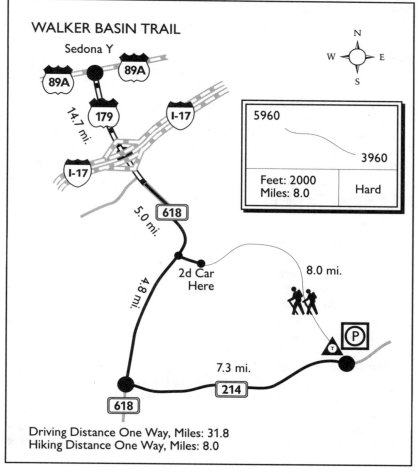

WALKER BASIN TRAIL

Sedona Y

89A 89A

14.7 mi.

179 I-17

I-17

5.0 mi. 618

5960

3960

Feet: 2000
Miles: 8.0 | Hard

2d Car Here

8.0 mi.

4.8 mi.

7.3 mi.

618 214

Driving Distance One Way, Miles: 31.8
Hiking Distance One Way, Miles: 8.0

WEST CLEAR CREEK TRAIL #17

General Information
Location Map G6
Buckhorn Mtn., Walker Mtn. USGS Maps
Coconino Forest Service Map

Driving Distance One Way: 29.5 miles *47.2 km* (Time 1 hour)
Access Road: All cars, Last 12.3 miles *19.7 km* good dirt road
Hiking Distance One Way: 1.0 miles *1.6 km* (Time 30 minutes)
How Strenuous: Easy
Features: Historic ranch, Permanent creek, Wide easy trail, Views

NUTSHELL: This easy trail starts from the West Clear Creek Campground 29.5 miles *47.2 km* south of Sedona and takes you through an interesting old ranch to a lovely creek in a deep scenic canyon.

DIRECTIONS:
From the Sedona Y Go:
    South on Highway 179 (toward Phoenix) for 14.7 miles *23.5 km*, to the I-17 Interchange. Instead of going onto I-17, go underneath it onto paved road FR 618. The paving ends at the Beaver Creek bridge. Follow FR 618. At the 24.5 mile *39.2 km* point, you will see a dirt road branching left to Cedar Flat. Keep going south on FR 618. At 26.5 miles *42.4 km* you will come to a road to the left (FR 215) to the West Clear Creek Campground. Turn left on FR 215 and go to the 29.5 mile *47.2 km* point, all the way to the end of the road. Parking for the trail is located there and signed.

TRAILHEAD: At the parking area you will see trail signs for the West Clear Creek Trail #17, and the **Blodgett Basin Trail.**

DESCRIPTION: This trail takes you across the old Bull Pen Ranch, which is now public property. (This trail is also called the Bull Pen Trail.) Go through the gate and walk the bygone ranch road The first part of the road is lovely, as it is quite close to the creek and passes through a lush riparian forest. Farther on it moves away from Clear Creek and opens up into typical scrub and cactus habitat.
    At 0.66 miles *1.1 km* you will come out into an open field, where you see a sight that sticks in the mind of every visitor to this place, a rock house with cactus growing on its roof. When you inspect this small structure, which is about 20 x 12 feet, you will see that the builders heaped dirt on the roof, an old trick in the Southwest. Prickly pears and agave got established in this dirt and have grown there for years. Behind the rock house, on the north side of

the canyon, there is a ledge of exposed red sandstone adding a welcome touch of color to the landscape. The ranch site is very beautiful.

You will continue along the road to the 1.0 mile *1.6 km* point where the fields end and the road dips down to the creek. There you will find some slickrock ledges just above the water that seem to have been placed there by nature as places to sit and take the sun and watch the creek gurgle by.

When the water is low enough, you can wade across the creek here and hike upstream on the opposite bank for another mile with relative ease. Beyond that point the hike gets pretty tough. There is a place at about 3.0 miles *4.8 km* where the trail lifts out of the canyon on the north wall, requiring a strenuous 2,000 foot climb to a point on FR 214 about 1.2 miles *1.9 km* above the Blodgett Basin trail terminus.

For an easy day hike we recommend stopping at the 1.0 mile *1.6 km* point.

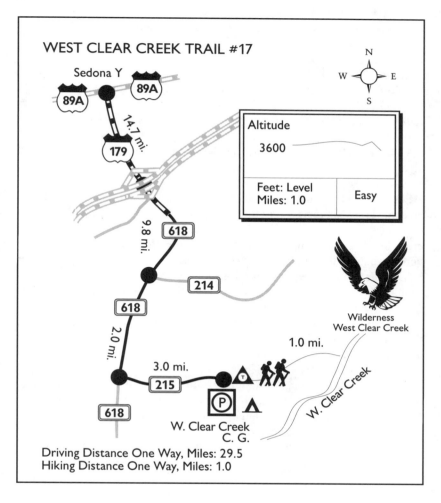

WEST CLEAR CREEK TRAIL #17

Sedona Y

89A   89A   89A

14.7 mi.

179

Altitude

3600

Feet: Level
Miles: 1.0

Easy

9.8 mi.   618

214

618

Wilderness
West Clear Creek

2.0 mi.

1.0 mi.

3.0 mi.

215

618

W. Clear Creek
C. G.

W. Clear Creek

Driving Distance One Way, Miles: 29.5
Hiking Distance One Way, Miles: 1.0

WEST FORK #108

General Information
Location Map B5
Dutton Hill and Munds Park USGS Maps
Coconino Forest Service Map

Driving Distance One Way: 10.5 miles *16.8 km* (Time 20 minutes)
Access Road: All cars, All paved
Hiking Distance One Way: 3.0 miles *4.8 km* (Time 90 minutes)
How Strenuous: Moderate
Features: Gorgeous canyon with stream

NUTSHELL: One of the best, most popular hikes in Arizona. The trailhead is located 10.5 miles *16.8 km* north of Sedona. **A personal favorite.**

DIRECTIONS:
From the Sedona Y Go:
    North on Highway 89A (toward Flagstaff) for a distance of 10.5 miles *16.8 km* (MP 384.7.) You will see a road sign for the parking area, which requires a sharp turn to your left (W). An entry fee is required.

TRAILHEAD: On the west side of the parking area loop, you will see a sign board. This marks the trailhead.

DESCRIPTION: This hike is so popular that a special parking area was created for it, complete with toilets. From the trailhead at the parking area, the trail goes west, to Oak Creek. You must climb down the east bank and cross the creek on some stepping stones. There are plans to build a bridge here, perhaps in the summer of 1997. Until then, it's the stones. Crossing can be a bit dicey when the stones are wet, and we have seen several people have trouble. Once over the creek, you climb up the opposite bank and turn left (S) on a wide sandy track. The clearing here is the site of the old Lolomai Lodge. Soon you will draw abreast of houses across the creek. Just beyond the last house, you will enter the ruins of Mayhews Lodge, where there are a few brick structures still standing. This point is 0.3 miles *0.48 km* from the beginning.
    The Dad Thomas family (**Thomas Point** namesake) built a home here, which was remodeled as a hunting and fishing lodge in the early 1900s. Carl Mayhew bought it in 1925 and enlarged it. Zane Grey immortalized the location in *The Call of the Canyon*. The owners of the lodge tried to raise as much of their own food as they could for guests. You can see areas where they had orchards and vegetable gardens and you will see the remains of

their chicken coop set into a shallow cave. The Forest Service bought the lodge in 1969 only to have it burn in 1980.

As you enter the West Fork canyon you become immediately aware of the charm of this place, with the gentle stream flowing through a lush habitat framed by tremendously high and colorful canyon walls. It is a magic place.

The path follows along the streambed, crossing back and forth over the water. At the crossings you will usually find stepping stones that allow you to get across without getting wet, but these are not foolproof. You should count on getting your feet wet. Some hikers prefer to wear old tennies or jungle boots and wade. You will find distance markers every half mile.

The canyon is narrow, so you are often right next to the cliffs. The stream has undercut them in many places, creating interesting overhangs. You really feel the majesty of the canyon on this hike, for the cliffs dwarf you.

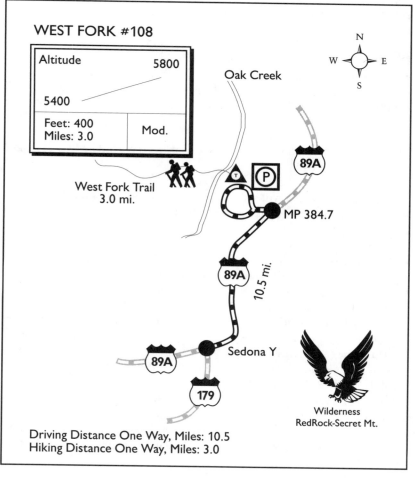

WEST FORK #108

Altitude 5800
5400
Feet: 400
Miles: 3.0
Mod.

Oak Creek

West Fork Trail
3.0 mi.

89A

MP 384.7

89A

10.5 mi.

89A

Sedona Y

179

Wilderness
RedRock-Secret Mt.

Driving Distance One Way, Miles: 10.5
Hiking Distance One Way, Miles: 3.0

WILSON CANYON #49

General Information
Location Map D5
Munds Park USGS Map
Coconino Forest Service Map

Driving Distance One Way: 1.1 miles *1.8 km* (Time 5 minutes)
Access Road: All cars, All paved
Hiking Distance One Way: 1.5 miles *2.4 km* (Time 1 hour)
How Strenuous: Moderate
Features: Views

NUTSHELL: Just 1.1 miles *1.8 km* north of Sedona, Wilson Canyon is spanned by Midgley Bridge. You can take a short easy stroll along the rim of the canyon or a longer hike up the canyon.

DIRECTIONS:
From the Sedona Y Go:
    North on Highway 89A (toward Flagstaff) for a distance of 1.1 miles *1.8 km* (MP 375.9). Go just across Midgley Bridge and turn left into the parking area.

TRAILHEAD: You will see a rusty sign at the parking lot. It reads, "Wilson Canyon #49."

DESCRIPTION: You will see the parking area just across the bridge. This is a very popular spot and you may not find a parking place open. If not, go up the road a bit. There are several wide shoulders for parking.
    The trailhead is easy to locate. Just walk toward the picnic tables at the end of the parking lot. There you will find the Wilson Monument, a bronze plaque set in stone, and two rusty signs. The sign to the left marks Wilson Canyon #49 and is the one you want for this hike. The other sign marks an uphill trail, Wilson Mountain #10, which we call **Wilson Mountain South**.
    The Wilson Canyon hike is little more than a leisurely stroll for the first 0.25 miles *0.4 km*. This may be as much of a hike as some readers want.
    Up to the 0.25 mile *0.4 km* point, the trail is as broad and flat as a road-way. It was a road. Turn around and look at Midgley Bridge and imagine what the road would have been without it. Drivers had to make a sharp turn and go up the canyon to a point where it narrowed and a bridge could readily be installed, cross over the canyon, then go back out and make another sharp turn. Old-timers tell us that the sharp unexpected turns were very dangerous. You will see the old bridge placements at the head of Wilson

Canyon. This is the place to stop for the short hike.

For the longer hike, you keep walking up the canyon, which is sometimes wet. The trail meanders from bank to bank There are many intersecting paths, but it is easy to stay on course if you keep paralleling the canyon. At about 0.5 miles *0.8 km* you will see a footpath going uphill to your left. This is part of the **Old Jim Thompson Road**. A few yards beyond that you will see an alternate branch of the Old Jim Thompson Road coming down to intersect your path.

The trail is a gradual uphill climb, quite gentle. In a few places the trail will seem to scramble up a steep bank and go to the top. Ignore these side trails and keep following the canyon bottom.

The canyon encloses you so that you can't see much outside it. At 1.5 miles *2.4 km* you will reach a place where a side trail goes uphill to the right. This goes up to a viewpoint and is the place to quit.

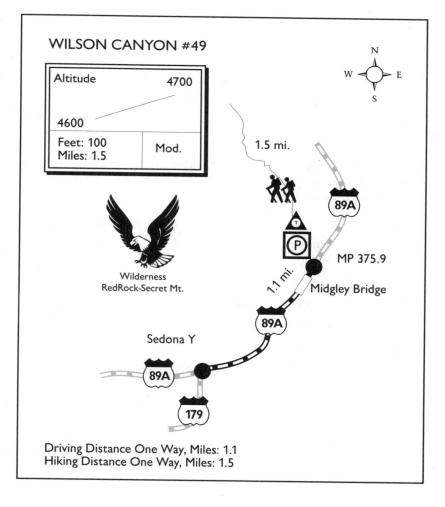

WILSON CANYON #49

N
W   E
S

Altitude	4700
4600	
Feet: 100 Miles: 1.5	Mod.

1.5 mi.

89A

T

P

MP 375.9

1.1 mi.

Midgley Bridge

89A

Wilderness RedRock-Secret Mt.

Sedona Y

89A

179

Driving Distance One Way, Miles: 1.1
Hiking Distance One Way, Miles: 1.5

WILSON MOUNTAIN NORTH #123

General Information
Location Map C5
Munds Park and Wilson Mt. USGS Maps
Coconino Forest Service Map

Driving Distance One Way: 5.3 miles *8.5 km* (Time 10 minutes)
Access Road: All cars, All paved
Hiking Distance One Way: 3.4 miles *5.5 km* (Time 4.0 hours)
How Strenuous: Hard
Features: Views

NUTSHELL: Located just north of Sedona, Wilson is the highest mountain in the area. This trail, originating at Encinoso Picnic Area, climbs Wilson's north face.

DIRECTIONS:
From the Sedona Y Go:
    North on Highway 89A (toward Flagstaff) for a distance of 5.3 miles *8.5 km* (MP 379.5), where you will see the Encinoso Picnic Area to your left. Park in the Encinoso parking lot.

TRAILHEAD: From the parking lot, walk up the canyon on the shoulder of the road about 100 yards. There you will see a trail sign reading, "Wilson Mt. #123" with the trail heading uphill.

DESCRIPTION: The trail climbs to the top of a small ridge at about 0.25 miles *0.4 km*, where you have a good vantage point to look across the canyon at the cliffs of the east wall. During spring runoff and after hard rains, the Encinoso Waterfall appears there and this is one of the best places from which to see it.
    From this ridge the trail climbs gently for another 0.75 miles *1.2 km* along a refreshing, wooded side canyon through a lovely mixed forest of pine, fir, spruce, oak and maple. The streambed here seldom carries any water, but when it does, it is delightful.
    At 1.0 miles *1.6 km* the serious work begins. Here the canyon pinches in and the trail begins a steep climb up the north face of Wilson. If you want an easy hike, the 1.0 mile point is the place to stop. The ascent beyond the 1.0 mile point is treacherous if the trail is slick with mud or snow. When dry, it is only strenuous. You will climb 1,300 feet in 0.5 miles *0.8 km*.
    After this hard haul, you top out on a flat flank of Wilson called First Bench. You will have great views to the north from here. Across Oak Creek

Canyon you will see a major tributary, Munds Canyon, which empties into Oak Creek at Indian Gardens.

Keep walking south along First Bench. At the 2.0 mile *3.2 km* point, at the edge of First Bench, you will intersect the Wilson Mt. South Trail coming up from Midgley Bridge. The junction is well marked with cairns. Take a look off the rim from here; it's great! You may want to quit here.

From this trail junction, you can go to the top of the mountain. See **Wilson Mountain South** for details. You have to hike 0.60 miles *1.0 km* to the Tool Shed, at the top of the mountain, 800 feet, then hike a level trail 0.80 miles *1.3 km* to the North Rim viewpoint, a total of 3.4 miles *5.5 km* from Encinoso. This hike is 0.60 miles *1.0 km* longer than the Wilson Mountain South Trail because of the walk across First Bench.

One way to do this hike is with 2 cars, parking one car at Midgley Bridge and the other at Encinoso. Go up from Midgley Bridge on the South Trail and then come back on the North Trail, doing both on one long hard day.

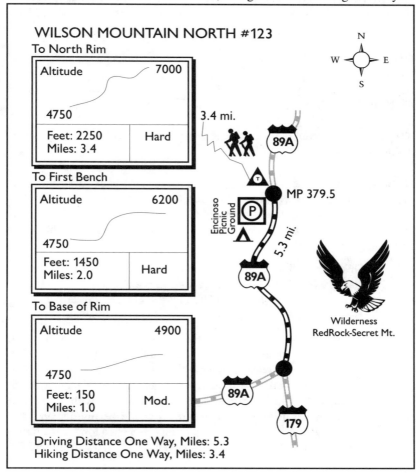

WILSON MOUNTAIN NORTH #123

To North Rim

Altitude	7000
4750	
Feet: 2250 Miles: 3.4	Hard

To First Bench

Altitude	6200
4750	
Feet: 1450 Miles: 2.0	Hard

To Base of Rim

Altitude	4900
4750	
Feet: 150 Miles: 1.0	Mod.

3.4 mi.

89A

MP 379.5

Encinoso Picnic Ground

5.3 mi.

89A

Wilderness RedRock-Secret Mt.

89A

179

Driving Distance One Way, Miles: 5.3
Hiking Distance One Way, Miles: 3.4

WILSON MOUNTAIN SOUTH #10

General Information
Location Map D5
Munds Park and Wilson Mt. USGS Maps
Coconino Forest Service Map

Driving Distance One Way: 1.1 miles *1.8 km* (Time 5 minutes)
Access Road: All cars, All paved
Hiking Distance One Way: 2.8 miles *4.5 km* (Time 3.5 hours)
How Strenuous: Hard
Features: Views

NUTSHELL: This popular hike starts at Midgley Bridge, north of Sedona, and goes up Wilson Mountain to the highest point in the area, then crosses the mountain top to a fabulous lookout point.

DIRECTIONS:
From the Sedona Y Go:
 North on Highway 89A (toward Flagstaff) for a distance of 1.1 miles *1.8 km* (MP 375.9). Just across Midgley Bridge is the parking area.

TRAILHEAD: You will see a rusty sign at the parking lot. It reads, "Wilson Mt. #10."

DESCRIPTION: The trailhead is easy to locate. Just walk toward the picnic tables. There you will find a bronze plaque set in stone, and two trail signs. The sign to the left is **Wilson Canyon #49.** The other, uphill, is Wilson Mountain #10, which we call **Wilson Mountain South** in this book, and is the trail you want to take.

 This hike is divided into three phases, each with a different feel:
Midgley Bridge to First Bench, 1.4 miles *2.3 km*, a 1,600' climb;
First Bench to Tool Shed, 0.60 miles *1.0 km*, an 800' climb;
Tool Shed to North Rim, 0.80 miles *1.3 km*, fairly level.

 Midgley Bridge to First Bench: This is a steep climb from the start. Ahead of you on the skyline you will see the saddle that is your destination. Along the way you have constantly enjoyable views of the formations of Wilson Mountain. You are in a high desert landscape, with juniper, manzanita and cactus. As you rise higher, you get into an area with little shade where you switchback to the top. This stretch would be murder on a hot sunny day. Finally you break over the top of First Bench, a long plateau running the length of the east side of the mountain. The views from here are very fine, though the bench itself is pretty drab and featureless.

First Bench to the Tool Shed: Take the path going left, toward the high cliffs. You will soon climb above First Bench and get into a heavy forest of pine and oak. This has a decidedly alpine feeling compared to the desert you have just been through. After a 500 foot climb you will come onto the top, where the land is pretty level, then make a modest 300 foot climb to the Tool Shed, where fire fighting tools are stored. The main trail goes ahead here, with a side trail to the left.

Tool Shed to North Rim: This is a delightful walk through a cool forest on nearly level ground, very easy compared to the first two phases of the hike. You are walking out to the mountain's north edge. When you come to a pond on the east side of the trail, you are almost at the end. Keep walking and you will come out onto a cliff face where you will find a soul-stirring view.

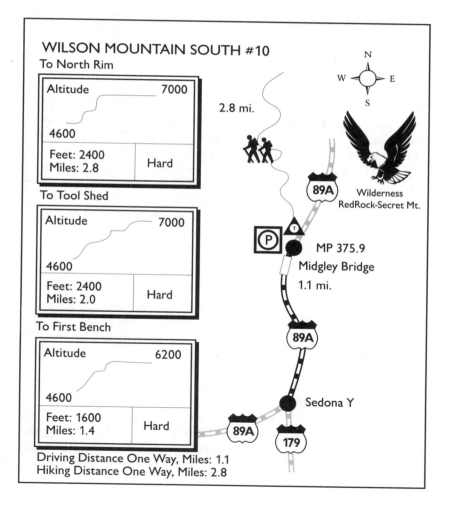

WOODCHUTE TRAIL #102

General Information
Location Map G1 (off the map)
Hickey Mtn. and Munds Draw USGS Maps
Prescott Forest Service Map

Driving Distance One Way: 36.1 miles *57.76 km* (Time 1 hour)
Access Road: All vehicles
Hiking Distance One Way: 3.75 miles *6.0 km* (Time 2.5 hours)
How Strenuous: Moderate to hard
Features: Jerome, Mountain trail through pine forests, Gorgeous views

NUTSHELL: You pass through Jerome and go up to Mingus Mountain. You then enjoy a hike that rewards you with remarkable views.

DIRECTIONS:
From the Sedona Y Go:
Southwest on Highway 89A. As you enter Cottonwood, do not turn on Highway 260, but keep going on Highway 89A. At the 23.2 mile *37.12 km* point, you will come to a stoplight where Highway 89A turns left. The sign is marked, "To Prescott." Take this left turn and keep going on Highway 89A, and you will soon begin to climb the long hill to Jerome. At 28.0 miles *44.8 km*, you will come to the stop sign in downtown Jerome. Turn right here, staying on Highway 89A. You will immediately begin to climb Mingus Mountain on a very winding road through a scenic canyon, where you will see ruins of old industrial structures. As you near the top of Mingus, you will see signs for the Potato Patch Campground to the right. Take the paved entrance to the campground at 35.6 miles *57.0 km* MP 336.3. In 0.3 miles *0.48 km* take the road to the left and follow it to the parking area.

TRAILHEAD: At the parking area you will see a green gate. If you are in a low-clearance vehicle, you may want to park in the parking area. If you have a high-clearance vehicle, you can drive to the trailhead. Walk or drive through the gate, and follow the primitive road for 0.6 miles *0.96 km* to the trailhead, which is signed.

DESCRIPTION: We decided to include a couple of the better hikes on Mingus Mountain in this edition of *Sedona Hikes* because they are not far from Sedona, and there are times in the summer when it is too hot for good hiking. Near the top of Mingus, where this hike starts, the altitude cools things off and you enjoy a refreshing pine forest. The inclusion of Mingus hikes also allows us to steer readers to Jerome, one of the must-see places in

Though it became an open-pit operation, at first the mining in Jerome was underground, and to shore up the tunnels, immense quantities of timbers were required. The forests of Mingus were the obvious source, and they were logged. In order to transport the timbers down to the town, a chute was built. Logs slid down the chute to a point on a railroad, where they were loaded into Jerome-bound cars, hence the name Woodchute Mountain.

You start hiking at the 7,000 foot level and work your way up to the top of Woodchute Mountain at the 7,700 foot level. The trail actually goes on for several miles, going downhill from the crest to end up at Sheep Camp, but we think this is too long for a good day hike. Going to the top of Woodchute, on the other hand, makes for a superior day hike. When you start the hike, the views are not very good, but soon the country begins to open up and at the end of the hike you will enjoy sweeping views over a huge area.

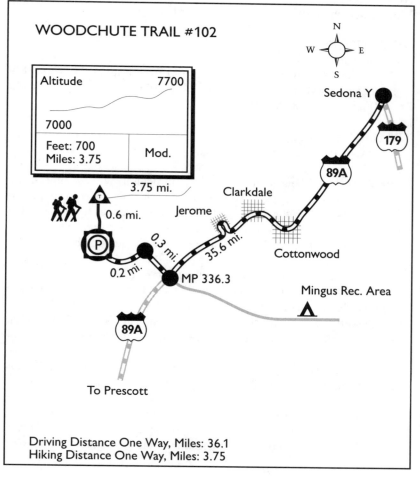

WOODS CANYON TRAIL #93

General Information
Location Map G5
Munds Mt. and Sedona USGS Maps
Coconino Forest Service Map

Driving Distance One Way: 8.7 miles *13.9 km* (Time 15 minutes)
Access Road*:* All cars, Paved except last 0.10 miles *0.16 km*
Hiking Distance One Way*:* 3.25 miles *5.2 km* (Time 90 minutes)
How Strenuous*:* Moderate
Features*:* Views

NUTSHELL: South of the Sedona Y 8.7 miles *13.9 km*, this trail follows Woods Canyon, through which Dry Beaver Creek flows.

DIRECTIONS:
From the Sedona Y Go:
    South on Highway 179 (toward Phoenix) for 8.6 miles *13.74 km* (MP 304.8) to an unmarked dirt road to your left. Turn left on the road, follow it for 0.10 miles *0.16 km* and park.

TRAILHEAD: At the road you will see a gate and a rusty sign reading, "Woods Canyon #93."

DESCRIPTION: The gate is unlocked. Go through it. We recommend that you park just beyond the gate. You can drive farther but the road conditions are dicey, especially if the road is wet. We have driven in as far as a mile but do not recommend this unless you are sure you and your vehicle can handle it. If you park near the highway as we recommend then this is a 3.25 mile *5.2 km* hike each way.
    To follow the trail just walk along the main jeep road. At 2.0 miles *3.2 km* from the highway you will come to a fence. Just beyond the fence you will find a sign for the Hot Loop Trail, where the **Hot Loop Trail** branches off to the left, going uphill. It looks like a road. The Woods Canyon trail forks to the right here and turns into a footpath descending to the bottom of the canyon.
    We recommend going to about the 3.25 mile *5.2 km* point on the Woods Canyon Trail, where the trail goes onto a sloping redrock shelf above the water.
    Dry Beaver Creek usually is dry, living up to its name. During the spring thaw it can carry a lot of water and we have seen it at times when it was strong. This hike is more interesting when water is running. Your best

chance of hiking it when water is running is in March or April. There is another stream nearby called Wet Beaver Creek, which runs year around.

Woods Canyon goes all the way to Interstate-17 just south of the Pinewood Country Club in the Munds Park area. When you are driving on Interstate-17 you will see a sign for an exit marked "Fox Ranch" where the highway bridges Woods Canyon. Woods Canyon and Munds Canyon, which is located to the north, are major lateral canyons that cut into Oak Creek Canyon. You can see why Interstate-17 is located where it is: it crosses these canyons at their heads, where they are narrow. Even so, the highway department built high bridges at both places. These canyons were a major obstacle between Sedona and Flagstaff in the old days and detouring around them added miles to the trip.

The developed part of the trail ends at the 4.0 mile *6.4 km* point, but we think the best stopping place is at 3.25 miles *5.2 km*. To hike the entire length of the canyon would mean going a rough 12.0 miles *19.2 km*.

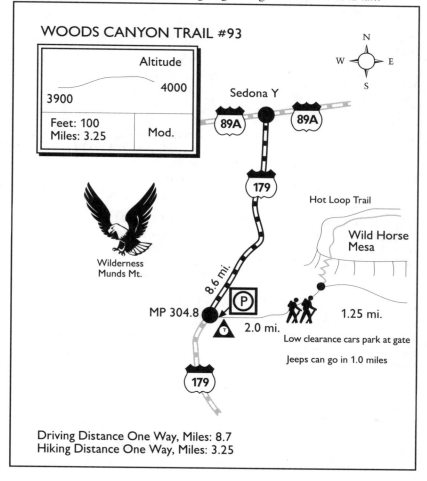

WOODS CANYON TRAIL #93

Altitude

4000

3900

Feet: 100
Miles: 3.25

Mod.

N
W—E
S

Sedona Y

89A   89A

179

Hot Loop Trail

Wild Horse
Mesa

Wilderness
Munds Mt.

8.6 mi.

MP 304.8

P

2.0 mi.

1.25 mi.

Low clearance cars park at gate

Jeeps can go in 1.0 miles

179

Driving Distance One Way, Miles: 8.7
Hiking Distance One Way, Miles: 3.25

INDEX

254

Yesterday

Sedona pioneers on the Thomas Point Trail

VORTEXES

Many persons claiming to be authorities have spoken about the Sedona Vortexes. Some of these people make very specific claims: that a particular Vortex is male, female, electric, magnetic, Yin, Yang, etc. These authorities don't always agree with each other.

We think it is a mistake to go to a Vortex expecting to find an antici-pated experience. If you do, you may set up a self-fulfillment trap, where you deceive yourself into thinking that you have found what you were *told* you would find, rather than having your own authentic experience. We rec-ommend that you approach a Vortex openly, seeking no pre-determined result.

The Vortexes are not hard to reach. You could easily visit all of them in a single day if you wish. Approach each one as a reverent seeker, open to what is there for you. Be quiet and unobtrusive so that you do not disturb others who are at the sites.

Experiences at the Vortexes range from negative, to neutral to cosmic. Each site is a place of beauty, worth visiting for aesthetic reasons; so your time will not be wasted even if you do not have a life-altering reaction. See the Index, pages 253- 254, for Vortexes that we recommend.

SCENIC DRIVES

Airport Hill: This is a very easy, short drive. The road is paved all the way. It takes you past one of the Sedona Vortex spots to the top of the hill where the Sedona Airport is located, an excellent viewpoint from which to see Sedona and some of its famous landmarks. When you get to the top, turn left and go toward the cross. You will find a fine lookout point there. See **Airport Saddle Vortex,** page 16.

Boynton Canyon: If your time is limited and you want to see some of the redrock back country, this is a nice, short drive over paved roads. See **Boynton Canyon**, page 42.

Loy Butte: You will drive over ten miles of good unpaved roads through some unspoiled country, allowing you to get away from town and see some great redrocks. At the end of the trip you will be within an easy walk from the best Indian ruin in the area. See **Loy Butte**, page 140.

Oak Creek Vista: By taking this drive you will travel the length of Oak Creek Canyon, a beautiful scenic area. At the end of the drive you will be at a high point from which you can see the canyon, take a nature walk and learn about the area. See Oak Creek Canyon Recreation Map, page 12.

Schnebly Hill Road: This is a favorite six mile drive that takes you through some beautiful redrock country to the top of a hill from where you can enjoy sweeping views. The road is paved the first 0.5 mile. The unpaved portion can be traveled by an ordinary car unless the road is wet and slippery. See **Schnebly Hill Trail**, page 192.

RULES OF THE TRAIL

Artifacts: Leave potsherds, arrowheads, and other artifacts where you find them.

Cabins: Northern Arizona's climate is hard on cabins and they are scarce. Treat the few remaining ones gently. Don't climb on them, pry boards off, or go digging for buried treasure.

Dogs: If you take your dog along on a hike, it should be on a leash.

Garbage: Pack it in, pack it out.

Rock Art: Do not touch it. Skin oils cause deterioration. Professionals don't even apply chalk in order to photograph rock art today, because it causes damage.

Ruins: Just look, don't touch. Preserve them. Don't pot hunt, climb walls or do anything else that might harm a ruin. Help them survive.

Trails: Stay on trails. They have been designed not only to provide access but also to bypass areas that can be harmed by people walking on them. Don't cut across switchbacks. It is disheartening to see how fast a trail can be destroyed by careless use.

Wilderness Areas: These are special places. The goal is to leave these lands unimpaired for future use and enjoyment. In the wilderness the hiker is king. No mechanized travel is permitted in Wilderness Areas, not even bicycles nor horses are allowed. Although Wilderness Areas may appear to be very rugged, they are quite fragile. Use them lightly. Leave no trace. They are a gift that we must all act to protect and preserve.